T0273991

Hiking Iowa

Hiking Iowa

A Guide to the State's Greatest Hiking Adventures

Second Edition

Seth Brooks

FALCONGUIDES

ESSEX, CONNECTICUT

To Mom and Dad, for always encouraging me to explore.

FALCONGUIDES®

An imprint of Globe Pequot, the trade division of
The Rowman & Littlefield Publishing Group, Inc.
4501 Forbes Blvd., Ste. 200
Lanham, MD 20706
www.rowman.com
Falcon and FalconGuides are registered trademarks and Make Adventure Your Story is a trademark of
The Rowman & Littlefield Publishing Group, Inc

Distributed by NATIONAL BOOK NETWORK

Copyright © 2024 The Rowman & Littlefield Publishing Group, Inc.

Photos by Seth Brooks unless otherwise noted.
Maps by The Rowman & Littlefield Publishing Group, Inc.

British Library Cataloguing in Publication Information available

Library of Congress Cataloging-in-Publication Data available

ISBN 978-1-4930-3652-3 (paperback)
ISBN 978-1-4930-3653-0 (e-book)

The author and The Rowman & Littlefield Publishing Group, Inc. assume no liability for accidents happening to, or injuries sustained by, readers who engage in the activities described in this book.

Contents

The Hikes

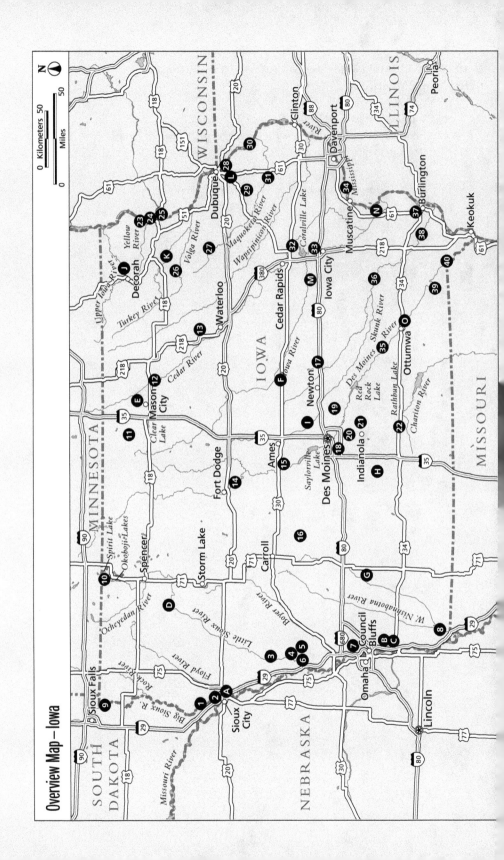

Overview Map – Iowa

Acknowledgments

There are numerous people to thank who helped bring this book to publication. Thank you to all the hikers, outdoor recreationists, and travelers who were curious about my project and shared my passion for the state of Iowa. I hope this book introduces more like-minded people to the natural beauty and cultural wealth that the Hawkeye State offers.

First, I must thank everyone at Globe Pequot and Falcon Guides. Mason Gadd, thank you for offering guidance, answering my questions, and encouraging me during this project. I am honored that you entrusted me with another Falcon Guides project. I must also thank Elizabeth Corcoran Hill. Her first edition of *Hiking Iowa* provided an excellent framework to update and revise the second edition.

A hearty thank you to the following park managers, rangers, biologists, naturalists, administrators, and inspirations who shared their knowledge to improve the accuracy of this guidebook or helped spark a curiosity: Michael Strauser at Pilot Knob State Park; Andy Roach at Pikes Peak State Park; Ryland Richards at Maquoketa State Park; Ben Marcus at Wildcat Den State Park; Ulf Konig at Geode State Park; Kaitlin Thompson and Fred MacVaugh at Effigy Mounds National Monument; Bruce Blair and Joseph Vastine at Yellow River State Forest; John Byrd at Shimek State Forest; Steve Pearson and Tanner Donovan at Madison County Conservation Board; Zach Rozmus at Washington County Conservation; Emma Kerns at Stephens State Forest; Heidi Reams at Floyd County Conservation; Zachary Scriver at the Coralville Lake Project; Keri Van Zante, Katie Cantu, and Greg Oldsen at Jasper County Conservation, Nate Detrich at Backbone State Park, Andy Bartlett at Ledges State Park, Justin Pedretti at Lacey-Keosauqua State Park, Nancy Corona at Neal Smith National Wildlife Refuge, Austin Lette at Volga River State Recreation Area; Friends of Blood Run; Andy Hockenson with Bremer County Conservation; Misty Conrad with Whiterock Conservancy; Kody Wohlers and Joe Jayjack with Iowa Natural Heritage Foundation; Chad Graeve at Pottawattamie Conservation; Matt Moles at Waubonsie State Park; Chris Lee with Des Moines County Conservation; Jeff Seago at the Loess Hills State Forest; Nick Beeck with Plymouth County Conservation; Sue Lueder with Fayette County Conservation; Micah Lee with Cass County Conservation; Lucas Wagner with Palisades-Kepler State Park; Brad Mormann with Jones County Conservation; Mark Wilson with Warren County Conservation; Jessica Lown with Polk County Conservation; Tami Krough with Marshall County Conservation; Shelly Eisenhauer; Sally "Iowa Park Lady" Ortgies; Lance Brisbois; Kelly Madigan; everyone at Golden Hills RC&D, as well as the countless unnamed who work in conservation across the state of Iowa.

Finally, and most importantly, I must thank my partner, Chelle, for your love, patience, and support. Thank you for being with me through the peaks and valleys. I could not have done and did not want to do this without you. I love you!

Meet Your Guide

Seth Brooks has been interested in travel and the natural world since an early age. Family trips were common growing up, including trips to Fort Robinson State Park in western Nebraska, a road trip to California, and visits to Wrigley Field in Chicago to root on the Cubs, among many other adventures. Seth frequently accompanied his father on business trips to Alaska, where the two braved the high seas to fish halibut and the giant mosquitoes on wild Alaskan rivers while fishing for king salmon.

Seth called the rainy, mystical region of Galicia in northwestern Spain home for seven years. He has worked in environmental education, conservation, outdoor recreation, and rural tourism since returning to the United States in late 2020. Seth enjoys spending time with his partner Chelle in the Loess Hills and exploring with his dog Jasper. He is also the author of *Hiking Nebraska* and *Hiking Kansas*, both published by Falcon Guides. To follow him on his adventures and see photography of his travels, you can find Seth on Instagram @sethfromsomewhere and his website, www.sethfromsomewhere.com.

Badger Ridge at Hitchcock Nature Center

Introduction

During the 2023 LoHi Trek, I overheard a group of hikers discussing the question, "What is a hike?" Does a hike have to be a rugged, multiday backpacking trek like the annual Loess Hills event organized by Kelly Madigan and Golden Hills RC&D? If so, that excludes a wide swath of people who are unable to undertake such a hike due to time or financial restraints or because of physical or age limitations. So what then, exactly, constitutes a hike?

In Iowa, the idea of a hike is shaped by the reality of land in the Hawkeye State. Due to the rich loess soil that covers much of the state, Iowa is the most altered state in the union. The state is neatly organized into ninety-nine counties, each of which are crisscrossed by innumerable, straight-as-an-arrow country roads. While the topography of some regions, like the Loess Hills or the Driftless Area, escaped the plough, nearly every possible acre of Iowa soil has been broken, even marginal land. The fertility and productivity of the land feeds millions and sustains rural communities, but it comes at a price.

Less than 1 percent of Iowa's original prairie remains, most of it in the Loess Hills.

Spend any time in conservation circles and you will hear a familiar refrain: the most altered state in the union; less than 1 percent of native prairie remains in Iowa; along with neighbors Kansas and Nebraska, the least amount of publicly accessible land. With all of these constraints and negative superlatives, where exactly can one hike in Iowa? What kind of hikes can you find in Iowa?

Thanks to its location, Iowa is the westernmost edge of the eastern hardwood deciduous forest. The state also happens to be the easternmost range for several western species, such as the yucca found in the Loess Hills. The largest tracts of remaining remnant prairie reside in western Iowa's unique landform, and there are several parks and preserves that are open to hiking. Prairie potholes, remnants of the last Ice Age, in the northern half of the state are hotspots for migratory waterfowl and shorebirds. Bird watchers should flock to these locations for hikes during spring and fall migrations. The Driftless Area in the northeast corner of the state avoided the glaciation that flattened much of Iowa. A fall hiking trip to Effigy Mounds, Pikes Peak, and other places should be on the bucket list of every Iowan. There are short but sweet prairie walks and hundreds of miles of forest trails throughout the state.

When considering Iowa hiking, don't let preconceived or uninformed biases detract from the countless number of excellent trails in the Hawkeye State. Hiking in Iowa is not the same as hiking in Colorado or California or Connecticut. For one, those states lack the biological diversity and sublime simplicity of Iowa's remnant prairies. Second, hiking is not a competition. The idea that it is, or that certain ecosystems are aesthetically more valuable than others, has led grasslands to become the most threatened ecosystem in North America because they were discredited aesthetically and disregarded ecologically. For decades, the National Park Service refused to consider grasslands for federal protection because they lacked the aesthetic appeal that places like Yosemite, Yellowstone, and other national parks deliver. However, as Willa Cather stated, "anybody can love the mountains, but it takes a soul to love the prairie."

Bottom line: Go take a hike! The forty featured hikes and fifteen honorable mentions described in this guidebook are an attempt at a balanced survey of some of the best and most unique hiking trails in the state of Iowa. There are countless other state parks and recreation areas, county parks, nature preserves, and other publicly accessible lands that are worthy of exploration. Whether you hike to watch birds, identify plants, connect with nature and disconnect from modern civilization, or simply for physical exercise, the Hawkeye State has numerous quality trails that are awaiting your footsteps. But remember, leave no trace!

Weather and Seasons

The four distinct seasons that annually grace Iowa are wonderful expressions of its placement in the Upper Midwest. Many Iowans are concerned with weather because of their agricultural roots, as they try to forecast, bet, or conjure the dates of the first fall and final spring frosts, which delineate the growing season. Our winters and summers contrast starkly, and while spring and fall have their own eye-opening

Wildflowers explode in summer, along with daily temperatures

differences, they serve mainly as transitions between very cold and very hot temperatures. Prairie vegetation tends to "green up late," and though certain plants bloom in early spring, wildflower forays are best done during the heat of the summer, as long as you wear a large sunhat and carry a supply of water.

The summer months, June to August, tend to be blisteringly hot and humid. Luckily, 70 percent of our annual precipitation falls between April and September. Once temperatures hit more than 100 degrees F, your only hope is for a thunderstorm with its whipping winds and cooling rain. Normally you can't "get caught" unintentionally in these storms, for their thunderheads—dark rolling cumulonimbus clouds—are always visible as they approach. However, should the sky turn an eerie purplish-green cast, you'll want to find a basement to huddle in as soon as possible. Between twenty and a hundred tornadoes and countless funnel clouds historically roll through Iowa each year, sometimes accompanied by violent hailstorms. With wind speeds of 100 to 500 miles per hour, they can cause destruction of property, injury, and even death.

As summer comes to an end and the cool of autumn arrives, prairie grasses turn rich gold and auburn, and changing leaves swirl into a spectrum of orange, amber, russet, and garnet. Although fall is beautiful everywhere in the state, northeast Iowa's forested bluffs offer an especially gorgeous palette of autumnal splendor. Hiking trips during fall usually elicit a strong feeling of nostalgia, causing many to love autumn in a special way.

When crisp fall breezes turn into icy northwesterly winds, winter has only begun. Snow constitutes only 10 percent of our annual precipitation but can blanket the state in a fluffy dreamland or fall on an ice-encrusted, subzero polar-scape. Estherville's local newspaper, the *Northern Vindicator*, claims to have first used the term "blizzard" to describe one hellacious snowstorm that blew through Emmet County in March 1870. Many of us keep our fingers crossed for as much snow as the sky will give, for cross-country skiing along the trails you hike during summer is the best way to spend winter.

As is the case throughout most of the northern temperate zone, spring's arrival is welcomed when it rolls around. Warming temperatures bring an array of spring wildflowers that bloom in the forests from April to June. Migratory birds begin heading north during this time, and a May morning spent looking at trout lilies and wood warblers is a real treat. Hiking is at its best during this not-too-hot, not-too-cold interval and should be enjoyed to the maximum extent.

Flora and Fauna

Iowa's lowest point (480 feet) lies in its southeast corner, which consequently receives more rainfall than anywhere else in the state. In the rising plains of the northwest corner is our high point (1,670 feet), situated in the driest part of the state. It's no mystery, then, that forests dominate the southeast, while prairie once covered the northwest.

Pasque flowers are one of the first wildflowers to bloom in early spring.

Iowa contains the westernmost extent of the deciduous forests of the East and the easternmost margin of the great plains of the West and before settlement was the heart of the tallgrass prairie. When Euro-American settlers arrived, three predominant ecotypes covered the state: about 80 percent prairie, 12 percent forest, and 8 to 11 percent wetland. The edges of these biomes were somewhat hard to define— wet hill prairies, marshy openings in forest, and oak savannas/grasslands were often interspersed.

The tallgrass prairies of Iowa are composed of three main plant families: *Poaceae* (grasses), *Asteraceae* (asters, or composites), and *Fabaceae* (legumes), with hundreds of others, from moonworts to orchids, filling in the dense maze of vegetation. Grassland birds and butterflies are entirely dependent on prairie grasses and wildflowers for food, nesting material, and breeding grounds. Goat prairies, which are forest openings or rock outcrops covered in prairie vegetation, are common in the eastern part of the state, as are sand prairies, which support prickly pear cactus, a surprising sight in Iowa to most people.

The deciduous forests of the Northeast begin to peter out in density as one crosses the Mississippi River into Iowa. Our woodlands, most widespread in the eastern part of the state, are for the most part undergoing a large-scale succession after having been logged entirely during the 1800s. Upland forests are dominated by oaks and hickories, while silver maple, basswood, and green ash grow in moist lowland sites. Twenty-one species of oaks live in Iowa and provide food and shelter for more than seventy

forest-associated animals. Riparian corridors are framed by willows, cottonwoods, and sycamores, which provide nesting habitat for many bird species, from wood warblers to bald eagles and great blue herons.

Due to the karst topography of the northeast corner, many holdovers from colder, glacial times are present. The most remarkable is the Iowa Pleistocene snail, a smaller-than-a-shirt-button snail thought to have been extinct for 10,000 years—until it was found eating birch leaves in northeast Iowa twenty-five years ago. Spring-fed trout streams meander through canyons dominated by balsam fir, eastern white pine, and yellow birch trees that grow over bunchberry and twinflower, plants with typically northern affinities.

Prairie hikes encourage slowing down and getting up close.

Iowa's Loess Hills provide habitat for plants and animals typically found in western states: yucca, cowboy's delight, ten-petaled mentzelia, blue grosbeak, black-billed magpie, prairie rattlesnake, and prairie skink. During the past 150 years, these once prairie-covered hills have succumbed to forest invasion, and expanding woodlands have pushed the ranges of some forest birds northward. In contrast, populations of many prairie and savanna species have declined sharply and in some cases have disappeared altogether.

During spring and fall, the Mississippi and Missouri Rivers serve as flyways for extraordinary numbers of migratory birds. Many of them—ducks and geese, shorebirds, and songbirds—stay to nest. The backwaters, sloughs, and islands in the Upper Mississippi River National Fish and Wildlife Refuge are veritable treasure troves of diverse freshwater and riparian organisms.

Recent glaciation of the north-central lobe left vast pothole marshes that serve as breeding grounds for countless thousands of waterfowl, as well as homes for amphibians and unusual aquatic plants. Bogs and fens also dot the state, and growing in their calcium-rich seepages are some curious plants: grass of Parnassus, bull sedge, upright sedge, swamp saxifrage, sensitive fern, and fringed gentian. In one spot near the Minnesota border, you can even find a fen that features the carnivorous sundew plant and a sphagnum moss mat.

Somehow, a large number of organisms manage to make their homes in fragmented young forests and croplands within the state. The "edge effect" has provided habitat for coyotes, white-tailed deer, and wild turkeys, whose populations are all soaring. Many species of birds tend to congregate around edges as well, and you'll be surprised at the diversity to be found in something as simple as a fencerow.

Wilderness Restrictions/Regulations

Land Ownership

Iowa has a total of seventy-one state parks and recreation areas, four major state forests, nearly 350 wildlife management areas, ninety-five state preserves, six national wildlife refuges, one national monument, two national historic trails, and one national historic site, in addition to hundreds of county parks. However, with more than 97 percent of its 56,276 square miles in private ownership, the percentage of publicly owned land is one of the lowest among the fifty states.

Native Lands

The state of Iowa is on the ancestral and traditional land of the Báxoje (Bah Kho-je) or Ioway, Sauk (Sac), and Meskwaki (Fox) peoples.

In 1976, Iowa became the first state in the country to enact a law to protect ancient burial sites. There are several trails in Iowa where burial mounds are visible. Pay your respects by staying on the trail and not disturbing any burial mounds.

Iowa Department of Natural Resources

The mission of the Department of Natural Resources was molded by the vision of some of the state's most intrepid conservationists. Iowa's "dean" of conservation, Professor Thomas MacBride, once said, "the park shall set us free." He and his colleagues Louis Pammel and Bohumil Shimek, as well as other academics and naturalists, created the Iowa Conservation Association (ICA) in 1917, and by 1920 Backbone and Lacey-Keosauqua State Parks had already been dedicated. During the 1920s, Iowa's park system was one of the most progressive in the nation, and by 1926 it included thirty-three sites managed by the ICA.

The Iowa DNR manages a total of seventy-one state parks and recreation areas. The signage at most state parks is excellent and the trails are well maintained. Signage does vary from park to park. Campgrounds and other amenities provide an opportunity for overnights to further explore the park and the region. There are no entrance fees to enter Iowa's state parks, with only two exceptions: Lake Manawa and Waubonsie in western Iowa require entry permits for out-of-state visitors.

County Parks

In 1955 the Iowa legislature enacted a law allowing voters to establish county conservation boards, which were meant to reduce the stress on state and federal agencies and to provide residents with the option to preserve land. Today, each of Iowa's ninety-nine counties has its own conservation board. Some hold large tracts of land, support nature centers, and even manage state parks and preserves; others care for small

Signage varies depending on the land manager, ranging from excellent to nonexistent.

remnants or undeveloped parcels. Many county parks aren't as heavily used as state-owned land and boast hiking trails and free camping. The online resource mycountyparks.com is an excellent tool to research hiking areas. The quality and amount of information varies by county but you can find trail maps and contact information for county conservation boards in every county in Iowa.

National Parks Service and National Wildlife Refuges
In the 1980s, the National Park Service investigated the creation of a national park in the Loess Hills. They determined it was not feasible because more than 90 percent of the land was privately owned. Instead, the NPS created a national natural landmark in Monona County. You won't find any information at the site, but at other NPS properties in Iowa you can expect to find friendly and helpful rangers, clean facilities and informative interpretive displays, and well-marked and maintained trails. The US Fish and Wildlife properties are of comparable quality.

Private Land, Nature Preserves, and Other Publicly Accessible Areas
There are several nonprofit organizations that allow public access to their land. The Nature Conservancy manages several reserves across the state. Iowa Natural Heritage Foundation also manages multiple properties in Iowa, but they are not open to public hiking. Like county and municipal parks, rules and regulations vary at each reserve. Dogs may be allowed at one place but are not permitted at another.

Before You Hit the Trail

Hiking Iowa focuses on some of the most scenic day hikes in Iowa. This guidebook is not comprehensive, however, as not every scenic trail in the state was able to be included. *Hiking Iowa* aims to provide a survey of the best trails in the state while balancing geography, difficulty, accessibility, and ecology. Effort was made to not saturate one area of the state at the expense of others while including hikes in different ecosystems. The hikes are organized into five sections based on the landform regions described in *Landforms of Iowa* (Prior, 1991). The fifty-five hikes covered in this book vary in difficulty to engage novice as well as experienced hikers. Use the overview map to locate the hikes nearest you. Detailed information is provided for each of the trails, with chapter sections explained below.

Start
This indicates the starting location for the hike.

Elevation gain
Elevation is generally the most important factor in determining a hike's difficulty. Total elevation gain in feet is listed, as well as the highest and lowest points reached on the hike. While there are sections of Iowa that are flat (Des Moines Lobe), other regions (Loess Hills and Driftless Area) have rugged topography.

Distance
The distance specified in each description is listed as a round-trip distance from the trailhead to the end of the route and back. Hike lengths have been determined by using the author's GPS unit. Some variability is to be expected between this measurement and those by the land manager or your own GPS device, however any discrepancies should be minimal.

Difficulty
Assessing a hike's difficulty is very subjective. Elevation, elevation change, and distance all play a role, as do trail conditions, weather, and the hiker's physical condition. The abundance of trail markers, or lack thereof, can also significantly affect a trail's difficulty. Trails that require constant navigation due to a lack of waymarking will be more difficult than a trail that has trail markers at every junction. The remoteness of a hiking area can also increase a trail's difficulty. With that being said, the author's subjective ratings will give some idea of difficulty. Difficulty is subjective and unique to each hiker and each hike itself; the best effort was made to provide a rating that takes into consideration the factors listed in this paragraph.

Despite cold temperatures, winter can be an excellent time to hike in Iowa (no bugs!).

Hiking time

Hiking time is a rough estimate of the time within which the average hiker will be able to complete the hike. Very fit, fast-moving hikers will be able to complete it in less time. Slow-moving hikers or those preoccupied with activities such as photography or field identification may take longer. To come up with this information, I estimated that most people hike at 2.5 miles per hour to take into account water breaks, photography, and other activities that add time to a hike. I also tried to consider other factors such as a rough trail or particularly large elevation changes. Carrying a backpack for overnight trips will add significantly to the time required.

Seasons/schedule

This section lists when hiking trails are open to the public. Most trails in Iowa are open year-round from sunrise to sunset. Some trails close on holidays or at specific times; always contact the land manager or visit their website to verify the status of the trails, not only for opening hours but also current conditions. Some trails may close during hunting seasons or important migration periods. Additionally, some agencies use prescribed burns to manage their land. Most prescribed fires occur in the spring (late April to early May) but they can occur throughout the year. Contact the land manager or check their website for updates and trail closures.

Fees and permits

The Iowa Department of Natural Resources requires entrance fees for nonresidents of Iowa at only two state parks: Lake Manawa and Waubonsie. Most parks and preserves in Iowa are free to the public, but some county parks require a daily vehicle permit. Some parks welcome donations. In general, organizations like The Nature Conservancy, the National Audubon Society, and other nonprofits do not require an entrance fee; however always check before you visit to avoid surprise entrance fees.

Trail contact

The trail contacts category lists the name, address, phone number, and website of the managing agency for the lands through which the trail passes. Call, write, or check the website for current information about the hike. The address listed is often not the physical address of the park or area where the hike and trailhead are located, rather it is the office or mailing address of the land manager.

Dog-friendly

This section describes whether dogs are allowed on the trail. Generally, dogs need to be leashed when they are allowed. Please be courteous and pick up your dog's waste and dispose of it properly.

Respect wildlife and land managers by leashing your pet when required.

Trail surface

Trail surface describes the material that makes up the trail. Most commonly it is simply a dirt path consisting of the native materials that were there when the trail was built. On occasion gravel is added or the trail may be paved. In a few instances the hike follows a paved road, dirt road, or a primitive two-track road.

Land status

The land status simply tells which agency, usually federal or state, manages the land in which the trail lies. In this book the Iowa DNR and county conservation boards are the most common land managers, along with federal, municipal, and private organizations.

Nearest town

The nearest town is the closest city or town to the hike's trailhead that has at least minimal visitor services. The listed town will usually have gas, food, and limited lodging available. In small towns and villages, the hours these services are available may be limited.

Maps

The maps in this guide are as accurate and current as possible. When used in conjunction with the hike description and the additional maps listed for each hike, you should have little trouble following the route.

Generally, two types of maps are listed. Most of the state parks have park or trail maps available free at the entrance station, headquarters, or online. Some of the park maps have a rudimentary map of trails, while other parks have more detailed maps. The US Forest Service has two different types of maps available. The motor vehicle use map lists the different types of roads within the national forests. They do not list, however, hiking trails and are not topographical maps. There are printable versions of these maps available on the Forest Service's website as well as digital maps available for download on the Avenza Maps app. The Forest Service website also has color, foldable brochures available for purchase. These are excellent maps that list forest roads as well as hiking trails. They are not topographical, however.

USGS topographic quadrangles are generally the most detailed and accurate maps available of natural features. With some practice they allow you to visualize peaks, canyons, cliffs, rivers, roads, and many other features. With a little experience, a topographic map, and a compass, you should never become lost. All the USGS maps noted in this guide are 7.5-minute quads. USGS quads are particularly useful for little-used trails and off-trail travel. Unfortunately, some of the quadrangles, particularly for less-populated parts of the state, are out of date and do not show many newer man-made features such as roads and trails. However, they are still useful for their topographic information. Most of the more developed hikes in this guide do not require a topo map. The state park maps, Forest Service maps, or maps made available by other land managers will suffice on most trails.

GPS (Global Positioning System) units, particularly those with installed maps, can be very useful for route finding when used in conjunction with paper maps. However, anyone that enters the backcountry should have at least basic knowledge in using a paper map and compass. Batteries die and GPS units get dropped. It's best not to be completely dependent on them in case of failure. A GPS unit with maps installed can be particularly helpful on off-trail hikes.

USGS quads can usually be purchased at outdoor shops or ordered directly from USGS at http://store.usgs.gov or from online companies such as www.mytopo.com or www.topozone.com. To order from USGS, know the state, the number desired of each map, the exact map name as listed in the hike heading, and the scale. You can also download USGS quads at https://apps.nationalmap.gov/downloader/#/ and print them yourself.

Other trail users

This describes the other users that you might encounter on the hike. Mountain bikers, equestrians, and hunters are the most common. On multiuse trails, bikers and hikers must yield to equestrians, while bikers must also yield to hikers.

Make sure every hiking partner wears blaze orange during hunting season.

Special Considerations
Unique elements of the trail that require extra preparation will be listed here. These might include water availability, drastic temperature changes, sun exposure, or hunting regulations.

Amenities available
This spec will address necessities like restroom availability, running water, shelter, first aid, vending machines, ramps, etc.

Maximum grade
This spec is a good indication of how hard the hardest part of the hike gets. This will tell you how steep the trail gets, and how long the steepest sections last.

Cell service
It's important to know if you can, or cannot, count on cell services before you head to the trail. If you are traveling with anyone with mobility or disability considerations, make sure all are aware of the communication channels available. If there is no cell service available, make extra sure to read the directions carefully and don't assume

you'll be able to follow your GPS. If you use your mobile phone for maps or to follow GPX tracks, download them before hiking to use them offline.

Finding the Trailhead

This section provides detailed directions to the trailhead. With a basic current state highway map or GPS unit, you can easily locate the starting point from the directions. In general, the nearest town or interstate exit is used as the starting point. Federal highways use the abbreviation US in this guide, while Iowa state highways are listed as IA in this guide. County roads are sometimes paved but often are gravel country roads; they are listed as CR in this guide.

Distances were measured using Google Maps. Be sure to keep an eye open for the specific signs, junctions, and landmarks mentioned in the directions, not just the mileage. The map services available on cell phone GPS systems are often inaccurate or nonexistent in remote areas so use them with care. In addition, many require decent cell service to work, further lessening their value. A current map is your best option for finding the trailhead.

Most of this guide's hikes have trailheads that can be reached by any type of vehicle. A few, as noted, require a high-clearance or four-wheel-drive vehicle. Rain or snow can temporarily make some roads impassable. Before venturing into the country, you should check with the land manager or other local services for current road conditions. On less-traveled back roads, you should carry basic emergency equipment such as a shovel, chains, water, a spare tire, a jack, blankets, and some extra food and clothing. Make sure that your vehicle is in good operating condition with a full tank of gas.

Try not to leave valuables in your car at all; if you must, lock them out of sight in the trunk. If I have enough room, I usually put everything in the trunk to give the car an overall empty appearance. In my many years of parking and hiking at remote trailheads, my vehicle has never been disturbed.

Trail Conditions

Not all hikes are created equally. Some hikes are well maintained and well marked with trail signs, markers, and more that make navigation incredibly simple. Other hikes have nonexistent trail infrastructure that can frustrate even the most experienced hiker and make your hike unexpectedly long, or worse, you get lost. This section addresses trail infrastructure such as waymarking, trail signage, and other helpful navigational assistance created by land managers and volunteers. This section also lists potential hazards that may be encountered on your hike. Sun exposure, ticks, and thunderstorms are the most common hazards you will encounter hiking in Iowa. Finally, an estimate of the foot traffic the hike receives gives you an idea of how popular the trails are in the area where the hike is located.

The Hike

All the hikes selected for this guide can be done by people in good physical condition. Scrambling is necessary for very few of the hikes, while none require any rock-climbing skills (rock climbing is permitted at several places in Iowa). A few of the hikes, as noted in their descriptions, travel on very faint trails. You should have an experienced hiker, along with a compass, map, and a GPS unit with your group before attempting those hikes.

The waymarking on trails depends on the agency that manages the land where the hike is located. Trail signage at Iowa DNR sites are generally similar but there are variations. State parks are typically the best marked trails, although there are exceptions. Trails at state recreation areas are well marked as well. Wildlife management areas and state preserves usually have very few, if any, trail markers or informational kiosks. Most of the time the paths are very obvious and easy to follow, but trail markers help when the trails are little-used and faint or when there are numerous intersecting trails throughout the park. Fresh snow can obscure footpaths, so always know the type of trail markers used where you are hiking and bring a map, compass, and GPS unit with fresh batteries. Be sure not to add your own trail waymarkings—it can confuse the route. Leave such markings to the official trail workers.

Possible backcountry campsites are often suggested in the descriptions. State parks and recreation areas do not allow backcountry camping (some do have hike-in campsites); some places, like the Loess Hills State Forest, allow dispersed camping. Check with the land manager to inquire about camping fees, registration, regulations, and other information.

After reading the descriptions, pick the hike that most appeals to you. Go only as far as ability and desire allow. There is no obligation to complete any hike. Remember, you are out hiking to enjoy yourself, not to prove anything.

Miles and Directions

To help you stay on course, a detailed route finder sets forth mileages between significant landmarks along the trail. The mileage may differ from official mileages of the land manager or your own personal GPS device. The author used both a mobile phone and GPS watch to track mileage; they rarely showed the same mileage but were usually within one-half mile of each other.

Trail Finder

Author's Favorites

6. Brent's Trail, Loess Hills State Forest Little Sioux Unit (Little Sioux)
7. Badger Ridge, Lotus Loop, and Westridge, Hitchcock Nature Center (Crescent)
29. Lost Canyon and Stream Bottom Trails, Whitewater Canyon Wildlife Management Area (Cascade)

Best Hikes for Scenic Views

15. Pea's Creek Canyon, Ledges State Park (Ames)
25. Pikes Peak to Point Ann, Pikes Peak State Park (McGregor)
28. Horseshoe Bluff Trail, Mines of Spain State Recreation Area (Dubuque)

Best Hikes for Families

12. Fossil and Prairie Loop, Fossil and Prairie Center (Rockford)
31. Maquoketa Caves Loop, Maquoketa Caves State Park (Maquoketa)
37. Flint River Trail, Starr's Cave Park and Preserve (Burlington)

Best Hikes for History

9. Blood Run Creek, Blood Run National Historic Landmark (Larchwood)
16. Long Creek Trail, Whiterock Conservancy (Coon Rapids)
24. Hanging Rock Trail, Effigy Mounds National Monument (Marquette)

Best Prairie Hikes

3. Sylvan Runkel State Preserve, Sylvan Runkel State Preserve (Onawa)
19. Tallgrass Trail, Neal Smith National Wildlife Refuge (Prairie City)
35. Sam Rodgers Educational Trail, Eddyville Dunes Sand Prairie (Eddyville)

Best Fall Hikes

8. Sunset Ridge, Waubonsie State Park (Hamburg)
10. Kettleson Hogsback Nature Trail, Kettleson Hogsback Wildlife Management Area (Spirit Lake)
32. Cedar Cliff Trail, Palisades-Kepler State Park (Cedar Rapids)

Best Hikes for Backpacking

5. Jones Creek Pond Ridge Loop, Loess Hills State Forest Preparation Canyon Unit (Pisgah)
22. Woodburn Unit Backpack Trail, Stephens State Forest (Chariton)
23. Yellow River Backpack Trail, Yellow River State Forest (Harpers Ferry)

Map Legend

Municipal

≡⟨35⟩≡ Freeway/Interstate Highway

≡⟨61⟩≡ US Highway

≡⟨1⟩≡ State Road

≡⟨18⟩≡ County/Paved/Improved Road

=== Improved Gravel Road Text

⊢——⊢ Railroad Text

——— Leader Line

Trails

------ Featured Trail

- - - - - Trail or Fire Road

⁞⁞⁞⁞⁞⁞ Steps/boardwalk

Water Features

⬭ Body of Water

⌇ River/Creek

≋ Waterfall

⚬⌐ Spring

Land Management

National Park/Forest

State/County Park

Reservation Area

National Monument/
Wilderness Area

Symbols

⬛ Boat Ramp

⌣⌢ Bridge

▪ Building/Point of Interest

⚐ Campground

▲ Campsite

⌃ Cave

→ Hike Arrow

▭ Inn/Lodging

▲ Mountain/Peak

🅿 Parking

⊞ Picnic Area

⊞ Restroom

⊠ Scenic View/Overlook

→ To Text

⓪⓪ Trailhead

○ Town (Hike Map)

⌖ Tower

Broken Kettle Grasslands

Loess Hills

Along the Missouri River floodplain, a ribbon of mysteriously wrinkled hills forms a narrow north-south band nearly 200 miles in length. Known as the Loess Hills, they are some of the most interesting and engaging of Iowa's landforms. To some they are the ridge where the western plains begin. Connie Mutel, author of Fragile Giants: Natural History of the Loess Hills, declared that she never felt like she was at home in Iowa until she first encountered the Loess Hills. Aside from being the deepest deposition of loess in the Western Hemisphere and thus some of the most dramatic topographic relief in the state, the Loess Hills harbor incredibly varied ecological communities. They act as an arm of western habitat extended into the Upper Midwest, rich with short-grass prairie and desert plants and animals. The ability for western species to thrive in the Loess Hills is due mainly to the characteristics of the yellow, silty matter that composes them.

Iowa's Loess Hills were formed by three major processes: They were ground by ice and deposited by wind, and are today still being sculpted by water. The name comes from the German word for loose ("loess," rhymes with bus), first given to massive silt deposits along the Rhine River. Originally hailing from Minnesota, the Dakotas, and Canada, the fine loess was created as continental ice sheets scoured the north, effectively grinding the bedrock into flour. During periods of warming, glacial meltwater carted this rock flour away and deposited it along the banks of the major drainages. Winters brought with them colder temperatures and greatly reduced the torrents of meltwater. When the water was low, powerful drafts swirled over the floodplains, lifting the loess and depositing it in huge hills on either side of the major river valleys. Loess can be found almost everywhere in Iowa, but nowhere to such depths as along the Missouri River. Only in China, along the Yellow River, named so for its loess, are the deposits deeper. The vulnerability of loess is demonstrated in China, where some of the highest erosion rates in the world occur. Able to stand at 90-degree angles when cut, loess is incredibly solid when undisturbed. However, loess loses its cohesive capabilities as soon as it becomes saturated or shifted.

The Loess Hills' fragility is their very essence. Because of the variance in slope gradient, aspect, and moisture content, the Loess Hills were historically less disturbed by agriculture and development. However, fire-suppression and grazing has, for now, determined the tumultuous relationship of prairie and forest on the once-bald hills. Forest cover has risen exponentially since the area's settlement in the 1840s and merited the creation of Loess Hills State Forest in 1986. The push to preserve tracts of land within the Loess Hills has been spurred by recognition of their exceptional and distinctive traits and communities. Today the Broken Kettle Grassland, Iowa's biggest prairie preserve, lies in the northern reaches. In 1986 the National Park Service designated nearly 10,000 acres in the north-central Loess Hills a national natural landmark.

Hiking the Loess Hills is the best way to experience their grandeur, and the bulk of the trails traverse prairie-covered ridgetops or cool, dark hollows. The native peoples who once lived here believed that by standing atop a ridge at dusk, one's soul would be transmitted to the ever after via the rays of the setting sun. After a long day spent walking the magnificent hills, it's hard to imagine otherwise.

1 Five Ridge Prairie

Named for the five ridges that dissect the preserve, this mixture of prairie and woodland in the far northern reaches of the Loess Hills is a gem. Old farm roads and mowed firebreaks provide ample space for wandering in a location where the land opens up to the Big Sioux River Valley and Northwest Plains of Iowa. An eastern outpost for many western species, it features plant and animal diversity that ranges from short- and tallgrass prairie plants to forest-loving neotropical migrants.

Start: Five Ridge Prairie West Entrance off IA 12

Elevation gain: 673 feet total gain; 1,149 (lowest) to 1,470 feet (highest)

Distance: 4.76-mile lollipop

Difficulty: Difficult due to steep climb to the cabin, rugged terrain, and often overgrown trails

Hiking time: 2-2.5 hours

Seasons/schedule: Trails open from 4 a.m. to 10:30 p.m.

Fees and permits: None

Trail contact: Plymouth County Conservation, PO Box 1033, Hinton 51024; (712) 947-4270; www.plymouthcountyparks.com

Dog-friendly: Yes, on leash

Trail surface: Natural (mowed grass)

Land status: Five Ridge Prairie State Preserve (Plymouth County Conservation)

Nearest town: Akron, 13 miles to the north, and Sioux City, 12 miles to the south

Maps: USGS Elk Point NE, IA, SD; trail map available online

Other trail users: None

Special considerations: Even though it is a state preserve, hunting is allowed. Check season dates and dress accordingly. Please be respectful if the camping cabin is occupied. Prescribed burns are used in spring, summer, and fall to manage the land. The road to the east entrance may be soft and impassable after heavy rain or snow melt.

Amenities available: None

Maximum grade: 24%; the steepest climb is from the trailhead to the camping cabin perched on the ridge above IA 12, gaining 150 feet over one-quarter mile. After the cabin, there is another climb of 150 feet over three-quarters mile, then a 250-foot climb over 1 mile along Ridge Three.

Cell service: Average to weak

Finding the trailhead: From exit 151 on I-29, head north on IA 12 for 13.5 miles. The west entrance parking area is located 3.5 miles after the junction with CR K18. GPS: N42° 40.299' W96° 33.106'

Trail conditions: The trails are fire breaks and mowed occasionally; you will likely encounter overgrown trails unless they have recently been mowed in preparation for prescribed burns. There are trail markers at important junctions, but not every junction is marked. The trail map and markers identify junctions using a combination of letters and numbers: "R" represents ridge, while "V" represents valley. The trails receive light traffic.

The Hike

As you drive north on IA 12 toward Five Ridge Prairie State Preserve, the world seems to open up. Loess deposits become shallower and the hills smaller, as they

Rustic cabin tops the ridge overlooking the Big Sioux River Valley.

gradually begin smoothing into the northwest Iowa plains. The thin deposits of loess, aided by the carving action of the Big Sioux River, have left Cretaceous-age bedrock exposed underneath. You'll find it on the east side of the Big Sioux River floodplain from Sioux City north. Outcrops along the highway expose the Dakota Formation's 80- to 90-million-year-old shale, limestone, and sandstone.

With assistance from The Nature Conservancy, the Plymouth County Conservation Board bought Five Ridge Prairie in 1981; it was dedicated as a state preserve five years later. Wild turkey reintroduction began in 1981, and now the preserve is open for most of the scheduled hunting seasons.

The preserve takes its name from the five prairie-covered ridges that lie between its borders, each of them parted by the deep fissures of forested valleys. Low precipitation and extreme weather in the northern hills give the prairies an edge over the invading woodlands, as shrubby growth is stunted by the harsh climate. However, you'll notice on the forest edge that large thickets of dogwood and sumac seem to be gaining ground on the prairie. The shrub creep is still a problem, but prescribed burns on the preserve have helped maintain large tracts of prairie. Several areas close to the parking area were cultivated at one time and now are riddled with invasive plants easily differentiated from the native prairie.

The south- and west-facing ridgetops are dominated by a mix of tall- and mixed-grass prairies. Little bluestem, sideoats grama, Indian grass, purple locoweed, New

Jersey tea, skeleton weed, prairie violet, silky aster, and rough blazing star can be found blooming through the summer. Here in the high and dry northern Loess Hills, twenty-five typically western organisms are at the very edge of their eastern range. Cut-leaf iron plant, yucca, plains muhly, blue grama, plains pocket mouse, northern grasshopper mouse, western kingbird, and blue grosbeak are a few of these species better known in the West.

Prairie makes up only half the preserve, and the bur oak woodlands in the valleys are just as impressive as the ridges they divide. Wide-stretching bur oaks towering above spring wildflower displays are a stunning sight. During summer look for such woodland birds as yellow- and black-billed cuckoos, indigo bunting, scarlet tanager, Bell's vireo, and ovenbird. Regal fritillary butterflies, obligates of prairie violets, have slowly been making a comeback in many preserved areas of the Loess Hills. On a tract of land close to Five Ridge Prairie, hundreds of such butterflies were found in one survey, reflecting their population growth as efforts intensify to preserve their habitat.

The trails, either old farm roads or mowed firebreaks, traverse four-fifths of the ridges in the park and dip into three of the valleys. The camping cabin perched precariously atop the ridge along the highway is available to rent for overnight stays. The only access to the cabin is a steep hike from the west entrance. While the east entrance of the preserve avoids this steep trail, climbs are inevitable in this ridge-and-valley trail system regardless of the trailhead. The tough climb from the west entrance to the cabin immediately rewards the effort with excellent views of the Big Sioux River Valley. From here, hike a pleasant loop along the third and fourth ridges (the ridges are counted beginning from the east entrance, not including the ridge where the cabin is located). You can also hike all of the ridge and valley trails in the preserve for more distance. Be sure to take ample water with you; the hiking is hard and on the ridges you'll be exposed to full sun. The trails may be overgrown depending on when they were mowed for fire season.

The Nature Conservancy's efforts to preserve tracts of land in the Loess Hills are extremely noticeable here, where from most of the ridges you can see only conserved land. In 2022, the organization purchased the 356-acre Joy Hollow Girl Scout Camp, which shares its southern boundary with Five Ridge Prairie. The trails will be open

BROKEN KETTLE GRASSLANDS

Broken Kettle is a place unto its own—the largest tract of remnant prairie in Iowa, the lone remnant population of prairie rattlesnakes, and one of the few bird conservation areas in Iowa. Just about everything that lives there is special: ten-petal blazing star, western kingbird, plains spadefoot, and Ottoe skipper, among countless other rare organisms. Intensive management efforts such as prescribed burns and a herd of bison protect the extensive and diverse prairie from encroaching woodlands. There are no trails but hiking is permitted south of Butcher Road and at Joy Hollow Scout Camp.

Five Ridge Prairie

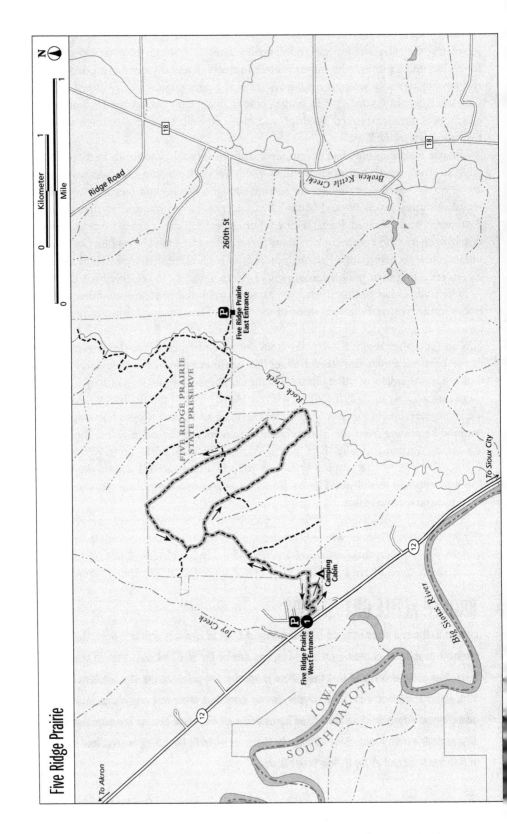

Hikers climbing up the ridge to the cabin

to the public when scouts are not using the camp, as TNC leased the property back to the Girl Scouts of Greater Iowa at no cost.

Miles and Directions

0.00 From the parking area, head west to begin the climb up the ridge.

0.10 Turn right (southeast).

0.20 Camping cabin.

0.30 Turn right (east).

0.40 Turn right (north).

0.80 Continue straight (northeast) at junction R5.

1.20 At junction R4-D, keep right (east).

1.40 Continue straight (southeast) at junction R4-C.

2.70 Continue straight (north) at junction R3-B.

3.60 Reach junction R4-E and keep left (south).

3.70 Turn right (south) at junction R4-D.

4.00 Continue straight (southwest) at R5.

4.40 Continue straight (west).

   Option: If this section is too overgrown, turn left (south) to return via the camping cabin trail.

4.76 Arrive back at the west entrance trailhead.

2 Mt. Lucia and Broken Toe Trails

Designated as an "urban wildlife sanctuary," Stone State Park seems so removed from the city that once you're hiking up Mount Lucia, you won't believe you're within Sioux City limits. Fifteen miles of trails around the park lead up dark, forested hollows to prairie-covered hilltops overlooking the Missouri and Big Sioux Rivers. The Dorothy Pecaut Nature Center, located adjacent to the southwest corner of the park, houses natural history exhibits and several miles of trails that connect to Stone State Park.

Start: Mark's Glen Trailhead northwest of Wah-kaw Shelter
Elevation gain: 591 feet total gain; 1,167 (lowest) to 1,394 feet (highest)
Distance: 4.27-mile loop
Difficulty: Difficult due to steep inclines
Hiking time: About 2 hours
Seasons/schedule: Park open from 4 a.m. to 10:30 p.m.
Fees and permits: None
Trail contact: Stone State Park, 5001 Talbot Rd., Sioux City 51103; (712) 255-4698; Stone@dnr.iowa.gov; iowadnr.gov/Places-to-Go/State-Parks/Iowa-State-Parks/Stone-State-Park
Dog-friendly: Yes, on leash
Trail surface: Natural (dirt)
Land status: Stone State Park (Iowa DNR)

Nearest town: Sioux City
Maps: USGS Sioux City North, IA, SD; park map available online
Other trail users: Equestrians and mountain bikers
Special considerations: Practice appropriate trail etiquette: Hikers and bikers yield to equestrians, while bikers also yield to hikers.
Amenities available: Restrooms, water, and camping in Stone State Park
Maximum grade: 19%; there are several notable climbs, beginning from the trailhead to Mt. Lucia (more than 200 feet over 1 mile) to two steep but short climbs on Broken Toe Trail (more than 100 feet gain over less than one-quarter mile)
Cell service: Average, although dense tree cover may restrict reception in places

Finding the trailhead: From the park office, head south on Pammel Road. Mark's Glen Trailhead is located near the T-junction with the road leading to Wahkaw Shelter and Pammel Shelter. GPS: N42° 32.886' W96° 27.877'

Trail conditions: The multiuse trails are well maintained and marked at important junctions. They can become soft and muddy after rain, so if your activity leaves marks, turn around to avoid trail degradation. The trails receive heavy traffic.

The Hike

Along IA 12, between the turnoffs for the Dorothy Pecaut Nature Center and Stone State Park, you'll find some of the few exposures of bedrock in the Loess Hills. The Missouri River southward bend cuts deeply into the hills on the east side of the floodplain. In the 90-million-year-old Cretaceous bedrock you'll see dark bands of lignite and iron oxide staining amid limestone, sandstone, and shale. Fossils of both

Big Sioux River and IA 12 from Dakota Point

marine and land-dwelling organisms have been found here, testament to the shifting shoreline of a shallow sea that once covered the Midwest.

Historical accounts of Stone State Park and adjacent Mount Talbot State Preserve from the 1800s describe the hills as being almost treeless, covered in billowing prairies. Today the endless prairies have been whittled down to south- and west-facing ridgetops. Although the prairie is diminished in size, you'll still find incredible diversity within the remnants. During May and June, look for large-flowered beardtongue, prairie larkspur, and prairie turnip. Both big and little bluestem serve as caterpillar hosts for crossline, dusted, and Ottoe skippers, aptly named for their bouncing flight.

Beginning in the 1880s, Daniel Talbot, a lawyer and amateur naturalist in Sioux City, acquired 7,500 acres along the Big Sioux River in Woodbury and Plymouth Counties. He grew crops, grazed livestock, and raised a plethora of exotic animals. When Talbot ran into financial problems, Sioux City banker Thomas Stone assumed Talbot's debt and the land. Stone's family deeded the land to the city in 1912, but it was transferred to the state soon after and became a state park in 1935. In 1989, 90 acres on the north side of the property were designated as Mount Talbot State Preserve for its diverse prairie ridgetops and butterfly species.

Mount Talbot State Preserve is on the northern end of Stone State Park.

The 15-mile multiuse trail system in Stone State Park facilitates an endless combination of trails for long or short hikes. While the trails in the northern section of the park are hiking-only, the best trails to hike are on the multiuse trails in the southern half of the park. Dakota Point and Elk Point Overlooks are worth a stop, but no visit to Stone State Park would be complete without a hike to Mount Lucia. The hike beginning near Wahkaw Shelter climbs more than 200 feet over 1 mile to Mount Lucia, which overlooks the Big Sioux River as it nears its confluence with the Missouri River.

The Dorothy Pecaut Nature Center is located in the extreme southwest corner of the state park. Its trail system connects with Stone State Park at Mount Lucia. You'll find stellar natural history exhibits about the Loess Hills inside. The nature center is the perfect place to bring a troop of kids on a summer afternoon. They'll delight in the indoor beehive and walk-under prairie and expend their energy on the short but satisfying trails and at the nature playscape.

From Mount Lucia, continue on Broken Toe Trail, Loess Trail, and Ruth's Ridge following pleasant, forested trails back to Wahkaw Shelter. The Carolyn Benne Nature Trail, named for the local environmental educator who started the Loess Hills Prairie Seminar, is an excellent trail that explores the northern part of the state park. This

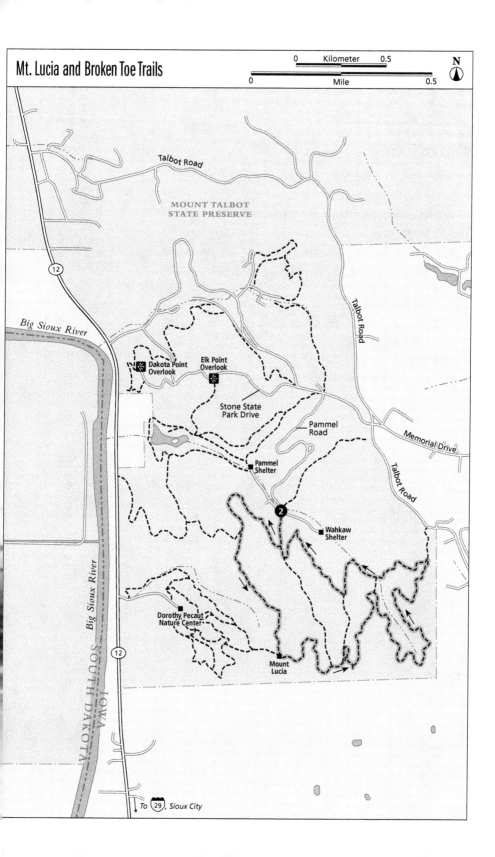

Mt. Lucia and Broken Toe Trails

0 Kilometer 0.5
0 Mile 0.5

N

Talbot Road

MOUNT TALBOT
STATE PRESERVE

Big Sioux River

12

Dakota Point
Overlook

Elk Point
Overlook

Talbot Road

Stone State
Park Drive

Pammel
Road

Memorial Drive

Pammel
Shelter

Talbot Road

2

Wahkaw
Shelter

Big Sioux River

12

Dorothy Pecaut
Nature Center

IOWA
SOUTH DAKOTA

Mount
Lucia

To 29, Sioux City

trail connects with the path that leads past Stone Lodge (built of Sioux quartzite from Gitchie Manitou State Preserve) and through Dakota Valley up to Dakota Point. From this overlook you can look west to Nebraska and South Dakota and see the Missouri and Big Sioux Rivers as well.

Miles and Directions

0.00 Begin at the trailhead and head south on Longfoot Trail.

0.10 Turn right (northwest) onto Mt. Lucia Trail.

0.60 Continue straight (south) on Mt. Lucia Trail.

1.10 Mount Lucia.

1.50 Continue on east Broken Toe at the junction with Mark's Glen.

1.60 Continue south on Broken Toe at the junction with Ruth Ridge.

2.10 Continue east, then south on Broken Toe at the junction with Loess Trail.

3.10 Left (west) onto Loess Trail.

3.40 Keep right (west) to stay on Loess Trail.

3.70 Turn right (northwest) to follow Ruth Ridge.

4.10 Turn right (north) onto Mark's Glen to return to the trailhead.

4.27 Arrive back at the trailhead.

3 Sylvan Runkel State Preserve

There's good reason this is home to the Loess Hills Prairie Seminar: Sylvan Runkel State Preserve and the surrounding Loess Hills Wildlife Management Area encompass some of the most incredible terrain for hiking and naturalizing in western Iowa. From your ridgetop perch, billowing bunchgrasses and prairie wildflowers of every hue encircle you. Dramatic, forest-covered hills extend to the south and east. To the west the wrinkled hills plummet down to a patchwork quilt of agricultural fields in the Little Sioux and Missouri floodplains.

Start: Sylvan Runkel State Preserve sign on Oak Avenue

Elevation gain: 430 feet total gain; 1,120 (lowest) to 1,357 feet (highest)

Distance: 2.76-mile out-and-back

Difficulty: Moderate due to rugged terrain

Hiking time: About 1.5 hours

Seasons/schedule: Trails open daily year-round

Fees and permits: None

Trail contact: Iowa Department of Natural Resources, Wallace State Office Building, 502 E. 9th St., Des Moines, 50319; (515) 669-7614; iowadnr.gov/Places-to-Go/State-Preserves

Dog-friendly: Yes, however, no dogs are allowed during nesting season from Mar 15 to July 15

Trail surface: Natural (narrow dirt footpath)

Land status: Sylvan Runkel State Preserve (Iowa DNR)

Nearest town: Onawa, 12 miles to the southwest

Maps: USGS Castana, IA

Other trail users: None

Special considerations: Hunting is permitted, so check season dates and dress accordingly.

Amenities available: None

Maximum grade: 19%; the steepest climb is at the beginning, gaining 200 feet over one-half mile; once you are on the ridge, there are ups and downs but shorter and less steep than the initial climb up the ridge

Cell service: Below average

Finding the trailhead: From Onawa, head north on CR L12. After 7.2 miles, keep right (northeast) onto Nutmeg Avenue and continue for 2 miles. Turn south onto Oak Avenue, then after 1.3 miles reach the Sylvan Runkel sign on the west side of the road. There is a small parking area opposite the sign on the east side of the road, or you can keep right (southwest) at the next fork onto 178th Street and turn into the parking area on the south side of the road (which also serves as the site of the annual Loess Hills Prairie Seminar). GPS: N42° 6.166' W95° 58.279'

Trail conditions: Since Sylvan Runkel is a state preserve, there are no established, maintained trails. However, there are "social trails" that are well-worn footpaths. The path is difficult to discern at the beginning, but once you reach the ridge, it is easier to follow. The footpaths are narrow dirt trails with no waymarkings. There is yucca along the trail, so either wear long pants or step around the sharp yucca leaves. The trail receives light traffic.

Catsteps are staircase-like features common on hillslopes of the Loess Hills.

The Hike

Originally acquired by the state in 1973, the 3,000-acre Loess Hills Management Area was selected in 1985 by the National Park System to be part of a 10,420-acre national natural landmark. In 1996, a 330-acre parcel of high-quality prairie in the area's northwestern corner was designated as the Sylvan Runkel State Preserve, commemorating one of the most respected naturalists to ever walk the Loess Hills. Sylvan Runkel's reverence for natural communities and ability to captivate audiences with his natural history teachings inspired many Iowans. Along with his many modes of conservation-oriented work, he was a cherished presenter at the Loess Hills Prairie Seminar until his death in 1995.

There are no established trails at the preserve, but a well-worn footpath follows the narrow, branching ridgeline covered with tall- and mixed-grass prairie. From atop a high point along the ridge, notice that woodlands thrive on the moist north- and east-facing slopes. Though the preserve is dominated by prairie, colonizing shrubs such as eastern red cedar, rough-leaved dogwood, and sumac climb up the ravines, which are soon invaded by woodlands. Looking at the hills from atop the ridges, note the terraced "catsteps," virtual staircases leading down the hills. These were created by loess's tendency toward slipping and slumping and were probably exacerbated by grazing cattle.

If you've visited native prairies throughout spring and summer, you know that the height of prairie plants usually depends on when they bloom. In early spring, when vegetation above ground hasn't had much of a chance to grow, blooming flowers don't need to be very tall to collect sunlight or be pollinated. The opposite occurs in autumn, when bunchgrasses and goldenrod are head-high, competing for sunlight and pollinators.

Pasqueflower is the first wildflower you'll see blooming, dotting the hillsides with shades of violet soon after the snow has melted. Take this time to look for the small soil lichens, hidden by tall vegetation during summer. Get down on your hands and knees to peer closely at the ground. Small, multicolored discs start coming into view. Spend a short time looking, and you'll begin to find the interlocking patterns of lichens colonizing the interface between earth and sky.

By May, a very tiny fern named prairie moonwort shoots up its fragile 2-to-3-inch-tall fiddleheads, which sporulate and disappear by early June. First discovered by Loess Hills Prairie Seminar attendees in 1982, prairie moonwort has since been found in several other Loess Hills locales, as well as in Minnesota and Nebraska.

To hike the state preserve, park in the parking lot at the Loess Hills Prairie Seminar campground (the only sign is an interpretive panel installed by Golden Hills RC&D) and head north on Oak Avenue. You'll see a brown state preserve sign on the west side of the road. The ridge you want to get onto lies directly behind (north of) the sign, and a small trail leads up to it. The first section of the trail leading up the hillside may be hard to discern, but once you reach the ridgeline, the footpaths are well defined. Follow the ridges to the northwesternmost point in the preserve with awesome views of the Missouri River floodplain.

To the south and east of Sylvan Runkel State Preserve, you'll find the more extensively forested Loess Hills Wildlife Management Area. Wide-spreading bur oaks intermingle with Kentucky coffee trees, American and slippery elms, white ash, and bitternut hickory. To explore the wildlife area, park at the southernmost access point, north of 205th Street. The trail will take you onto a ridge; it will likely require

LOESS HILLS PRAIRIE SEMINAR

Since 1977, when a small group who wanted to study the unique landform first began to meet, the Loess Hills Prairie Seminar has exalted the natural, cultural, historical, and aesthetic value of western Iowa's corrugated, pie-crust ridges and dark, hidden hollows. The annual event has grown considerably over the years as the public has become aware of the ecological and recreational value of the Loess Hills. A temporary campground is set up on Oak Avenue near Sylvan Runkel State Preserve. Field sessions, events, guided hikes and bike rides, and lectures fill one weekend in early summer.

Sylvan Runkel State Preserve

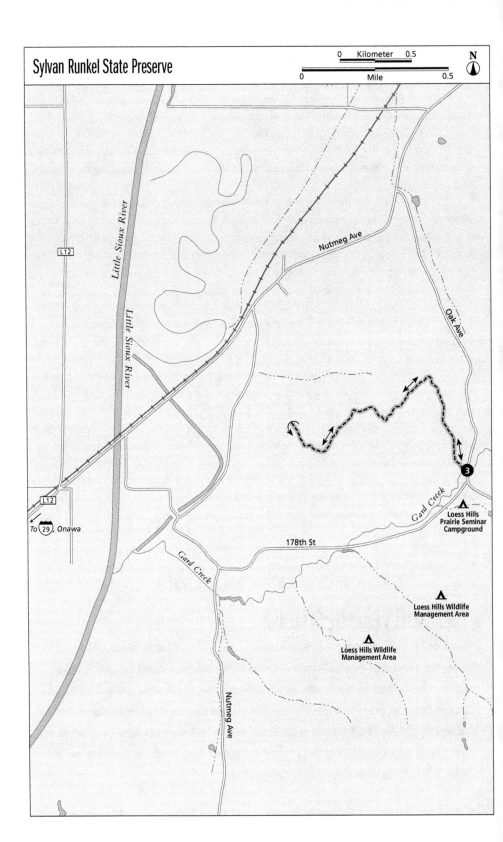

Fall is a beautiful and quiet time to hike at Sylvan Runkel.

bushwhacking and wayfinding to reach the ridge, but once you do, enjoy the wide prairie-covered ridgetop with sweeping views of the Loess Hills in Monona County.

Miles and Directions

0.00 Begin at the Sylvan Runkel State Preserve sign on Oak Avenue, heading northwest up the ridge.

0.46 Turn left (southwest).

Option: You can explore the two ridges heading northeast and northwest, but you will have to return to this junction and continue along the ridge heading southwest.

0.78 Turn right (northwest).

Option: Explore the ridge heading south, then return to this junction.

1.38 Reach the top of a ridge; you can explore the spur ridges here, then turn around and follow the same path to the trailhead.

2.76 Arrive back at Oak Avenue Trailhead.

4 Loess Hills Scenic Overlook Trail

If you've seen photos of the Loess Hills, you have likely seen one of the Loess Hills Scenic Overlook. Dubbed "The Spot" by local legend Walter Ordway, a narrow footpath leads south along a prairie ridge from the photogenic scenic overlook. The trail descends the ridge and crosses restored prairie, then climbs another ridge to complete a short 1-mile loop that pays dividends: This is one of the best hikes in Iowa for scenic views.

Start: Loess Hills Scenic Overlook
Elevation gain: 171 feet total gain; 1,296 (lowest) to 1,479 feet (highest)
Distance: 0.95-mile double loop
Difficulty: Moderate due to rugged terrain and steep climbs up ridges
Hiking time: 1–1.5 hours
Seasons/schedule: The state forest is open daily, year-round.
Fees and permits: None
Trail contact: Loess Hills State Forest, PO Box 158, 206 Polk St., Pisgah 51564; (712) 456-2924; LoessHills_Forest@dnr.iowa.gov; iowadnr.gov/Places-to-Go/State-Forests/Loess-Hills-State-Forest
Dog-friendly: Yes, on leash
Trail surface: Natural (grass, dirt)

Land status: Loess Hills State Forest Preparation Canyon Unit (Iowa DNR)
Nearest town: Moorhead, 6 miles to the east
Maps: USGS Moorhead NW, IA; trail map available online
Other trail users: None
Special considerations: Hunting is allowed in the state forest, so check season dates and dress accordingly. Prescribed burns are used as a conservation practice, so check the state forest website for updates.
Amenities available: None
Maximum grade: 15%; there is a steep section where a footbridge used to cross a road cut, in addition to two steep climbs up ridges, the first nearly 150 feet over one-third mile and the second almost 200 feet over nearly one-half mile
Cell service: Average

Finding the trailhead: From Moorhead, head southwest on IA 183 for 2 miles. Turn west onto 314th Street, then after 2 miles turn northwest to continue on 314th Street. After 1 mile, keep right (west) onto Oak Avenue, following the signs for the Loess Hills Scenic Overlook. The parking area is one-half mile ahead on the north side of Oak Avenue; the Loess Hills Scenic Overlook is on the south side of the road. GPS: N41° 54.314' W95° 56.746'

Trail conditions: The trails are narrow dirt footpaths atop the ridges and mowed grass trails in the valley; they are easy to follow but there are no waymarkings. The section descending and immediately climbing out of the road cut in the first ridge is steep and will be very slippery after rain or with snow and ice; use caution and trekking poles are recommended. The trail receives moderate traffic.

The Hike

In 1986, the National Park Service studied the possibility of establishing a national park in the Loess Hills, but because 95 percent of the hills are privately owned, it

A narrow footpath along the ridge begins at the scenic overlook.

wasn't feasible. Instead, the National Park Service designated two areas in Harrison and Monona Counties as national natural landmarks.

State and county agencies were left with the major responsibility of protecting and managing the future of this uniquely Iowan treasure. When state lottery monies became available through REAP grants in the late 1980s, the Department of Natural Resources began acquiring land and established this state forest. One day, it is hoped, the parcel will encompass 20,000 acres of the Loess Hills. Thus far, the forest includes 11,484 acres purchased by the DNR and divided into four units (Little Sioux, Mondamin, Pisgah, and Preparation Canyon). Hundred of acres have been replanted to red and white oaks, green and white ashes, and black walnut; hundreds of additional acres have been replanted to native prairie. Prescribed burns are used annually, and invasive woodlands are cut down.

Start your tour of the forest with a visit to the Loess Hills Scenic Overlook, located just off 314th Street at the north end of the Preparation Canyon Unit. The overlook is perched atop a narrow prairie-covered ridge that extends southward toward the panorama of valleys and hilltops that make up the unit. This is one of the most photographed views in the Loess Hills. A monument at the entrance to the overlook notes that it was dubbed "The Spot" by Walter Ordway Jr., a local legend and world traveler. Ordway designed the original logo for the Loess Hills National Scenic Byway and founded the Loess Hill Hospitality Association.

A 0.75-mile loop trail follows the ridge south from the overlook and drops down into a valley with restored prairie. Ascend the next ridge to the east, where the trail turns north, bringing you back up to the overlook. On either side of the ridges during summer, a spectrum of wildflowers draws hundreds of nectar-seeking butterflies. There are additional trails that connect to the scenic overlook, so you can lengthen your hike if the 1-mile loop is too short.

Additionally, a maze of mowed firebreaks and ridgetop trails in the Mondamin and Pisgah Units can be explored with intrepid motivation and the aid of a compass. Keep in mind that you're never far from a road; as long as you keep to the ridgetops,

PREPARATION CANYON STATE PARK

During the 1850s, this valley was home to a group of Mormon settlers, who described it as their "school of preparation for the life beyond." Today, the state park trails can be hiked in preparation for longer, steeper, more exhausting hikes in the neighboring Loess Hills State Forest. Trails totaling 6.68 miles miles lead through cool hollows and ascend steep ridges that overlook the 4,068-acre Preparation Canyon Unit adjacent to the south and west. Ten hike-in campsites provide a welcome respite from state park camping often dominated by recreational vehicles. Sarah's Trail connects to state forest trails, including the Jones Creek Pond Ridge Loop described in the next chapter.

Loess Hills Scenic Overlook Trail

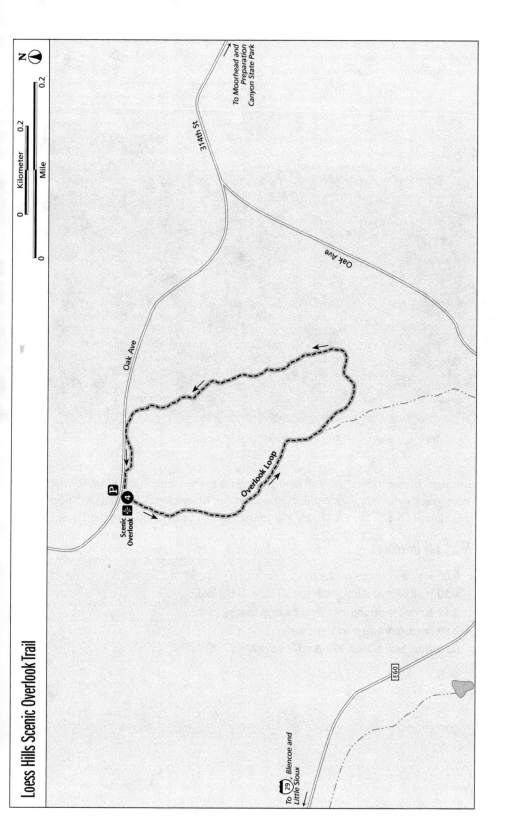

N

Kilometer
0   0.2   0.2

Mile
0   0.2

314th St

To Moorhead and
Preparation
Canyon State Park

Oak Ave

Oak Ave

Overlook Loop

P

Scenic
Overlook

4

E60

29

To Blencoe and
Little Sioux

"The Spot" is one of the classic viewpoints in the Loess Hills.

the vistas in every direction will help guide your movements. The trail up the narrow, steep razor ridge from the south trailhead of the Mondamin Unit (located near the junction of IA 127 and IA 183) is one of the author's favorite hikes in the Loess Hills.

Miles and Directions

0.00 From the overlook, head south.

0.20 Head southwest downhill to hike a shorter 1-mile loop.

0.40 Turn left (east) and then climb the ridge heading north.

0.80 Reach Oak Avenue and head west.

0.95 Arrive back at Loess Hills Scenic Overlook.

5 Jones Creek Pond Ridge Loop

Nestled in the Loess Hills between the Little Sioux and Soldier Rivers, the Preparation Canyon Unit contains some of the most remote trails in the Loess Hills State Forest. A devastating wildfire in 2023 burned over 2,400 acres of state forest land, but the fire has given the prairie a chance to fight back against woody invaders like eastern red cedar, dogwood, and sumac. Forest trails around Jones Creek Pond give access to trails along ridges with serene vistas of prairie and forest fighting a slow battle. Combine this loop with other trails in the state forest and adjacent state park for one of the best backpacking hikes in Iowa.

Start: Jones Creek Pond picnic shelter and parking area
Elevation gain: 643 feet total gain; 1,121 (lowest) to 1,447 feet (highest)
Distance: 6.6-mile loop
Difficulty: Difficult due to distance, rugged terrain, and wayfinding in sections
Hiking time: 2.5–3 hours
Seasons/schedule: The state forest is open daily, year-round.
Fees and permits: None
Trail contact: Loess Hills State Forest, PO Box 158, 206 Polk St., Pisgah 51564; (712) 456-2924; LoessHills_Forest@dnr.iowa.gov; iowadnr.gov/Places-to-Go/State-Forests/Loess-Hills-State-Forest
Dog-friendly: Yes, on leash
Trail surface: Natural (grass, dirt) and gravel road
Land status: Loess Hills State Forest Preparation Canyon Unit (Iowa DNR)
Nearest town: Pisgah, 3.5 miles to the south

Maps: USGS Moorhead NW, IA and USGS Pisgah, IA; trail map for Jones Creek Pond and the Preparation Canyon Unit are available on the state forest website; the most up-to-date trail map is available on Golden Hills RC&D's website (goldenhillsrcd.org/lhsf.html)
Other trail users: None
Special considerations: Hunting is permitted in the state forest, so check hunting season dates and dress accordingly; Iowa DNR uses prescribed fire to manage the state forest, so check the website for updates
Amenities available: Picnic shelter at the Jones Creek Pond parking area; dispersed camping is allowed throughout the state forest
Maximum grade: 14%; the steepest climbs are from the south end of Jones Creek Pond to the trails west of the pond and the climb from CR E60 to another ridge on the northern end of the loop; both climb nearly 100 feet over a short distance; the hike along the west ridge to CR E60 climbs 250 feet over 2 miles
Cell service: Weak to average

Finding the trailhead: From Pisgah, head north on IA 183 for 2.3 miles. Turn left (west) onto 340th Street, then after 0.7 miles turn right (north) onto CR E60. Keep left (northwest) at the next fork, then turn left (west) to enter the parking area at Jones Creek Pond. GPS: N41° 52.267' W95° 55.523'

   Trail conditions: The trails are generally in good condition, although they can become slightly overgrown in summer. There are many intersecting trails in the state forest, so take a map (the map on the Golden Hills website is more accurate than the maps on the state forest website) and follow a GPS tracker. Trail markers provide directional information but not trail names. The trail along the eastern ridge is more difficult to follow than the western ridge. The trails receive light traffic.

Frozen Jones Creek Pond in winter

The Hike

On April 13, 2023, a catastrophic wildfire ignited in the Preparation Canyon Unit of the Loess Hills State Forest. The fire started near Jones Creek Pond, and strong winds carried embers north into old stands of bur oak timber. The fire burned 2,400 acres of state forest land and 3,770 acres total in Monona County. The interagency effort to contain the large wildfire in two days exemplified the cohesion fostered during the Loess Hills Cooperative Burn Week, an annual fire management training event that brings together conservation professionals from various agencies.

This hike traverses two ridges that rise near Jones Creek Pond; both ridges suffered damage during the wildfire. There is a parking lot and a shelter on the east side of the pond, an ideal place to have a picnic after finishing the hike. This loop can be followed in either direction but clockwise leaves the easiest part at the end. Beginning at the picnic shelter, the trail borders the southern end of Jones Creek Pond before entering the woods on the western side of the pond. You can explore the trail system of Jones Creek Pond as it meanders through a young forest of basswood, bur oak, bitternut hickory, black walnut, and other woodland species. Eventually, take the trail named Prairie Pass (trail markers do not have trail names, only directional information) as it heads south to the forest's edge. Here, the trail turns west and climbs uphill to reach the first ridge of this hike.

Once you reach the top of the ridge, the trail heads north along a classic example of the prairie ridges that once dominated the Loess Hills. Today, unfortunately, it is becoming exceedingly difficult to encounter prairie remnants in the Loess Hills. Enjoy the uninterrupted path along the ridge's crest with expansive views west. Both ridges this hike follows provide clear examples of the encroaching woodlands as they move uphill, particularly on their eastern slopes. As you walk north along the western ridge on this loop, notice bur oak and other trees on your right as the woodland comes right up to the ridgetop. On your left, you will find the invasive eastern red cedar, either solitary or in dense stands, that are the target of the prescribed burns and chainsaws of state forest staff because it shades out native prairie grass. Several skeletal remains of dead eastern red cedars dot the western slope of the first ridge.

After 2 miles, the trail descends from the ridge through some trees to CR E60 and, after crossing the road, climbs to reach a clearing. Your initial instinct is to follow the ridge on your right heading south. Instead, continue ahead through a broad prairie heading due northeast. The trail bends southeast and becomes less open. Eventually, you will reach a confusing intersection. Don't take the hard right that descends west to the cornfield. Also, resist the urge to continue straight on the wide path under trees; this leads to another cornfield on the eastern side of the ridge. You want to stay on top of the ridge, so look for a narrow footpath cut deep into the earth that climbs up onto the grassy ridge. This intersection sorely needs a trail marker to point hikers in the right direction.

Once on top of the ridge, the trail comes and goes but the path is simple: Continue atop the ridge heading southeast. The occasional Iowa DNR trail marker will confirm that you are on the right track. When you reach a deep roadcut in the ridge, the plan is the same: Climb down, then back up to continue along the crest of the ridge heading southeast. Eventually, the prairie is overtaken by eastern red cedar on both sides of the ridge. This forested section is an excellent spot to encounter wildlife, from a whitetail buck that snorts at you then gallops down the ridge, to dozens of turkey vultures taking flight from the red cedar tops as you walk along the trail below. The trail descends under the canopy of cedar trees until it reaches a cornfield. Head southwest toward a gravel road, following it to reach a gate and a small parking turnout off CR E60. Cross the road with Jones Creek Pond ahead of you, staying on the trail on the eastern side of the pond.

Combine this loop with additional trails in the state forest and in the adjacent state park to create one of the best backpacking experiences in Iowa. Water sources are extremely scarce in the Loess Hills, making extended backpacking treks difficult. Park in the overnight lot at Preparation Canyon State Park, then hike to one of the ten hike-in campsites. You can hike back to your car if you need water the following day. Filtering or boiling water from Jones Creek Pond is another option.

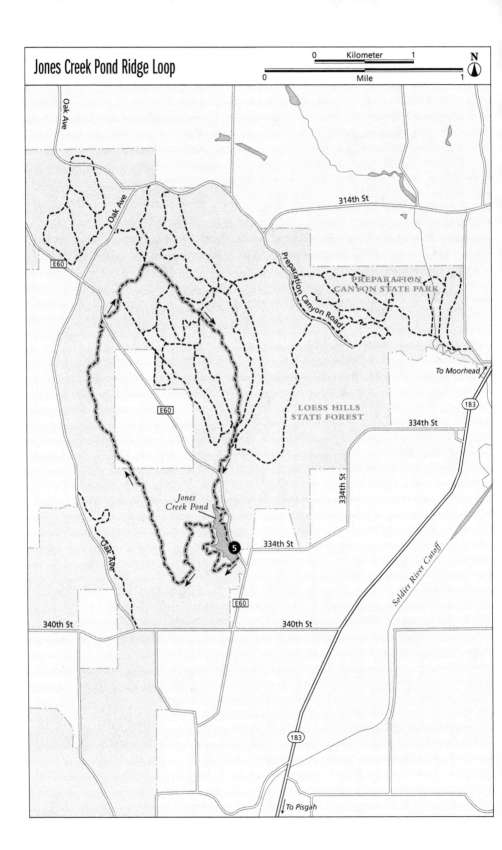

Jones Creek Pond Ridge Loop

0   Kilometer   1

0   Mile   1

N

Oak Ave

314th St

Oak Ave

E60

PREPARATION
CANYON STATE PARK

Preparation Canyon Road

To Moorhead

E60

LOESS HILLS
STATE FOREST

183

334th St

334th St

Jones
Creek Pond

334th St

5

Oak Ave

Soldier River Cutoff

340th St

340th St

E60

183

To Pisgah

Miles and Directions

0.00 Begin at the trailhead for Oak Trail and head southeast. Turn right (southwest) at the boat launch.

0.60 Turn right (east) at the trail marker.

1.00 Turn left (south) at the trail marker to follow Walnut Trail uphill heading south.

1.20 Keep straight (southwest) past a trial marker to continue on Walnut Trail West.

1.30 Continue straight (south) past a trail marker; Walnut Trail West becomes Prairie Pass.

1.40 Reach an open prairie and turn right (southwest) at the trail marker to continue uphill.

1.60 At the ridge top, turn right (north) to follow the trail north along the ridge.

2.90 Continue straight (north) at a crossroads.

3.60 Cross CR E6, pass through the gate, and continue northwest uphill.

3.70 Turn left (north) at the trail marker.

3.90 Continue straight (east) past the trail marker.

4.10 Continue straight (northeast) past the trail marker.

4.40 Follow a narrow rut heading south that climbs uphill just to the right of the wide trail. At the top in a clearing, continue southeast following along the top of the ridge.

4.70 Reach a cliff cutting the ridge in half. Descend through the trees to your right, cross the road, and climb the ridge again at the trail marker to continue southeast along the ridgetop.

5.00 Continue straight at the trail marker, heading due south.

5.60 Reach a field and turn left (south) at the trail marker. Follow the gravel path south toward the road.

6.00 Continue straight (south) through a gate and parking area, cross the road, and take the trail that leads back to Jones Creek Pond.

6.10 Continue straight (south) at the trail marker, passing the wooden bridge on your right.

6.60 Arrive back at Jones Creek Pond picnic shelter and parking area.

6 Brent's Trail

Iowa DNR forester Brent Olson envisioned a long-distance hiking trail across the Loess Hills similar to the Appalachian Trail. Three years after the long-time state forester passed away, Brent's Trail was opened to fulfill his dream. The 8-mile rugged trail traverses some of the most beautiful terrain in the Loess Hills, including two incredible road cuts. A fall hike under golden canopies and 6-foot-tall big bluestem is one of the best in Iowa.

Start: Murray Hill Scenic Overlook
Elevation gain: 1,407 feet on the original 8-mile trail; 1,893 feet on the 11-mile extension
Distance: 8-mile or 11-mile point-to-point
Difficulty: Very difficult due to rugged terrain, distance, and rough trails
Hiking time: At least 4 hours
Seasons/schedule: The state forest is open daily year-round.
Fees and permits: None
Trail contact: Loess Hills State Forest, PO Box 158, 206 Polk St., Pisgah 51564; (712) 456-2924; LoessHills_Forest@dnr.iowa.gov; iowadnr.gov/Places-to-Go/State-Forests/Loess-Hills-State-Forest
Dog-friendly: Yes, on leash
Trail surface: Natural (dirt, grass) and gravel roads

Land status: Loess Hills State Forest Little Sioux Unit (Iowa DNR) and Gleason-Hubel Wildlife Area (Harrison County Conservation)
Nearest town: Pisgah, 4.5 miles to the east
Maps: USGS Little Sioux, IA, NE and USGS Pisgah, IA; official trail map available online at goldenhillsrcd.org/brentstrail.html
Other trail users: None
Special considerations: Since it is a point-to-point hike, you will either need two cars or hike back on Brent's Trail or Larpenteur Memorial Road.
Amenities available: None
Maximum grade: 23%; there are numerous steep ascents and descents throughout the entirety of the trail
Cell service: Average to above average along ridges, below average in road cuts and forested valleys

Finding the trailhead: From Pisgah, head west on CR F20. After 4.3 miles, turn south into the parking area at Murray Hill Scenic Overlook. From I-29, take exit 95 and head west toward River Sioux on Easton Trail, which becomes Vinte Street in River Sioux. After 1.2 miles, turn north onto Main Street in Little Sioux. Main Street becomes Easton Trail/CR F20 as you leave Little Sioux. Continue northeast for 1.5 miles, then turn north to stay on Easton Trail. At the next fork, keep right (northwest), then turn south into the parking area for Murray Hill Scenic Overlook. GPS: N41° 50.335' W96° 0.012'

Trail conditions: The trail is well marked with steel bur oak trail markers. Hikers frequently complain about overgrown trails, but Brent's Trail was envisioned as a natural trail, so expect tall grasses and overgrown conditions. There are no safe water sources, so bring plenty of water. The trail receives heavy traffic near Murray Hill and Gleason-Hubel, but you can find solitude on most of the trail.

Prairie and forest trails in the Little Sioux Unit

The Hike

After opening in 2019, Brent's Trail quickly became one of the best trails in Iowa. The 8-mile trail was the vision of the late Brent Olson, a long-time state forester who passed away after a battle with cancer. Brent envisioned a long-distance hiking trail through the Loess Hills. In 2019, Harrison County Conservation and the Iowa DNR opened Brent's Trail in honor of Olson's dream. The 8-mile hike connects Murray Hill Scenic Overlook and Gleason-Hubel Wildlife Area; an extension to the southern end of the state forest's Little Sioux Unit offers an 11-mile option. A section of trail is remnant, native midgrass prairie that is mowed once in the late spring or early summer to allow uncommon forbs a chance to persist.

Brent's Trail presents logistical challenges in addition to its physical demands. If you are hiking with others, simply park one car where you intend to finish, then drive to your starting point and begin your hike (don't forget the other car!). Intrepid solo hikers can hike the entire trail twice, or pick a point to turn around and return where they began. For example, start from Murray Hill Scenic Overlook and hike to Fountainbleu Cemetery, then take 124th Trail west and CR F20 north to rejoin Brent's Trail back to Murray Hill Scenic Overlook (3 miles total). Additionally, the parking lot at 1715 138th Trail is roughly 4 miles from either Murray Hill or Gleason-Hubel, so you could start from either trailhead for an 8-mile out-and-back.

LOHI TRAIL

After the outbreak of the COVID-19 pandemic in 2020, Kelly Madigan decided to hike the entirety of western Iowa's Loess Hills. With the help of her partner, volunteers, and conservation professionals, Kelly hiked from Akron to Hamburg in the fall of 2020. The following year, Kelly partnered with Golden Hills RC&D to hold the first LoHi Trek. The event was created in the spirit of Kelly's trailblazing journey the year before: connecting with the Loess Hills through observation, contemplation, and community. The trek was such a success that two more were held in 2022 and one in 2023. Plans are to continue the tradition, rotating to different regions of the Loess Hills every year, with the ultimate goal of creating a long-distance thru-hike similar to the Appalachian Trail. For more information visit www.visitloesshills.org/lohi.html.

There are numerous ways to "hike" Brent's Trail, but everything being equal, hiking south from Murray Hill Scenic Overlook provides the best views. Hiking the steep terrain near Murray Hill with fresh legs is another advantage to starting at the northern trailhead. The hike begins with a steep climb immediately from the parking lot, reaching a picnic table and, later, a bench with stunning views south of the Loess Hills and Missouri River floodplain. Instead of following the ridge, the trail descends steeply down the south face of Murray Hill (hiking poles come in handy on this section). Follow the bur oak trail markers across the meadow, then look for a line of markers climbing a steep spur ridge. Brent's Trail descends and ascends steeply in this area because part of the main ridge east of Murray Hill is private property; without an easement, the trail had to be routed down and then back up to stay on state forest land.

During the first 1.5 miles, the trail traverses spur ridges that form three horseshoe-shaped valleys. At the mouth of the third valley is Fountainbleu Cemetery; the namesake of Larpenteur Memorial Road, an early settler and French fur trader, is buried here. South of the cemetery is 124th Trail, an excellent example of a primitive Loess Hills road. This section is no longer maintained by the county (named a Level C road in Iowa), so hikers have the dirt track to themselves. Road cuts in the Loess Hills have to be nearly vertical because loess soil slumps at lesser grades. Roots hang from 30-foot or higher road cuts, while the tree canopy forms a stunning tunnel of golden leaves in fall.

Brent's Trail leaves 124th Trail once it becomes suitable for vehicles again—look for trail markers here and in the following section as there are several intersecting state forest trails over the next few miles. The junction with state forest trail LS-2 (2.8 miles from Murray Hill; LS-2 is marked on the official trail map) was one of Brent Olson's favorite views in the entire Loess Hills State Forest: The Little Sioux and Missouri Rivers are visible to the southwest. Enjoy the 6-foot-tall big bluestem during a fall hike down the ridge to the parking lot at 1715 138th Trail, which is a great spot to take a break underneath the shade of the large cottonwood.

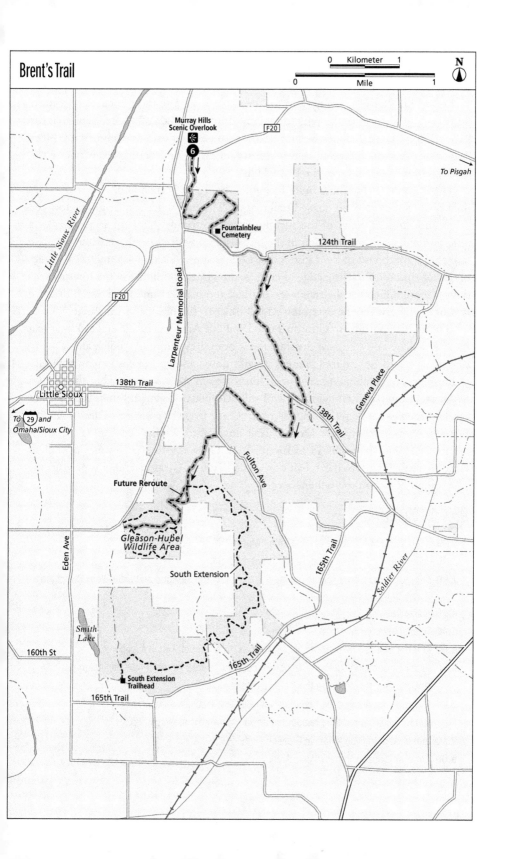

Brent's Trail

0 Kilometer 1
0 Mile 1

N

Murray Hills
Scenic Overlook

6

To Pisgah

Little Sioux River

F20

Fountainbleu
Cemetery

124th Trail

Larpenteur Memorial Road

F20

138th Trail

Little Sioux

To 29 and
Omaha/Sioux City

138th Trail

Geneva Place

Fulton Ave

Future Reroute

Gleason-Hubel
Wildlife Area

Eden Ave

South Extension

165th Trail

Soldier River

Smith
Lake

160th St

South Extension
Trailhead

165th Trail

165th Trail

Continue north on 138th Trail, then turn west at the "1700" blue 911 sign. The tough, 200-foot climb is followed by 2 miles along ridges and Fulton Avenue, a classic Loess Hills "Level B" minimum maintenance road. The most fascinating section, however, is just north of the junction where Brent's Trail joins Fulton Avenue. At the "1368" blue 911 sign, continue north to the junction of Fulton Avenue with 138th Trail. The razor-thin spine of yellow soil separating the two dirt roads is one of the most memorable oddities in the Loess Hills.

Head south on Fulton Avenue to rejoin Brent's Trail, then after nearly one-half mile turn west at an easily missed trail marker. The trail heads south along a forested ridge with limited views of the surrounding countryside. After three-quarters of a mile, you will reach the junction of the original trail with its southern extension. The trail to the south end of the Little Sioux Unit is approximately 4.5 miles. Two miles of the extension follows the edge of crop fields, while wayfinding in the forested sections is more difficult as the trail is less defined and markers are spread out. If distance is your goal, however, the extension adds 3 miles to the original 8-mile hike.

Those that continue to Gleason-Hubel Wildlife Area will be pleased to know that the trail will be rerouted near the state forest boundary with the wildlife area. Due to lack of an easement, the trail plunges straight down a steep hill without switchbacks to immediately climb an equally steep hill to rejoin the ridge but avoid the section of private property. The new route will still take hikers down and then back up, but at a less steep grade than the original route. Once Brent's Trail enters Gleason-Hubel Wildlife Area, it follows the Orange Trail down into a valley leading to the parking lot and southern trailhead of Brent's Trail. There is a total of 3 miles of trails at Gleason-Hubel. The southern half of the Red Trail in Gleason-Hubel is perhaps the best stretch of trail in the wildlife area.

Miles and Directions

0.00 Head south uphill at the parking lot for Murray Hill Scenic Overlook.

1.70 Fountainbleu Cemetery and 124th Street road cut.

2.80 Brent Olson's favorite spot in the state forest; both the Missouri and Little Sioux Rivers are visible to the west.

4.10 138th Trail.

5.40 Fulton Avenue.

5.80 At a bur oak trail marker that is easy to miss, turn west off Fulton Avenue.

6.50 Junction: Continue south to Gleason-Hubel Wildlife Area for the 8-mile original route.

   Option: Turn east to follow the 11-mile extension route.

6.60 Two steep sections at the boundary with Gleason-Hubel Wildlife Area.

   Note: This section will be rerouted nearby to lessen the steep grades.

7.10 Turn west onto Orange Trail in Gleason-Hubel Wildlife Area.

8.00 Arrive at Gleason-Hubel Wildlife Area.

7 Badger Ridge, Lotus Loop, and Westridge

Just 20 minutes northeast of the Omaha–Council Bluffs metro, Hitchcock Nature Center is popular and busy yet enchanting. Thirteen miles of trails wind through restored prairie and dark hollows, then climb steep loess bluffs to ridgelines with fabulous views. Each fall, Hitchcock HawkWatch holds a count from the Loess Hills Lodge, from which thousands of raptors can be seen. Summer wildflowers on the ridgetop prairies are especially pretty, and seven hike-in campsites make the area a perfect overnight destination.

Start: Badger Ridge Trailhead
Elevation gain: 761 feet total gain; 1,030 (lowest) to 1,308 feet (highest)
Distance: 5-mile loop
Difficulty: Difficult
Hiking time:
Seasons/schedule: Trails open daily, year-round from 6:00 a.m. to 10:00 p.m.
Fees and permits: $5 per vehicle, payable with exact change or check at the park gate; annual memberships are also available online or at the front entrance (passes mailed at a later date)
Trail contact: Hitchcock Nature Center, 27792 Ski Hill Loop, Honey Creek 51542; (712) 545-3283; pottconservation.com/parks/hitchcock_nature_center/
Dog-friendly: Yes, on leash (please pack out dog waste)
Trail surface: Natural (dirt and grass)
Land status: Hitchcock Nature Center (Pottawattamie County Conservation)

Nearest town: Crescent, 5 miles to the south
Maps: USGS Hitchcock orvia Avenza Maps; trail maps available online and at Fox Run Ridge, Badger Ridge, Iowa West Foundation Equal Access Nature Trail/Boardwalk, and Hohneke Trailheads, or at the Loess Hills Lodge
Other trail users: None
Special considerations: Prescribed fire may occur in the park during your visit or stay (particularly during November). Please check Hitchcock's website or Facebook page for updates and details.
Amenities available: Water; restrooms at Loess Hills Lodge available 365 days a year from 6 a.m. to 10 p.m.; modern campground and hike-in campsites
Maximum grade: 19%; the 200-foot climbs up Westridge and The Chute are the steepest sections of the hike
Cell service: Below average

Finding the trailhead: From Crescent, head north on Old Lincoln Highway for 4.2 miles. Turn southwest onto Page Lane, then northwest onto Ski Hill Loop. Enter Hitchcock Nature Center and follow the signs for the Loess Hills Lodge. Badger Ridge Trailhead is located in the parking area below Loess Hills Lodge. GPS: N41° 24.802' W95° 51.442'

Trail conditions: The trails are some of the best maintained in the state of Iowa. There are trail markers with maps at each junction; trail maps are posted at the trailheads. If trails are muddy and your activity leaves a mark, turn around to prevent trail erosion and degradation. There is poison ivy alongside the trails. The trails receive heavy traffic.

View from Dorie's Bench on Badger Ridge

The Hike

A 20-minute drive from downtown Omaha, Hitchcock Nature Center lies directly beneath the flight path of the city's airport and within earshot of trains lumbering along the tracks at the park's western edge. With these urban reminders screaming at you from every direction, it might seem hard to believe that a hike in Hitchcock could be anything close to a wilderness experience, especially considering the nature center's history. In 1990, a landfill proposal on the site of the present-day Hitchcock Nature Center prompted a local citizens' group to take action to preserve the area. With help from the Iowa Natural Heritage Foundation and a Resource Enhancement and Protection (REAP) grant from the state, the Pottawattamie County Conservation Board assumed ownership of the area in 1991. Since the first edition of this guidebook was published in 2005, Hitchcock Nature Center has nearly doubled in size from 800 to 1,500 acres. It has been expertly managed over the years to restore native habitat. Many of the southwest-facing ridges in the preserve are covered in native prairie plants, such as purple prairie clover, leadplant, skeleton plant, whorled milkweed, and ground plum.

To truly appreciate the work of Pottawattamie Conservation, you should explore as much of the nature center as possible. Walk the innumerable trails to fully understand the steepness of the slope gradients of the Loess Hills. From atop the steep ridges, you'll notice the encroachment of "woodland creep" on the hilltop prairies. Below, forests in the drainages are dominated by bur oak, hackberry, green ash, and ironwood, with sumac and dogwood pushing out the edge onto the prairie. Reintroduction of fire into the preserve has slowed the shrub creep and has been a saving grace for many plants and prairie-dependent animals. In recent decades it has become evident that the Loess Hills' unique ecosystems are imperiled. Restoration projects at Hitchcock, such as prescribed burns and plantings, are critical to the continuation of this incomparable landform.

Equally important is the preservation of large tracts of land; fragmentation of the hills has contributed to the loss of habitat and species. That's why the additions of 400 adjacent acres, centered around Mount Crescent, were such important steps in Pottawattamie Conservation's long-term plan. The county purchased Mount Crescent Ski Area and the first season in 2022–23 was a resounding success. The transfer of additional land from a local landowner secured a serene pond and beautiful prairie for future generations to enjoy and protect. New trails connect Badger Ridge and Westridge with the Mount Crescent area, with the lotus-covered pond in between. There are countless combinations of trails to hike at Hitchcock; a loop following Badger Ridge to Westridge via Lotus Loop is an author favorite.

The trail south along Badger Ridge is the best in the nature center. Dorie's Bench is a popular photo spot one-half mile from the trailhead. The valley below the bench will one day be home to bison, as Pottawattamie Conservation hopes to reintroduce the keystone species to Hitchcock. Shortly after Dorie's Bench, you'll reach a junction. Take Blazing Star Trail back to the Badger Ridge Trailhead for a popular short loop hike, or head down into Hidden Valley to return via The Chute. To continue the longer hike, stay on Badger Ridge and pass the hike-in campsite to reach Lotus Loop.

The trails south of this junction were added after the acquisition of land around the pond and the ski area. Keep left (south) to reach the pond, which is covered with beautiful lotus flowers in summer. Southeast past the pond is Prairie Clover Pass, a pleasant prairie trail that heads north to connect with Blazing Star Trail. As you continue around Lotus Loop, you will pass Crescent Ridge Trail, which leads up to the eponymous ski hill with views of the Omaha skyline.

For more impressive views of Omaha and the Missouri River floodplain, take Westridge to climb more than 200 feet in one-half mile. Westridge is the most remote and rugged trail at Hitchcock and has two hike-in campsites with incredible sunset views. If you're interested in camping at one of the sites, watch the forecast for a calm night as the ridge gets pounded by strong westerly winds. Descend Westridge to follow the wooded Wildwoods and Heritage Trails to the final push up The Chute. As you hike up the steep tunnel-like trail, you will realize why this is a popular sledding route in winter. Once you reach the top of The Chute, it's a short hike back to the parking lot. If you want a little more distance, follow Fox Run Ridge to Hohneke Pond, then hike through a beautiful oak savanna on Oak Avenue to return to the main parking lot via Moonseed Path and Lodge Trail. Stop in at the Loess Hills Lodge for exceptional environmental education, interpretive displays.

The Missouri River floodplain has always served as a migration corridor for thousands of ducks and geese that arrive in spring on their way north. From mid-September

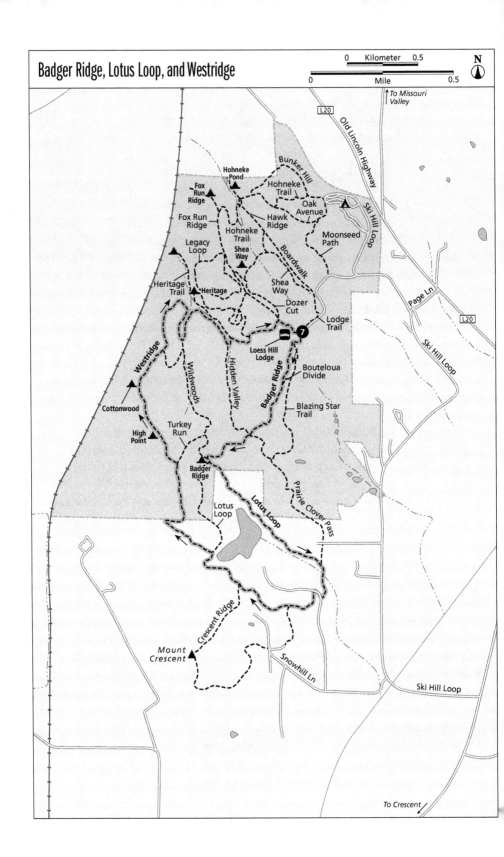

Badger Ridge, Lotus Loop, and Westridge

0   Kilometer   0.5

0   Mile   0.5

N

To Missouri Valley

L20

Old Lincoln Highway

Ski Hill Loop

Bunker Hill

Hohneke Pond

Fox Run Ridge

Hohneke Trail

Oak Avenue

Page Ln

L20

Ski Hill Loop

Fox Run Ridge

Hawk Ridge

Moonseed Path

Hohneke Trail

Legacy Loop

Shea Way

Boardwalk

Heritage Trail

Heritage

Shea Way

Dozer Cut

Lodge Trail

7

Westridge

Wildwoods

Hidden Valley

Loess Hill Lodge

Bouteloua Divide

Badger Ridge

Cottonwood

Turkey Run

Blazing Star Trail

High Point

Badger Ridge

Lotus Loop

Lotus Loop

Prairie Clover Pass

Crescent Ridge

Mount Crescent

Snowhill Ln

Ski Hill Loop

To Crescent

Keep dogs leashed at Hitchcock Nature Center.

to mid-December, cold fronts and winter weather in northern breeding grounds push the birds south in large groups. This southward movement, viewed from the Loess Hills Lodge, can be just as impressive as the springtime migration.

In the preserve, you may see birds rarely observed in Iowa, including prairie falcon, merlin, black vulture, northern goshawk, and ferruginous hawk. Hitchcock HawkWatch, associated with the Hawk Migration Association of North America, is held each fall to monitor the vast numbers of raptors that travel the Missouri River Valley "hawk highway." Around twenty species of raptors/vultures are seen every year, with an average of 13,000 migrating raptors counted annually.

Miles and Directions

0.00 Head south from Badger Ridge Trailhead.

0.60 Continue southwest on Badger Ridge.

    Option: Turn southeast onto Blazing Star to return to Badger Ridge Trailhead.

0.90 Turn south toward Lotus Loop, then keep left (south) at the next fork.

1.50 Continue south on Lotus Loop.

    Option: Turn north onto Prairie Clover Pass to hike back to Badger Ridge Trailhead via Blazing Star.

1.90 Continue west on Lotus Loop.

    Option: Turn south onto Crescent Ridge.

2.50 Turn northwest onto Westridge.

4.10 Turn north onto Wildwoods.

4.70 Keep right (east) onto The Chute.

4.80 Turn east onto Fox Run Ridge toward Loess Hills Lodge.

5.00 Arrive at Fox Run Ridge Trailhead.

8 Sunset Ridge

One of the southernmost protected areas in Iowa's Loess Hills, Waubonsie State Park serves as a refuge. Common species of southern and western plants, butterflies, birds, mammals, and reptiles—many of which are listed in Iowa as rare, threatened, or endangered species—are present at Waubonsie. Eight miles of trails in the hiking unit and an additional 8 miles in the equestrian unit wind up steep ridges, through mature woodlands, and onto ridgetop prairie remnants. They can be enjoyed in an intense hike or a mellow stroll. For naturalists who visit Waubonsie, binoculars and the appropriate field guides are absolute necessities.

Start: Scenic overlook parking area
Elevation gain: 804 feet total gain; 1,025 (lowest) to 1,273 feet (highest)
Distance: 5.2-mile loops and out-and-backs
Difficulty: Moderate
Hiking time: 2–3 hours
Seasons/schedule: Park open daily from 4 a.m. to 10:30 p.m.
Fees and permits: None for Iowa residents; entrance fee of $5 per out-of-state vehicle
Trail contact: Waubonsie State Park, 2585 Waubonsie Park Rd., Hamburg 51640; (712) 382-2786; Waubonsie@dnr.iowa.gov; https:// www.iowadnr.gov/Places-to-Go/State-Parks/ Iowa-State-Parks/Waubonsie-State-Park
Dog-friendly: Yes, on leash
Trail surface: Natural (dirt and grass)
Land status: Waubonsie State Park (Iowa DNR)

Nearest town: Sidney, 7 miles to the north, and Hamburg, 6 miles to the south; there are also services 6 miles west at I-29 exit 10
Maps: USGS Sidney, IA; park map available online
Other trail users: None (there are equestrian trails north of IA 2 that are open to hikers)
Special considerations: The shower building in the modern campground can be used as an emergency shelter if necessary during severe weather.
Amenities available: Water, restrooms, and modern campground and cabins in the state park
Maximum grade: 18%; the descent from Sunset Ridge on the southern part of the loop is very steep, dropping nearly 200 feet over one-tenth of a mile, while the climb out is also steep; there are two climbs of more than 150 feet on Bridge and Valley Trails
Cell service: Below average to weak

Finding the trailhead: From the junction of US 275 and IA 2 in Sidney, take US 275/IA 2 south, turning west onto IA 2 when the road forks. Turn left (south) onto IA 239, and follow the signs for the overlook. GPS: N40° 40.536' W95° 41.373'

Trail conditions: The hiking trails are well maintained and well marked. Steep sections can be very slippery after rain or snow. Be aware of poison ivy alongside the trail. Trails receive moderate to heavy traffic.

The Hike

In July 1804, while explorers Meriwether Lewis and William Clark camped near the Missouri River west of present-day Waubonsie State Park, Clark described in his

Hikers on Sunset Ridge Shelly Eisenhauer

journal a scene far different from that of today: "A large prairie . . . which we called Baldpated prairie . . . a ridge of naked hills which bound it, running parallel with the river as far as we could see."

Woody invasion of the southern Loess Hills would parallel Euro-American settlement, and the prairie and oak savanna that once dominated the rugged hills were replaced by extensive woodlands. The usual suspects were fire suppression, agricultural cultivation, extermination of once-numerous hoofed grazers, and the subsequent overgrazing by domestic cattle. All of these factors permanently altered the landscape seen by Lewis and Clark two centuries ago. Today west-facing ridgetop prairie remnants and woodland openings offer only scattered reminders of Iowa's once "bald hills."

Waubonsie comes from the name of an honored chief of the Potowatomi tribe (pronounced Wah-bon-sey, meaning "Break of Day"), who originally came from the Great Lakes region. During the early 1800s, waves of white settlement forced tribe members to abandon their homes in Michigan. From 1837 to 1848, up to 2,000 Potowatomi occupied a reserve in southwest Iowa. Chief Waubonsie traveled to Washington, DC, to meet with presidents Andrew Jackson and James Polk to assure peace between his tribe and settlers. However, Iowa statehood in 1846 resulted in federal seizure of Potowatomi lands, and the tribe was pushed into Kansas. It's said that Chief Waubonsie died in 1848 as the last of his people left Iowa.

The main overlook is a relatively safe spot for watching dramatic midsummer thunderstorms approach from the west, but on clear days a jaunt down the sunset

Bench overlooking Waubonsie State Park SHELLY EISENHAUER

ridge trail is a must. From the westernmost ridge in the park, your eyes will strain to push the horizon beyond the Missouri River floodplain into infinity. Here you'll find a ridgetop prairie dense with big and little bluestem, Indian grass, sideoats grama, pale purple coneflower, lead plant, fringed puccoon, and the endangered biscuit root.

Many woodland animals, such as the summer tanager, chuck-will's-widow, Keen's myotis, and woodland vole, are expanding their typically more southern range into the northward-expanding forests. The pawpaw tree serves as a host to the stunning zebra swallowtail, the most abundant of North American "kite swallowtails," named for their triangular wings and long, sharp tails. The savanna-like openings are refuge for other rare butterflies, including the Olympia marble, hoary edge, white-M hair-streak, and Henry's elfin.

To make the most of the park's lengthy hiking-only trails, a figure-eight pattern is recommended. Start at the overlook parking lot, and follow the Sunset Ridge Trail down the finger ridge. From here a smaller footpath leads south and east into a valley, where you'll find a dug-out cave used as a root cellar by settlers in the early 1900s. Climb up the ridge to the southernmost picnic area, and follow the trail parallel to the road or the Mincer Nature Trail north back up to the main overlook. Complete the trails north of the park office by following the Ridge Trail north through well-developed forests dominated by the gnarled and fissured bodies of bur oaks. Turn around to connect with the Bridge and Valley Trails, where cross sections of

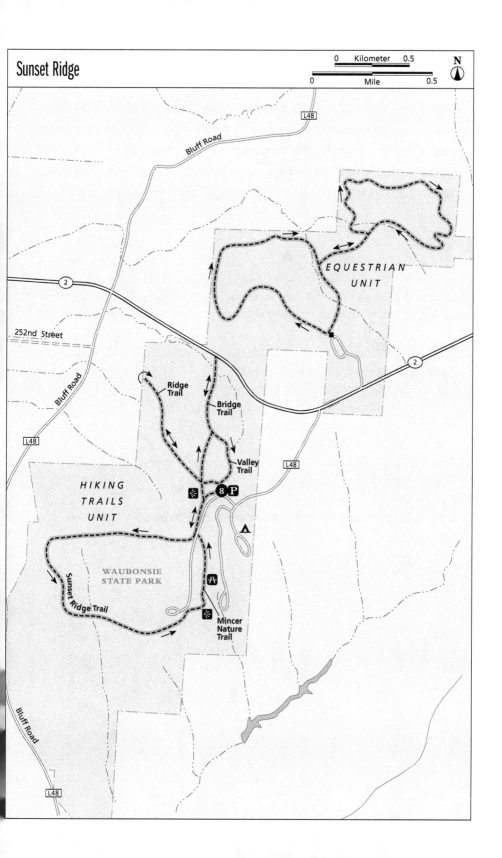

Sunset Ridge

0 Kilometer 0.5
0 Mile 0.5

N

Bluff Road

L48

EQUESTRIAN
UNIT

2

252nd Street

Bluff Road

Ridge
Trail

Bridge
Trail

Valley
Trail

L48

2

L48

HIKING
TRAILS
UNIT

8 P

WAUBONSIE
STATE PARK

Sunset Ridge Trail

Mincer
Nature
Trail

Bluff Road

L48

LOESS HILLS NATIONAL SCENIC BYWAY

Majestic views are the hallmark of a trip on the Loess Hills National Scenic Byway. Stretching from Akron in Plymouth County at the northern reach to the Missouri border in Fremont County at the southern end, the 220-mile paved main route (or "spine") has received national designation as one of America's Byways. There are 185 additional miles of optional excursion loops, ranging from interstate highways to gravel roads for the more adventuresome.

underground root systems are visible in the trail cuts that lead you back up to the parking area.

If you want a grueling hike and a long day, continue walking the equestrian trails on the north side of the highway. They'll wear you out with their steepness but won't offer as picturesque a view, and they are seriously eroded from excessive horse traffic. No matter what, bring binoculars—you'll need them.

Miles and Directions

0.00 Begin at the scenic overlook and head south.

0.30 Turn right (west) onto Sunset Ridge.

1.80 Continue east through the picnic area alongside the park road.

2.50 At the scenic overlook, continue north on Overlook Trail.

2.60 Keep left (north) onto Ridge Trail.

3.10 Reach the end of Ridge Tail; turn around and return to the junction with Bridge Trail.

3.50 Turn left (northeast) onto Bridge Trail.

3.70 Continue north on Bridge Trail.

4.10 Reach the end of Bridge Trail; turn around and return to the junction with Valley Trail.

4.40 Turn left (northeast) onto Valley Trail.

5.20 Arrive back at the scenic overlook parking area.

Honorable Mentions

A Sioux City Prairie

Together, Sioux City Prairie, Stone State Park, and Riverside Bluffs probably account for the largest amount of prairie within an urban boundary in the country. Adjacent to Briar Cliff College, the 157-acre prairie was rescued from development after serving as a golf course. Look for regal fritillaries dancing over yucca plants and the rare prairie moonworts poking their fiddleheads up in spring. Listen for eastern meadowlarks and grasshopper sparrows or yellow-breasted chats, also sometimes found here. Footpaths lead over the predominantly prairie-covered hills from Briar Cliff to Talbot Road, which borders the west side of the prairie.

Start: Trailhead on the north side of McCoy Arnold Center at Briar Cliff University
Elevation gain: Variable
Distance: There are no established trails, but hiking is allowed on worn footpaths and off-trail.

Difficulty: Moderate due to rugged terrain
Hiking time: Variable
Seasons/schedule: Trails are open year-round from sunrise to sunset.
Fees and permits: None

Sioux City Prairie is one of the largest urban prairies in the United States.

Trail contact: The Nature Conservancy in Iowa, 505 5th Ave. Suite 630, Des Moines 50309; (515) 244-5044; iowa@tnc.org; nature.org/en-us/about-us/where-we-work/united-states/iowa/

Dog-friendly: Leashed dogs and under the direct control of the owner are permitted.

Trail surface: Natural (dirt and grass)

Land status: Sioux City Prairie (The Nature Conservancy)

Nearest town: Sioux City

Maps: USGS Sioux City North, IA, SD

Other trail users: None

Special considerations: No collecting or consumption of plants, seeds of plants, animals, mushrooms, antlers, berries in whole or in part; no removal of any natural feature.

Amenities available: None

Maximum grade: Variable; there are steep but short inclines up the ridges

Cell service: Excellent

Finding the trailhead: From the intersection of Stone Park Boulevard and Hamilton Boulevard in Sioux City, go northwest on Stone Park Boulevard to Clifton Avenue (there is a sign for Briar Cliff College). Take IA 12 north to CR K18. Turn left onto Clifton Avenue and then left again onto Rebecca Street. Turn right onto College Road, which will go up the hill to the meeting place in the Briar Cliff College western parking lot, adjacent to the northeast corner of Sioux City Prairie. GPS: N42° 31.603' W96° 25.702'

Trail conditions: There are no established trails at Sioux City Prairie, rather there are "social trails" that are well-worn footpaths. Off-trail hiking is also permitted. The footpaths are narrow dirt single-track. The trails receive moderate to heavy traffic.

B Folsom Point Preserve

Folsom Point Preserve protects one of the largest remaining contiguous prairie remnants in the southern Loess Hills. Purchased in 1999, the prairie provides a valuable habitat for grassland animals, particularly in an area where the prairie community has largely disappeared. The terrain is quite rugged with steep slopes. There are no official trails at the preserve but there are several well-traveled footpaths that lead up to and along the ridges, allowing sweeping views of the Missouri River floodplain and the Loess Hills.

Start: 50365 Brohard Ave.

Elevation gain: Variable; 997 (lowest) to 1,265 feet (highest)

Distance: There are no established trails, but hiking is allowed on worn footpaths and off-trail; a 2-mile loop is the most common trail.

Difficulty: Moderate due to rugged terrain

Hiking time: Variable

Seasons/schedule: Trails are open year-round from sunrise to sunset.

Fees and permits: None

Trail contact: The Nature Conservancy in Iowa, 505 5th Ave. Suite 630, Des Moines 50309;

(515) 244-5044; iowa@tnc.org; nature.org/en-us/about-us/where-we-work/united-states/iowa/

Dog-friendly: Leashed dogs and under the direct control of the owner are permitted.

Trail surface: Natural (dirt and grass)

Land status: Folsom Point Preserve (The Nature Conservancy)

Nearest town: Council Bluffs, 11 miles to the north

Maps: USGS Council Bluffs South, IA, NE

Other trail users: None

Special considerations: No collecting or consumption of plants, seeds of plants, animals, mushrooms, antlers, berries in whole or in part; no removal of any natural feature. The preserve is used for research by local students; visitors should avoid flags and other markers.

Amenities available: None
Maximum grade: Variable; there are steep but short inclines up the ridges
Cell service: Excellent

Finding the trailhead: Take I-29 south of Council Bluffs to IA 370. Go east on IA 370 approximately 1 mile and turn right on Alcorn Avenue. Turn left on Brohard Avenue. Go to 50365 Brohard Ave. A red gate and small yellow Nature Conservancy sign mark the entrance to the preserve. GPS: N41° 9.301' W95° 48.204'

Trail conditions: There are no established trails at Folsom Point Preserve, rather there are "social trails" that are well-worn footpaths. Off-trail hiking is also permitted. The footpaths are narrow dirt single-track. The trails receive light to moderate traffic.

○ West Oak Forest

West Oak Forest, less than 30 minutes from Omaha, has one of the most spectacular views overlooking the Missouri River floodplain in the Loess Hills. If the view does not take your breath away, the climb up to the ridge from the parking lot surely will. More than 4 miles of trails traverse green valleys, hilltop prairie remnants, and heavily forested upland hardwood timber including bur oak, red oak, ironwood, basswood, scattered black walnut, and shagbark hickory.

Late fall at Folsom Point Preserve

Start: 55877 195th St. Pacific Junction, IA

Elevation gain: Variable; 1,016 (lowest) to 1,253 feet (highest)

Distance: Variable; the hike from the parking area to the scenic viewpoint is 1.3 miles one-way

Difficulty: Moderate due to steep climb from the parking area and rugged terrain

Hiking time: Variable

Seasons/schedule: Park open daily from 5:30 a.m. to 10:30 p.m.

Fees and permits: None

Trail contact: Mills County Conservation, 56235 Deacon Rd., Pacific Junction 51561; (712) 527-9685; conservation@millscounty iowa.gov; millscountyiowa.gov/191/ Conservation-Parks

Dog-friendly: Yes, on leash

Trail surface: Natural (dirt and grass)

Land status: West Oak Forest (Mills County Conservation)

Nearest town: Glenwood, 5 miles to the southeast

Maps: USGS Pacific Junction, IA, NE; trail map posted at the trailhead kiosk

Other trail users: None

Special considerations: None

Amenities available: None

Maximum grade: Variable; there are steep but short inclines up the ridges, the steepest climb from the parking area to the top of the ridge

Cell service: Above average

Finding the trailhead: From the I-29 and US 34/275 interchange, head east on US 34/275. Turn north onto CR L31/195th Street. After 2 miles, turn east into West Oak Forest. GPS: N41° 4.524' W95° 48.685'

Trail conditions: The trails follow dirt footpaths and mowed grass trails. They are easy to follow but are not waymarked; take a photo of the trail map posted at the trailhead kiosk. The trails in the northern section of the park are extensive and game trails can confuse hikers. The trails receive light to moderate traffic.

The Missouri River floodplain from West Oak Forest

Northwest Plains and Des Moines Lobe

Three of Iowa's distinct landform regions are covered within this over-arching category: the Northwest Plains, Des Moines Lobe, and Iowan Surface. The common link among these protected areas is their presence as islands within a sea of modern agriculture. The locations are a blend of geologically and biologically unique areas and a testament to the richness of Iowa's northern and central regions, places that most people find entirely uninteresting.

Beginning with the youngest landscape in the state, you'll find the descriptively named "knob and kettle" terrain in the north-central tongue of Iowa. The Des Moines Lobe of the Wisconsinan glacier finally removed its icy grip from Iowa a short 10,500 years ago, leaving in its wake vast amounts of glacial till. Also left behind were interesting formations called kames, also known as knobs. Pilot Knob in Hancock County is one of the best representations of these glacial-debris domes, deposited when silt- and gravel-laden meltwater drained through holes and crevices in the receding glacier. Kettles—usually marsh-filled bowl-like dimples—were created when isolated blocks of ice broke off the glacier and melted into place. Drainage networks never developed, and the kettles are annually filled with snowmelt, rain, interesting plants, and tons of ducks.

Each spring and summer the vast pothole marshes are breeding grounds for hundreds of thousands of waterfowl. At Fossil and Prairie Park Preserve in Floyd County, you can learn how during the 1800s the bulk of Iowa's wetlands were drained with clay tiles, and then walk outside and hike around a restored wetland—a transformation that's appreciated by the blue-winged teals that spend summers there.

The geologic grandparent to north-central Iowa resides just next door, to the east, and is known as the Iowan Surface. Located in Tama County, Casey's Paha in Tama County ("paha" is the Dakota Sioux word for "hill" or "ridge") was deposited by the Pre-Illinoian glaciers 500,000 years ago. For some reason, while the rest of the landscape was being wiped away by the intense erosive forces of nearby glaciers, the paha stood fast. More than one hundred paha can be found in Benton, Linn, and Tama Counties and for the most part make up the few isolated tracts of upland forest to be found in those areas.

Canyon Drive at Ledges State Park

To some it is surprising that Iowa's highest point is found in the topographically challenged Northwest Plains. Deposits of loess become shallower the farther from the Missouri River you travel, and a gently tilting land is revealed. Unlike the deeply wrinkled deposits of the southern hills, the Northwest Plains wear the loess as a smooth blanket. The lowest point in the state, at 480 feet, is found in extreme southeast Iowa at the confluence of the Des Moines and Mississippi Rivers, near Keokuk. Hawkeye Point, 1,670 feet, is located on a ridge pushed into place by the outer margins of the Des Moines Lobe ice sheet, in Osceola County near the Minnesota border. The two corners of the state are also diametrically opposed with regard to the amounts of annual precipitation and forested areas. Comparatively, the northwest corner is overwhelmingly lacking, receiving less than 25 inches of yearly precipitation and marked only by trees growing along creeks or in windbreaks planted by settlers. Historically, the Big Sioux, Rock, Floyd, Ocheyedan, and Little Sioux Rivers were the forested bands winding through a mixed-grass prairie wonderland.

In the extreme northwest corner of Gitchie Manitou State Preserve, the state's oldest exposed rock, Sioux quartzite, lies in outcrops along the Big Sioux River. Just above the Sioux quartzite lie deposits of the state's youngest rocks, Cretaceous-age shales and limestones. The gap in the rock sequence between the quartzite and the limestones spans just over 1.5 billion years! South of Cherokee sits Pilot Rock, one of the state's largest glacial erratics. The Sioux quartzite boulder measures nearly 180 feet around and 14 feet tall. Standing atop the ancient boulder yields a view of the Little Sioux River Valley.

9 Blood Run Creek

One of the most beautiful places in the Northwest Plains is located at the confluence of Blood Run Creek and the Big Sioux River. A Native American ancestral village straddling the Big Sioux River in both Iowa and South Dakota was probably one of the largest trade centers in the region and the site is one of the oldest villages of long-term habitation in the United States. Pottery resembling that of the Oneota culture has been uncovered at Blood Run, and more than 250 burial mounds surround the site. A 1.7-mile trail takes hikers past three burial mound groups and an old homestead.

Start: 1 mile south of 1001 120th St., Larchwood, IA 51241

Elevation gain: 118 feet total gain; 1,269 (lowest) to 1,332 feet (highest)

Distance: 1.73-mile loop

Difficulty: Easy

Hiking time: About 1 hour

Seasons/schedule: Grounds open sunrise to sunset

Fees and permits: None

Trail contact: State Historical Society of Iowa, 600 E. Locust St., Des Moines 50319; (515) 281-4221; history.iowa.gov/history/sites/blood-run-national-historic-landmark

Dog-friendly: Yes, on leash

Trail surface: Mowed grass

Land status: Friends of Blood Run, friendsof bloodrun@yahoo.com; history.iowa.gov/history/sites/

Nearest town: Larchwood, 8 miles to the east

Maps: USGS Klondike, IA, SD; walking tour map available online

Other trail users: None

Special considerations: Please respect the burial mounds and only hike on trails. There is little shade along the trail and no amenities, so plan and pack accordingly.

Amenities available: None

Maximum grade: 10%; the biggest climb is a short 50-foot incline after crossing the footbridge over Blood Run Creek

Cell service: Above average

Finding the trailhead: From Larchwood, head northwest on IA 9 for 4 miles. Turn south onto Beech Avenue, then immediately west onto 120th Street. Cross CR K10, then turn south to reach the end of 120th Street and the parking lot at Blood Run National Historic Landmark. GPS: N43° V' W96° 34.572'

Trail conditions: The trails are well maintained, mowed grass paths. There are no trail markers, but it would be difficult to get lost. Please respect the burial mounds and do not hike off-trail. The trails receive light traffic.

The Hike

Ancestors of the Omaha, Ponca, Iowa, and Oto-Missouria tribes, all practitioners of the Oneota culture, have all been attracted by the abundant game, fertile soil, and access to pipestone along the Big Sioux River on the present-day border of Iowa and South Dakota near Sioux Falls. Blood Run National Historic Landmark was once the location of a large village and ceremonial site for the aforementioned native peoples.

Wide mowed trails along Blood Run Creek and the Big Sioux River

Archaeological evidence suggests the site was inhabited from 900 to approximately 1720; the site served as a major trading site during the 1500s until the 1700s.

The village that straddled the Big Sioux River in northwestern Iowa and on the South Dakota border was probably one of the largest trade centers in the region. Pottery resembling that of the Oneota culture of northeast Iowa and the Des Moines River Valley has been uncovered at Blood Run, and more than 250 burial mounds surround the site. Pipestone quarries to the north were a source of the malleable red mudstone, used to make sacred figurines, ornaments, and pipes.

Time and the Big Sioux River and Blood Run Creek have sculpted this corner of Iowa. The area is covered in loess, but not to the

GITCHIE MANITOU STATE PRESERVE

The preserve contains outcrops of Sioux quartzite, the oldest bedrock in Iowa. Designated a state preserve in 1969, Gitchie Manitou is bordered on the north by the South Dakota–Iowa state line and on the west and south by the Big Sioux River. A visit offers a day filled with birding along the river and rock-hopping on the exposures. Hikers are treated to beds of Sioux quartzite that abound with western flowers, mosses, and lichens.

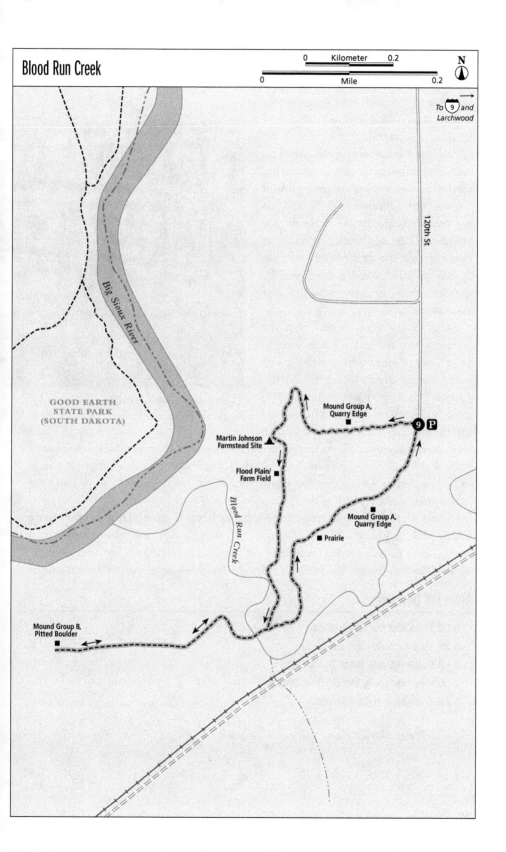

Blood Run Creek

0   Kilometer   0.2

0   Mile   0.2

N

To 9 and
Larchwood

120th St

GOOD EARTH
STATE PARK
(SOUTH DAKOTA)

Big Sioux River

Blood Run Creek

Mound Group A,
Quarry Edge

9 P

Martin Johnson
Farmstead Site

Flood Plain/
Farm Field

Mound Group A,
Quarry Edge

Prairie

Mound Group B,
Pitted Boulder

depths like the hills to the south that were described in the previous section. The waterways have eroded the loess deposits and rearranged the gravel and sand deposits, carving a widening path through the rolling landscape. Prairie grasses and trees help keep erosion in check. Quarrying remains an ever-present danger—while it has uncovered numerous artifacts, it has also destroyed considerable archaeological evidence. There is a wealth of information about the site on the State Historical Society of Iowa's website, describing the Oneota culture in depth as well as past excavations.

The national historic landmark is managed by the Iowa DNR.

The 1.7-mile trail begins from the parking area at the end of 120th Street in Lyon County. Head west toward the first burial mound group, then reach Martin Johnson's farmstead site, where crumbling buildings are being taken over by the prairie. The trail heads south, then west again as it crosses Blood Run Creek. Currently, as of February 2024, visitors must wade across the creek (a new bridge is planned). The trail ends with an impressive view of the Big Sioux River Valley. On your return to the trailhead, you will pass another burial mound to the south of the trail.

Good Earth State Park, across the Big Sioux River in South Dakota, offers more hiking trails. A bistate advisory committee is currently working on implementing a management plan developed for Blood Run National Historic Site. For local information on the area contact the Friends of Blood Run (friendsofbloodrun@yahoo.com).

Miles and Directions

0.00 Head west from the trailhead.

0.29 Martin Johnson farmstead site.

0.63 Footbridge over Blood Run Creek.

1.00 View overlooking the Big Sioux River.

1.73 Arrive back at the trailhead.

10 Kettleson Hogsback Nature Trail

The Des Moines Lobe ice sheet that covered northern Iowa more than 13,000 years ago created one of the most unique and ecologically diverse regions in the state. Kettleson Hogsback Wildlife Management Area takes its name from a narrow ridge that separates West Hottes Lake and Marble Lake in Iowa's Great Lakes region. Birding enthusiasts will relish the nearly 3-mile nature trail that traverses one of the most bird-rich locations in the entire state.

Start: 11471 240th Ave., Spirit Lake, IA 51360
Elevation gain: 141 feet total gain; 1,404 (lowest) to 1,456 feet (highest)
Distance: 2.79-mile out-and-back
Difficulty: Easy with some short inclines
Hiking time: About 1.5 hours
Seasons/schedule: Open daily, year-round
Fees and permits: None
Trail contact: Iowa DNR Great Lakes Wildlife Unit, (712) 330-4543
Dog-friendly: Yes, on leash
Trail surface: Natural (grass, dirt)

Land status: Kettleson Hogsback Wildlife Management Area (Iowa DNR)
Nearest town: Spirit Lake, 4.5 miles to the south
Maps: USGS Okoboji, IA
Other trail users: Mountain bikers
Special considerations: Hunting is allowed, so check season dates and dress accordingly
Amenities available: None
Maximum grade: 7%; there are several small inclines, and the biggest incline is at the southern end of the out-and-back with a climb of just under 50 feet
Cell service: Average, but reception may be limited under tree cover

Finding the trailhead: From Spirit Lake, head north on IA 276/Hill Avenue. After 1.6 miles, turn west onto 140th Street. After 0.5 miles, keep right onto 240th Avenue. Continue north for 2.6 miles, then turn west at the blue 11471 sign. GPS: N43° 28.897' W95° 7.663'

Trail conditions: The trail from the trailhead is narrow and can be overgrown in summer. It widens and becomes less overgrown as you continue on the trail. There are no trail markers, but the trail is easy to follow. There are two alternative trailheads; you can begin from either and hike the same trails, but the hike from the trailhead between Sunken Lake and Marble Lake is atop a narrow hogsback ridge and is recommended. The trails receive light traffic.

The Hike

The Iowa Great Lakes straddles the border of Iowa and Minnesota, drawing recreationists from both states and beyond. The lakes are the largest natural lakes in the Hawkeye State, remnants of the Des Moines Lobe ice sheet that probed into northern Iowa more than 13,000 years ago. Spirit Lake is Iowa's largest natural lake, while West Okoboji Lake is known for its deep blue waters. Outdoor recreation and tourism are year-long affairs in the region, and hiking its trails is excellent any time of year.

At Kettleson Hogsback Wildlife Management area, spring and fall are wonderful times to hike the eponymous nature trail. The oak timber attracts twenty-eight

Marble Lake

species of warblers, while waterfowl and shorebirds stop over during both spring and fall migrations. Nearly 300 species of birds have been identified here, making it one of the most bird-rich sites in Iowa. The unique geology of the area makes Kettleson Hogsback Nature Trail one of the best hikes in northwestern Iowa.

There are three trailheads to access Kettleson Hogsback Nature Trail—this hike begins at the trailhead located on a narrow ridge separating Sunken Lake and East Hottes Lake. The trailhead is marked by a sign indicating that no bikes are allowed, although this sign, and the trail itself, will likely be obscured by vegetation in summer. Once you get past the initial overgrown section, the trail becomes a clearly defined and beautiful footpath for one-quarter mile along the narrow, wooded ridge separating the two lakes. Once you reach the quarter-mile mark, you will have left Sunken Lake behind you but East Hottes Lake remains to the north. The trail heads south away from East Hottes Lake, then heads west once it reaches Marble Lake. You will reach an excellent view of Marble Lake at the half-mile mark of the hike.

Shortly after the viewpoint, reach a fork and keep right to take the higher path along the narrow ridge that gives the hike and wildlife management area its name. As the Des Moines Lobe melted, two large blocks of ice separated and formed Marble and West Hottes Lake, while glacial till and gravel were pushed together forming

West Hottes Lake

the ridge that resembles a hog's back. The hogsback ridge rises 40 feet and separates Marble Lake and West Hottes Lake.

As you continue west, you will come across a path at the three-quarter mile mark that heads north. Follow this path and you may see beavers, or at least the evidence of them, where West Hottes Lake flows into East Hottes Lake. The main trail curves southwest, then heads directly south to reach a fork after 1 mile of hiking. Before you take the right fork, find the island in West Hottes Lake to see if the great blue heron rookery is occupied.

The fork at the 1-mile mark is the junction of a short, half-mile loop. Keep right to reach an alternative trailhead, then continue south through a small prairie. The buildings you see to the southwest are Iowa DNR headquarters for the wildlife management area. Follow the loop back north to the junction, and then when you reach the next junction at 1.7 miles, take the right fork for the lower trail along the north shore of Marble Lake. Enjoy the views of Marble Lake through the trees as you make your way east and approach 2 miles on the hike. The final stretch takes you past a trail that leads to another trailhead, then along a roller-coaster section with three small inclines before reaching the trailhead.

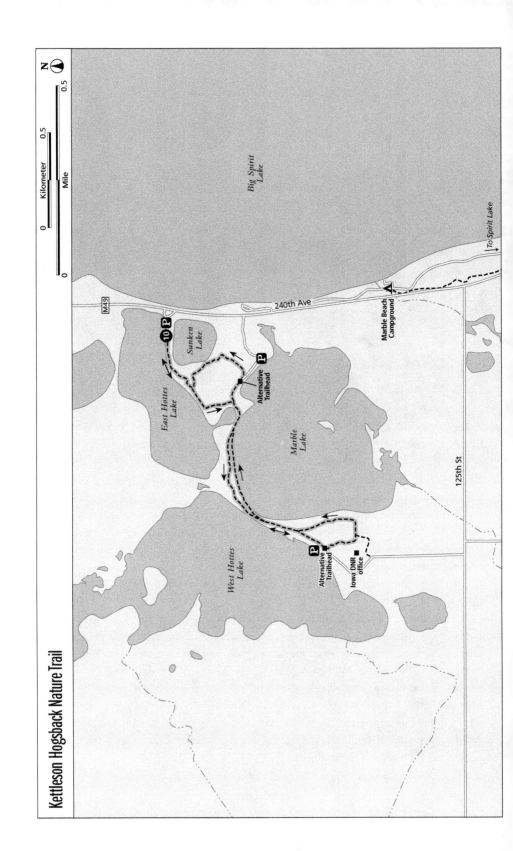

Kettleson Hogsback Nature Trail

There are several additional hiking areas worth exploring in the Iowa Great Lakes region. Located on West Okoboji Lake, Gull Point State Park is the principal state park in the region. The Barney Peterson Memorial Trail is a 1.5-mile self-guided interpretive trail where visitors can learn about the natural and cultural history of the lakes region. There are also several buildings constructed by the Civilian Conservation Corps. Horseshoe Bend Wildlife Area has an extensive trail system through forest, meadows, oxbows, and marshes along the Little Sioux River. Fort Defiance State Park, located near Estherville 13 miles east of Spirit Lake, has a pleasant 3-mile loop along School Creek and through upland prairie.

Miles and Directions

0.00 Head west at the trailhead.

0.23 Keep left (west).

0.42 Turn right (west).

0.53 Reach a junction; continue straight and take the right fork heading west.

0.73 Keep left (southwest).

0.90 Continue straight (south).

1.05 Reach a fork and keep right (southwest).

1.17 Turn left, then immediately left to continue south.

1.30 Keep left (east).

1.54 Keep right to continue north.

1.69 Turn right (northeast) onto the lower trail next to Marble Lake.

1.81 Continue straight (east).

2.03 Continue straight (east).

2.14 Keep right (east).

2.25 Turn left (northeast).

2.54 Turn sharp right (east) onto the narrow footpath back to the trailhead.

2.79 Arrive back at the trailhead.

11 Pilot Knob Lake and Dead Man's Lake Loop

As settlers heading west crossed the expansive, undulating prairies and wetlands of north-central Iowa in the 1800s, they used Pilot Knob as an indelible beacon. The park contains a fen, home to many rare plants as well as a floating mat of sphagnum moss. Trails wind through beautifully mature forests, around Dead Man's and Pilot Knob Lakes, and through an area dominated by wetlands. On a clear day, you'll be able to see 30-plus miles from the observation tower built atop Pilot Knob by the Civilian Conservation Corps.

Start: Plum Alley Trailhead at the south end of the parking loop
Elevation gain: 220 feet total gain; 1,312 (lowest) to 1,450 feet (highest)
Distance: 2.68-mile loop
Difficulty: Easy, although the climb on Tower Trail is moderately steep
Hiking time: 1–1.5 hours
Seasons/schedule: Park open daily from 4 a.m. to 10:30 p.m.
Fees and permits: None
Trail contact: Pilot Knob State Park, 2148 340th St., Forest City 50436; (641) 581-4835; Pilot_Knob@dnr.iowa.gov; iowadnr.gov/Places-to-Go/State-Parks/Iowa-State-Parks/Pilot-Knob-State-Park
Dog-friendly: Yes, on leash
Trail surface: Natural (dirt and grass)

Land status: Pilot Knob State Park (Iowa DNR)
Nearest town: Forest City, 5 miles to the west
Maps: USGS Miller, IA and USGS Pilot Knob, IA; park map with trails available online
Other trail users: None (there are other multi-use trails in the park)
Special considerations: Option to extend the hike on other trails in the state park.
Amenities available: Restrooms and water at the campground; restrooms at the observation tower and Dead Man's Lake
Maximum grade: 9%; the biggest climb is from the beginning of Tower Trail to the Observation Tower, gaining more than 100 feet over one-third of a mile. There are 50 steps to reach the top of the Observation Tower.
Cell service: Adequate throughout the state park

Finding the trailhead: From Forest City, head east on IA 9 for 3.3 miles. Turn south onto IA 332/205th Avenue, then after 4.3 miles turn east into Pilot Knob State Park. Take the second right into the parking area. The trailhead is located on the south end of the loop. GPS: N43° 15.193' W93° 33.884'
   Trail conditions: The trails are well maintained and marked at junctions. This hike follows hiking-only trails; there is another hiking-only trail (Three Bridges Trail) and multiple multiuse trails to extend your hike. The natural surface trails can be soft and muddy after rain; if your activity is leaving a mark, turn around. The trails receive moderate traffic.

The Hike

Pilot Knob is a classic glacial kame—a landform associated with retreating glaciers, in this case the Des Moines Lobe around 12,000 to 14,000 years ago. Meltwater poured

Observation Tower

off the edge or into crevices and chambers in the deteriorating ice sheet, leaving behind large deposits of sand and gravel that now appear as isolated, fairly conical hills.

The forests that cover Pilot Knob are dominated by bur, northern pin, and red oaks, elm, ironwood, and hazelnut. The woods serve as a haven for migratory birds during spring, with many species staying to nest. Look for various flycatchers and warblers, veery, scarlet tanager, and the black-billed cuckoo. Hidden among the trees are small, marshy depressions dominated by sedges and rushes, but you'll also find arrowhead, smartweed, marsh fern, monkey flower, swamp milkweed, and blue flag iris.

Pilot Knob State Park owes its creation to local preservation efforts. More than 150 residents of nearby Forest City campaigned and raised funds to purchase the land surrounding Pilot Knob, including Dead Man's Lake. The land was purchased in 1921 with a matching grant from the state and in 1924 was dedicated as a state park. In 1934, Civilian Conservation Corps workers spent four months developing Pilot Knob's recreational facilities. During winter months, this is one of the best places to cross-country ski in Iowa. The trails are gently sloped and well maintained, and the warming house is a nice incentive to spend some time in the cold.

During the rest of the year, the trails attract hikers to the observation tower and the unique Dead Man's Lake. Seven miles of hiking and multiuse trails in the state park, plus an additional 1.5 miles in the adjacent wildlife management area to the north, provide a day's worth of hiking at Pilot Knob. For a pleasant loop around Pilot Knob Lake and Dead Man's Lake, take Plum Alley Trail heading southwest in the parking area next to the unnamed pond by the park office. The trail weaves through the wooded north shore of Pilot Knob Lake for two-thirds of a mile before reaching the campground. Continue heading south on the east end of the lake for another one-quarter mile before reaching Tower Trail.

Pilot Knob Lake and Dead Man's Lake Loop

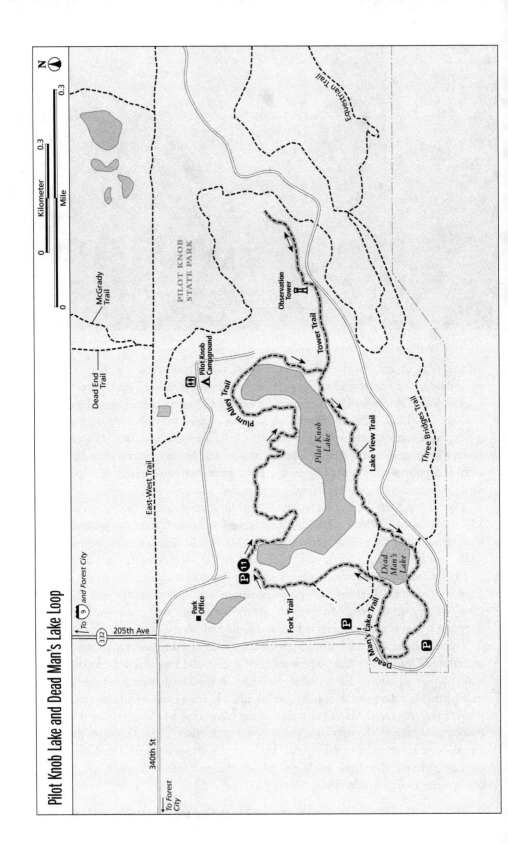

N

Kilometer
0   0.3   0.3

Mile
0   0.3

PILOT KNOB STATE PARK

To 9 and Forest City

340th St

To Forest City

205th Ave 332

McGrady Trail

Dead End Trail

East-West Trail

Park Office

Pilot Knob Campground

Plum Alley Trail

Fork Trail

Pilot Knob Lake

Tower Trail

Observation Tower

Lake View Trail

Three Bridges Trail

Equestrian Trail

Dead Man's Lake Trail

Dead Man's Lake

P 11

P

P

Tower Trail climbs 125 feet over one-third mile, passing through a parking area before reaching the observation tower at 1,450 feet. The climb is not over, however, as fifty steps up the metal staircase inside the tower await. The final push is worth the effort, as the view of northern Iowa stretches for miles from atop the CCC (Civilian Conservation Corps)-built tower. After catching your breath and taking in the view, head back down Tower Trail to follow Lake View Trail along the south shore of the lake to finally reach Dead Man's Lake.

A number of legends, many with headless horsemen and drowning victims, describe the origin of the lake's name. However, the accepted explanation dates to when the Winnebago tribe inhabited the region. Winnebago means "people of the stinking water" and possibly refers to the attributes of nearby wetlands, where large amounts of decomposing organic matter release fumes. The story tells of a Winnebago member who was excommunicated from the tribe, and thus considered dead, who came to live near the lake.

Dead Man's Lake is the only sphagnum bog in the state of Iowa. Earlier, the lake was a much larger floating mat of sphagnum moss, but excessive harvest of peat in the 1920s left only a remnant. This fen is the only home in the state to several rare northern plants, including cordroot sedge and the carnivorous sundew. Three species of water lilies live in the lake; one of them, commonly known as watershield, is known only from this site in Iowa. Because of the area's incredibly sensitive nature and exceptional plant community, do not walk off the trail surrounding the lake.

Continue on Dead Man's Lake for one-quarter mile until reaching Fork Trail. Head north, passing two spur trails that lead west to a picnic area, to reach the south end of the pond where you began the hike. Pass the warming house to reach the parking area.

Miles and Directions

0.00 At the south end of the parking area, head southwest on Plum Alley Trail.

0.61 Continue straight (east), passing the campground to the north.

0.85 Turn left (east) onto Tower Trail.

1.04 Observation Tower parking area; continue east onto Tower Connector Trail.

1.18 Observation Tower.

1.54 Continue west onto Lake View Trail.

1.89 Turn left (south) onto Dead Man's Trail.

  Option: Keep right (east) to follow Dead Man's Trail on the north side of Dead Man's Lake.

1.97 Continue straight (west).

2.12 Continue straight (west).

2.28 Continue straight (east).

2.40 Keep left (north) onto Fork Trail.

2.51 Keep right (north) on Fork Trail.

2.68 Arrive at the warming house and parking area.

12 Fossil and Prairie Loop

A visit to Fossil and Prairie Park will give you an expansive look into north-central Iowa's past, as well as the chance to take a little piece of it home with you. Outside Rockford at the bottom of an old quarry turned park, a 350-million-year cross section of Iowa is visible. To the west of the quarry, a virgin prairie tract is home to several rare species. Juniper Hill is the only recorded site in Iowa for creeping juniper, a species more commonly found in Minnesota and Canada.

Start: Next to the restrooms and maintenance shed

Elevation gain: 259 feet total gain; 993 (lowest) to 1,222 feet (highest)

Distance: 4.47-mile loop

Difficulty: Moderate

Hiking time: 1.5-2 hours

Seasons/schedule: Open year-round from sunrise to sunset

Fees and permits: None

Trail contact: Fossil & Prairie Park Preserve, 1227 215th St., PO Box 495, Rockford 50468; (641) 756-3490; fpcenter@myomnitel.com; fossilcenter.wordpress.com

Dog-friendly: Yes, on leash

Trail surface: Natural (grass, dirt, rock) and gravel road

Land status: Fossil & Prairie Park Preserve (Floyd County Conservation)

Nearest town: Rockford, 1.5 miles to the east

Maps: USGS Rockford, IA; trail map provided in park packs at the center's front door (when available) and a trail map displayed outside the center

Other trail users: None

Special considerations: Fossil collection is allowed, but resale is prohibited

Amenities available: Restrooms and water at the parking area east of the center

Maximum grade: 11%; one short climb of 75 feet and another in the northwest corner of the prairie that climbs 100 feet over one-third mile

Cell service: Adequate coverage with spots of weak reception on the prairie trails

Finding the trailhead: From Rockford, head south on 8th Street SW/CR B47. After one-half mile, keep right to head west on 215th Street/CR B47. Turn north after 1.5 miles, then take the next right into the parking area near the shelter and maintenance shed. The trail is located on the west side of the maintenance shed where the restrooms are. GPS: N43° 2.837' W92° 58.736'

Trail conditions: The trails are in excellent condition. Most of the junctions are marked, but take a picture of the trail map displayed next to the center or grab a park pack if they are available. The prairie trails are mowed and wide. There are long sections without shade, so wear a hat and bring plenty of water on sunny days. The fossil trails receive heavy traffic, while the prairie trails get less traffic.

The Hike

Rockford Brick and Tile Co. began mining the clay deposits in Floyd County in 1910, producing bricks and drainage tile to supply Iowa's "black gold" rush as farmers drained the waterlogged marshland of north-central Iowa to plant crops in the highly

Fossil collecting is permitted at Fossil and Prairie Center.

fertile soil beneath the wetlands. Rockford Brick and Tile mined the quarry until 1976, all the while exposing Devonian fossils. The rush to drain north-central Iowa's wetlands took an immense toll, unfortunately—between 1780 and 1980, the state lost an estimated 89 percent of its wetlands.

In 1989, word spread that the quarry might become a dump site for a local foundry. Conservationists lobbied for protection, and in 1990 the Floyd County Conservation Board received the state's first REAP (Resource Enhancement and Protection) grant, which funded the purchase of the 109-acre Rockford Brick and Tile property and an adjoining 47 acres of virgin prairie. A nature center was opened in 2001 and trails were installed. The visitor center is open most afternoons; exhibits cover the history of the site, natural history of the prairie, geology and paleontology, and the Euro-American settlement of Iowa and its effects.

East of the visitor center is another parking area, with a large picnic shelter and restrooms in the maintenance shop to the north of the parking lot. Begin your hike on the trail near the restrooms and head north. The first one-third mile passes through a barren, desert-like landscape. You will likely see people of all ages hunched over hunting for fossils in this area. If you've come to not only hike but hunt for fossils, explore off trail for the best chance of finding ancient treasures. Be prepared to hop around on the rocks and eroding slopes of the pits, and watch out for sludgy clay at the bottom. A closer look at the side slopes will fill you with awe as fossils seem almost to pop out: solitary and colonial corals, sea lilies, many species of brachiopods and mollusks, and, if you're lucky, the teeth of *Ptyctodus*, a primeval fish. Modest fossil collection is allowed, but only for personal use, not commercial sale.

Continuing east from the fossil area, you'll encounter beehive kilns in which millions of bricks and tiles were fired during the 1900s. Follow the gravel road east past the kilns to reach a footbridge over the Winnebago River (a trail connects the town of Rockford to the footbridge). Hike back to the kilns but continue south along the gravel road past a pond on your left. Before you reach CR B47, turn west off the gravel road. The trail will bend to head north, but you can take a side-trip at the sign indicating fishing access. The footpath leads to the pond that you saw earlier from the fossil area. Back on the main trail, you will reach the kilns once again and head west back toward the fossil area. If you plan to continue your hike and don't need water or the restrooms, there is a shortcut to the prairie just before the fossil area overlook.

The three main prairie types in Iowa—wet, dry, and mesic—occur here in unlikely places. Because of the soil's high clay content, groundwater and seepage accumulate and spit out in springlike fashion in the middle of the hills, creating wet prairies on hillsides. You'll pass an old farm pond that now drains into a wetland, where Canada geese and blue-winged teals spend much of the summer. Look for monarch butterflies sipping nectar from the bright fuchsia flowers of swamp milkweed nestled among sedges and cattails. At the north end of the prairie, a wetland mitigation project straddles the dike and the Winnebago River, which you can see to the north. As a result, water entering the river from the park goes through several filtration stages before entering the river.

There are five trails that weave and meander throughout the prairie. As you explore the prairie trails, you will be astonished by the drastic change of landscape compared to the eastern edge of the park where the quarry was active. Creeping Juniper Trail is named after the matted evergreen shrub, normally found thriving on open dunes in northern Minnesota and Michigan. Juniper Hill at Fossil and Prairie Park is the only place in Iowa where creeping juniper can be found.

Miles and Directions

0.00 Begin next to the restrooms and head north.

0.40 Continue straight (southeast).

0.48 Beehive kilns.

0.75 Winnebago River.

0.97 Keep left (south) to continue on the gravel road.

1.20 Turn right (west).

1.37 Continue straight (north).

 Option: Turn left (west) onto the spur trail leading to a pond.

Fossil and Prairie Loop

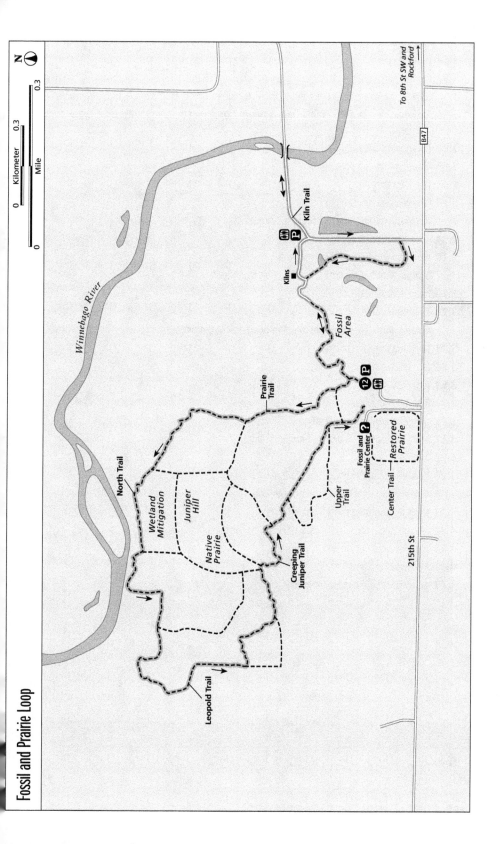

1.54 Turn left (west).

1.82 Continue straight (south).

> **Option:** If you are hiking the entire route, turn right (west) onto a shortcut to Prairie Trail.

1.90 Turn right (west) onto Prairie Trail. **Bailout:** Continue straight (south) toward the parking area.

1.93 Turn right (north).

1.99 Shortcut joins on your right.

2.03 Turn right (north).

2.24 Bench; continue straight (north).

> **Option:** Turn right (west) toward the pond.

2.54 Keep right (northwest).

2.79 Turn right (north) onto Leopold Trail.

> **Option:** Turn left (south) to continue on North Trail.

3.05 Keep right (west).

3.23 Turn left (south).

> **Option:** Turn right (north) to hike the perimeter of the prairie.

3.28 Continue straight (south).

3.55 Turn left (east).

3.62 Turn right (south).

3.72 Turn left (east).

3.78 Continue straight (northeast).

3.87 At a junction with a bench, turn right (south).

4.01 Turn right (south).

4.06 Turn left (east) to stay on Prairie Trail.

> **Option:** Turn right (west) onto Upper Trail.

4.25 Keep left (southeast) on Prairie Trail.

4.32 At the bench, turn right (south) toward the visitor center.

4.38 Turn left (east) at the visitor center.

4.42 Jon Tumilson Memorial.

4.47 Arrive back at the parking area.

13 Joey Schmidt Orienteering Course

Ingawanis Woodland, north of Cedar Falls and Waterloo, has seven flat and tranquil miles of forested trails along the Cedar River. The timber is popular with mountain bikers, but an orienteering course developed by an Eagle Scout will test the navigational prowess of hikers of all experiences. Load up your GPS device or use an old-fashioned map and compass to navigate 140 acres of hardwood forest.

Start: Lower Access Path Trailhead (1681 260th St., Janesville)
Elevation gain: 269 feet total gain; 886 (lowest) to 958 feet (highest)
Distance: 5.87-mile loop
Difficulty: Difficult due to length and orienteering course
Hiking time: About 2.5 hours
Seasons/schedule: Trails open year-round from sunrise to sunset
Fees and permits: None
Trail contact: Bremer County Conservation; 1104 S. Main St. PO Box 412, Tripoli 50676; (319) 882-4742; https://www.bremercounty.iowa.gov/
Dog-friendly: Yes, on leash
Trail surface: Natural (dirt)
Land status: Ingawanis Woodland (Bremer County Conservation)

Nearest town: Denver, 4 miles to the east
Maps: USGS Waverly, IA; trail map available online and posted at the trailhead and along the trails
Other trail users: Mountain bikers
Special considerations: There are 2 trailheads, one on 260th Street where this hike begins and the other at 2588 Hawthorne Ave. It is popular with mountain bikers, so don't hike with earbuds or headphones so that you are aware of surroundings.
Amenities available: Portable toilet and private clothes changing structure available at the 260th Street trailhead.
Maximum grade: 5%; there are ups and downs but no substantial inclines on the trails
Cell service: Average to below average due to the tree canopy

Finding the trailhead: From Denver, head west on CR C50/260th Street for 1.5 miles. Turn north, then immediately west to continue west on 260th Street. After 3.5 miles, the road curves to head south and becomes Hawthorne Avenue. Turn west onto 260th Street, then turn north after one-third mile into the parking area. GPS: N42° 40.302' W92° 25.283'

Trail conditions: The trails are well maintained. There are trail markers at each junction, and there are trail maps at certain junctions. Since it is a mountain bike trail, the trails are winding and curvy and often another section of trail is right alongside another trail. To monitor or report trail conditions, visit the Ingawanis Woodland Trails group on Facebook. The trails receive moderate traffic.

The Hike

Ingawanis Woodlands is another example of both the Iowa Natural Heritage Foundation and the Resource Enhancement and Protection (REAP) grant program creating outdoor recreation opportunities for the public. The project was opened to the public in 2016, after four years of planning, fundraising, and grant applications.

Deer are plentiful at Ingawanis Woodland.

INHF initially purchased the property, while Bremer County Conservation raised funds and applied for grants to complete the transfer. The award from the Iowa DNR's REAP grant was the largest the project received. The 142-acre timber tract sits on the Cedar River north of Cedar Falls and Waterloo. The woodland was originally owned by the Winnebago Council of Boy Scouts of America. The council wanted to sell a portion of the timber but instead have protected the park and opened it to the public. The trails pass through Camp Ingawanis, including the

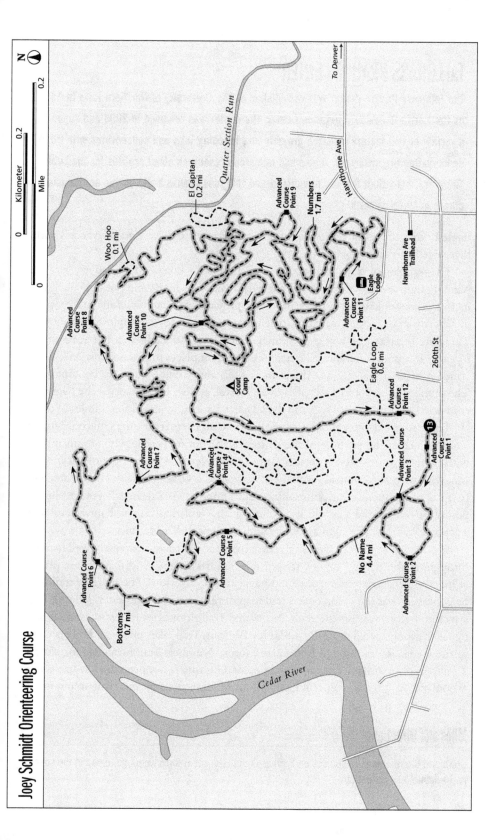

Joey Schmidt Orienteering Course

TALLGRASS PRAIRIE CENTER

The Tallgrass Prairie Center was established at the University of Northern Iowa in 1999 as the Native Roadside Vegetation Center. The center was renamed in 2006 and supports a variety of UNI faculty research projects and teaching labs and collaborates with other conservation organizations. It also has numerous resources about prairies for the public. There are more than 5 miles of wetland and tallgrass prairie trails on the southeastern corner of UNI's campus.

Eagle Lodge, the scout camp, and other scout structures. There are two access paths that have been incorporated into the trail system.

The 7 miles of trails are popular with mountain bikers. The relatively flat and winding trails are nice forest tracks, but what makes this hike stand out to be included in this guidebook? That answer has been provided by Joey Schmidt of Troop 90 in Waverly, Iowa. Joey created an orienteering course for an Eagle Scout project. There are three course levels—beginner, moderate, advanced—that test your ability to navigate a trail. Mountain bike trails are excellent places to practice this skill, as the winding maze of narrow dirt single-track trails and wildlife trails can be confusing. The number of waypoints increases in each level, as does the distance—the beginner course is 1 mile, moderate is 3, and the advanced course winds along 5 miles of trails.

There is an extensive training guide available on Bremer County's mycountyparks .com webpage. The purpose of the courses is to educate people who are unfamiliar with orienteering and GPS devices. You can complete the courses the old-fashioned way, with map and compass, or you can download a GPS map with coordinates and navigate to the various waypoints using your phone or GPS device. There are control points, or trail markers, at the waypoints on the trail that list the course level and waypoint number. The signs are white and orange and hard to miss.

In addition to the orienteering course markers, the trail is extremely well marked throughout the entire 7-mile system. Each trail has a name, and markers are placed at junctions that state trail names and navigational directions. The maze of trails can be confusing, but the color-coded trail map displayed at the trailhead is helpful; snap a picture before you hit the trails. No Name Trail dominates the woodland, as it is by far the longest trail at nearly 4.5 miles. Bottoms Trail takes hikers and bikers close to the Cedar River through bottomland forest. Numbers Trail meanders for almost 2 miles in the southeast corner of the timber. Hunting is not permitted at Ingawanis Woodland. As a result, you will likely see more deer at Ingawanis than at any other 150-acre tract in Iowa.

Miles and Directions

Download the orienteering courses on Bremer County Conservation's webpage (listed in the specs) for navigational information.

14 Boneyard Trail

The Pennsylvanian sandstone outcrops that people flock to view at Ledges State Park are also exposed at Dolliver Memorial State Park, towering 100 feet above Prairie Creek. Seven miles of trails wind over forested bluffs above the Des Moines River. Several Woodland period burial mounds sit atop these bluffs. Explore Boneyard Hollow, in the northern reaches of the park, where early settlers found tremendous amounts of bison bones in the canyon.

Start: Trailhead near North Shelter off Dolliver Park Avenue

Elevation gain: 715 feet total gain; 941 (lowest) to 1,119 feet (highest)

Distance: 4.9-mile double loop

Difficulty: Difficult due to rugged terrain and numerous steep inclines

Hiking time: About 2 hours

Seasons/schedule: Park open daily year-round from 4 a.m. to 10:30 p.m.

Fees and permits: None

Trail contact: Dolliver Memorial State Park, 2757 Dolliver Park Ave., Lehigh 50557; (515) 359-2539; Dolliver@dnr.iowa.gov; iowadnr.gov/Places-to-Go/State-Parks/Iowa-State-Parks/Dolliver-Memorial-State-Park

Dog-friendly: Yes, on leash

Trail surface: Natural (dirt and grass), paved roads, and wood chips

Land status: Dolliver Memorial State Park (Iowa DNR)

Nearest town: Fort Dodge, 10 miles to the northwest

Maps: USGS Evanston, IA; park map available online

Other trail users: None

Special considerations: There are multiple trailheads, as well as various options to cut the hike shorter.

Amenities available: Restrooms and water throughout the park, as well as campgrounds

Maximum grade: 24%; there are five substantial climbs, the steepest gains more than 150 feet over one-quarter mile

Cell service: Adequate to below average

Finding the trailhead: From Fort Dodge, head south on Quail Avenue for 3.7 miles. At the junction with US 20, continue south on CR P59/Nelson Avenue. After 6 miles, turn east onto 255th Street. Keep south onto Dolliver Street, then keep east onto 260th Street/Dolliver Park Avenue. Enter the state park, then park on the loop adjacent to the North Shelter. The trailhead closest to the restrooms lead to the river; the trailhead farther southwest leads to Boneyard Hollow. GPS: N42° 23.954' W94° 4.661'

Trail conditions: The trails are well maintained. Copperas Trail is marked and there are trail markers at recreation areas. Take a park map and follow a GPS unit to assist navigation. Most of the trails are wide and clean. The trails in Boneyard Hollow are narrow and rugged. The trails receive moderate to heavy traffic.

The Hike

Dolliver Memorial State Park, and Ledges State Park in the following chapter, buck the trend of relatively flat terrain in the Des Moines Lobe. The two parks share more

Copperas Beds

BRUSHY CREEK STATE RECREATION AREA

Brushy Creek contains 45 miles of multiuse trails and offers a multitude of recreational opportunities, including hunting, fishing, boating, and equestrian and hiking trails. A controversial 1967 proposal to flood Brushy Creek's stunning forested canyon led to a twenty-year struggle over future development. In the end, the Iowa Department of Natural Resources created a state preserve to protect an extremely sensitive tract, impounded a smaller lake than earlier proposed, and acquired additional land to build more equestrian trails. Though not every group involved was satisfied with the outcome, many people now enjoy the multiuse aspect of Brushy Creek.

in common with the hikes in the Bluffs over Rivers section of this guidebook, as both overlook the Des Moines River Valley with towering sandstone bluffs. However, their geographic location places them in the southern reaches of the Des Moines Lobe in central Iowa. Dolliver Memorial State Park consists of nearly 600 acres of rugged trails, historic Native American burial mounds, unique sandstone outcroppings, and the eerily named and visually spectacular Boneyard Hollow.

There are multiple places to begin hiking at Dolliver Memorial State Park, and multiple loops or other routes to hike. Beginning at the northern end allows you to first explore Boneyard Hollow, then hike along a beautiful quarter-mile trail along the Des Moines River. If you aren't up for hiking to Copperas Bends on the southern end of the park, you can take the upper trail back through Boneyard Hollow. It is thought that previous inhabitants of the area drove herds of bison off the cliffs or into the narrow canyon in order to kill them for food, clothing, and tools. If you continue south, you will climb more than 100 feet up a ridge above the park road and Des Moines River (tree cover limits your view of both) then plunge back down to the park road.

Cross the road, then a footbridge over Prairie Creek to reach Indian Trail. The staircase leads up 200 steep feet to reach the broad ridgetop above. There are several burial mounds throughout the upland hardwood forest; stay on the trails and respect the mounds. These Native American mounds from the Woodland culture were once used for ceremonial and burial purposes. There are also numerous primitive lean-tos constructed alongside Indian Trail. The timber is an ideal spot to hear, and hopefully see, a pileated woodpecker.

Indian Trail descends the ridge to cross the road once again near the South Lodge. Continue west through the parking area to reach the trailhead for the 1-mile Copperas Beds Trail. The trail gets its name from mineral deposits on the unique sandstone formations along Prairie Creek. The second half of the loop climbs up a steep ridge on the creek's north bank. The official trail is a wide gravel trail, but there is a narrow footpath along the steep ridgetop for the more adventurous. You will have to descend

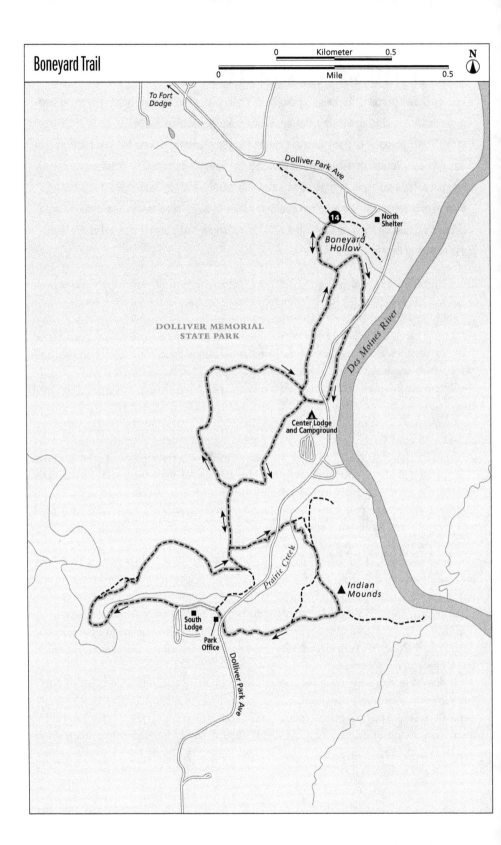

Boneyard Trail

Kilometer
0   0.5

Mile
0   0.5

N

To Fort
Dodge

Dolliver Park Ave

14

North
Shelter

Boneyard
Hollow

DOLLIVER MEMORIAL
STATE PARK

Des Moines River

Center Lodge
and Campground

Prairie Creek

Indian
Mounds

South
Lodge

Park
Office

Dolliver Park Ave

and climb up Center Trail once again. Take the western offshoot of Center Trail to hike through upland forest and then along a crop field to reach Boneyard Hollow.

Miles and Directions

0.00 Begin at the trailhead and head west.

0.03 Keep right (northwest).

0.26 Turn left (northeast).

0.45 Cross the road and continue southeast onto River Trail.

0.63 Keep left (south).

0.75 Cross the road heading west, pass the center lodge, and continue west.

0.82 Keep left (southwest).

> **Bailout:** Keep right (north) onto Boneyard Trail to return to Boneyard Hollow.

1.00 Continue straight (south).

> **Bailout:** Turn right (northwest).

1.36 Turn left (west).

1.45 Reach a recreation area; continue west toward the road, cross the road, and head toward the footbridge.

1.76 At the fork, keep left (southeast).

1.88 Keep right (southwest).

2.07 Continue straight (west).

> **Option:** Turn right (north) to follow Indian Trail back to Prairie Creek.

2.27 Cross the park road heading west, following the sign for South Lodge.

2.42 Copperas Beds Trailhead; continue west.

2.65 Footbridge over Prairie Creek; cross it after viewing Copperas Beds.

2.74 Reach a fork and turn right (north).

2.83 Continue north on the narrow footpath along the edge of the cliff, or follow the wider parallel trail on your left.

2.92 Continue east as the two paths rejoin.

3.36 Turn sharp left (north) onto Center Lodge Trail.

3.44 Continue straight (north) and cross the stone footbridge.

3.60 Keep left (north).

4.25 Keep left (north).

4.61 Continue straight (north).

4.90 Arrive back at Boneyard Trailhead.

15 Pea's Creek Canyon

Picturesque sandstone bluffs line the canyon of Pea's Creek just before it enters the Des Moines River. Hike into the canyon, climb up to Crow's Nest for views of the Des Moines River, hike back down to wade in the creek, then climb up to Table Rock for more splendid views. If you like climbing stairs or just want a nice steep hike, this is the place. If you want a more leisurely jaunt, take the loop around the upland prairie reconstruction or the interpretive trail around Lost Lake.

Start: Hog's Back Trailhead opposite Oak Woods Shelter

Elevation gain: 453 feet total gain; 867 (lowest) to 1,072 feet (highest)

Distance: 2.12-mile loop

Difficulty: Difficult due to numerous steep inclines and rugged terrain

Hiking time: 1–1.5 hours

Seasons/schedule: Park open daily from 4 a.m. to 10:30 p.m.

Fees and permits: None

Trail contact: Ledges State Park, 1515 P Ave., Madrid 50156; (515) 432-1852; Ledges@dnr .iowa.gov iowadnr.gov/Places-to-Go/State -Parks/Iowa-State-Parks/Ledges-State-Park

Dog-friendly: Yes, on leash

Trail surface: Natural (dirt, rock) and paved roads

Land status: Ledges State Park (Iowa DNR)

Nearest town: Boone, 5 miles to the north

Maps: USGS Madrid NW, IA; park map available online

Other trail users: None

Special considerations: The trails pass by steep bluffs and involve numerous stairs and steep climbs.

Amenities available: Restrooms near the trailhead and water pumps and other restrooms throughout the state park

Maximum grade: 28%; this is one of the steepest hikes in this guidebook; the steepest climb is from the park road to Crow's Nest, climbing over 200 feet in less than one-quarter mile

Cell service: Adequate coverage in most of the park, although tree cover and canyon walls may restrict reception in places

Finding the trailhead: From US 30 south of Boone, head south on CR R27/Quill Avenue. After 2.8 miles, turn west onto 250th Street. After entering the state park, turn south at the Oak Woods Shelter and park. Hog's Back Trailhead is on the west side of the park road. GPS: N41° 59.714' W93° 52.834'

Trail conditions: The trails are well maintained and have excellent trail markers at major junctions. The steep trails and steps will be slippery after rain. Some trails pass by steep bluffs, so caution must be taken. The trails receive heavy traffic.

The Hike

The Pennsylvanian sandstone for which Ledges State Park is so well known was deposited some 300 million years ago, when Iowa was located just south of the equator. Large rivers flowed northeast-southwest through the state, draining into the shallow sea that covered much of the western United States. The sea's coastline was

The climb to Crow's Nest

constantly in flux, migrating back and forth between Oklahoma and Illinois, periodically flooding the coastal swamps and tropical forests of Iowa (the source of our coal deposits). The rivers deposited clay, mud, and sand, which today can be found in the park's Pennsylvanian rock record of sandstone, shale, coal, and limestone.

In geologic time, the sandstone was sculpted into the ledges overlooking Pea's Creek Canyon much more recently, only 12,000 to 13,000 years ago. As the Des Moines Lobe of the Wisconsinan ice sheet was melting, massive amounts of water drained off it. The routes the meltwater took carved out the steep-sided Pea's and Davis Creek valleys. Over 4 miles of trails lead hikers up and down the steep canyon, but for those looking for a gentler hike, there is a fully accessible interpretive trail to Lost Lake on the south end of the park. In late summer, you'll find abundant fungi growing on rotting wood around the lake: coral tooth (*Herecium corraloides*), chicken-of-the-woods (*Laetiporus sulphureus*), and honey mushrooms (*Armillariella mellea*) are three edibles that are quite common during wet summers. For wildflower enthusiasts, there is a trail through the prairie south of Oak Woods Shelter. A summer stroll around the prairie reconstruction will give you a look at yellow and purple coneflowers, rattlesnake master, big bluestem, Indian grass, Missouri goldenrod, and several species of gentian.

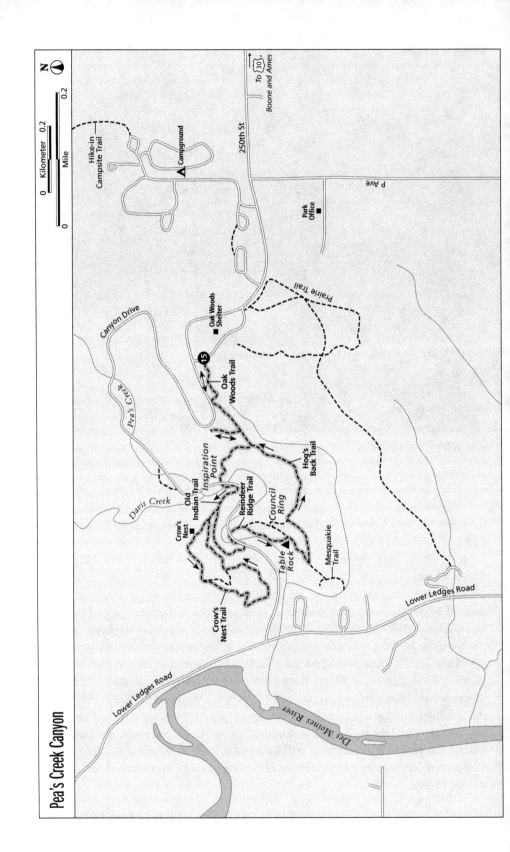

Pea's Creek Canyon

N

0 — Kilometer — 0.2
0 — Mile — 0.2

Canyon Drive

Pea's Creek

Davis Creek

Hike-in Campsite Trail

Campground

250th St

To 30,
Boone and Ames

P Ave

Park Office

Oak Woods Shelter

Prairie Trail

15

Oak Woods Trail

Old Indian Trail

Inspiration Point

Crow's Nest

Reindeer Ridge Trail

Council Ring

Hog's Back Trail

Table Rock

Mesquakie Trail

Crow's Nest Trail

Lower Ledges Road

Lower Ledges Road

Des Moines River

There are several places to begin your hike in Pea's Creek Canyon, and the aforementioned Oak Woods Shelter is as good as any. Head down Hog's Back Trail to shortly reach a parking area. Follow the sign toward Inspiration Point—there is not a formal overlook, but the view from the park road of the Des Moines River valley is inspiring. Continue down Oak Woods Trail, then take a right down steep steps to Canyon Road. Cross Pea's Creek, then take a breather before heading up Old Indian Trail.

There are two junctions before reaching Crow's Nest, ideal stops to catch your breath. When the trees have shed their leaves, it's a perfect spot to see the canyon, but during spring and summer the view is a splendid wall of green. Take a rest on the bench, then make one final push uphill. Take the trail heading west along the northern rim of the canyon. As the trail curves southwest, you will begin another descent into Pea's Creek Canyon. On your way down, you will pass the Hutton Memorial, placed in honor of Murray Lee Hutton, a strong conservationist and first director of the Iowa State Conservation Commission in 1935.

Continue downhill until reaching a large sandstone outcropping (heed the sign and do not climb on the rock). Instead of continuing to the road, keep left to head east along the canyon until reaching Old Indian Trail. Follow the stairs down, then take the next right to head west along the canyon. This "switchback" down the canyon avoids a longer walk along Canyon Road. Once you finally reach the road, take the opportunity to wade in ankle-deep Pea's Creek along sandstone bluffs. After drying your feet, turn south onto Reindeer Ridge Trail for the final climb of the hike. Your efforts will be rewarded with incredible views at Table Rock. Continue uphill toward Council Ring, then Inspiration Point to take Hog's Back Trail back to Oak Woods Shelter.

Miles and Directions

0.00 Start at Hog's Back Trailhead; head southwest.

0.03 After crossing the footbridge, turn left (southwest).

0.15 Inspiration Point and Hog's Back Trail parking.

0.17 Turn right (north) to reach Inspiration Point.

0.32 Turn right (north) onto Canyon Drive.

0.44 Turn left (south) onto the park road.

0.48 Turn right (north) onto Old Indian Trail and climb the stone steps.

0.57 Continue straight (northwest) toward Crow's Nest.

0.62 Crow's Nest.

0.65 Keep left (southwest) at the fork.

0.72 Turn left (south).

0.77 Hutton Memorial.

0.95 Pass the sandstone outcropping and turn left (north) at the wooden handrail.

1.04 Turn right (northeast).

Table Rock

1.16 Turn right (southeast) and go down the steps.

1.18 Turn right (southwest).

1.31 Turn left (north) onto the road toward the sandstone cliff.

1.37 Turn right (southeast) onto Reindeer Ridge Trail and climb the steps toward Table Rock Overlook.

1.49 Table Rock.

1.50 Turn right (south).

1.58 Turn left (east) toward Council Ring.

1.70 Council Ring; turn right (east).

1.90 Continue straight (northeast) toward Inspiration Point.

2.12 Arrive at Oak Woods Trailhead.

Honorable Mentions

D Prairie Heritage Center

The headquarters of O'Brien County Conservation, the Prairie Heritage Center is a great place to enjoy educational and interactive displays, hike the trails, savor the wildflowers, and engage in bird and wildlife watching. Observe a small herd of bison before hiking 5 miles of trails through prairie along the Little Sioux River. After the hike, drive the 36-mile Glacial Trail Scenic Byway to see how glaciers shaped the Hanging Valley and wildflowers blooming at Waterman Prairie.

Start: Trail access from Prairie Heritage Center and Yellow Avenue

Elevation gain: Variable

Distance: 5 miles of hiking trails

Difficulty: Easy

Hiking time: Variable; 2.5–3 hours if you hike the entire trail system

Seasons/schedule: Trails open daily from sunrise to sunset

Fees and permits: None

Trail contact: Prairie Heritage Center, 4931 Yellow Ave., Peterson 51047, (712) 295-7200; occb@obriencounty.iowa.gov; prairieheritagecenter.org/prairie-heritage -center/

Dog-friendly: Yes, on leash

Trail surface: Natural (dirt and grass)

Land status: Prairie Heritage Center (O'Brien County Conservation)

Nearest town: Peterson, 4.5 miles to the east

Maps: USGS Sutherland East, IA; trail map available online

Other trail users: None

Special considerations: None

Amenities available: Restrooms and water in the Prairie Heritage Center when open (check website for hours)

Maximum grade: Variable

Cell service: Adequate

Finding the trailhead: From Peterson, head west on IA 10. After 4 miles, turn north onto Yellow Avenue. Prairie Heritage Center is one-half mile down the road. GPS: N42° 56.072' W195° 25.120'

    Trail conditions: The trails are mowed grass paths. They are easy to follow, but ask the center for a trail map or download it from the center's website. The trails receive light traffic.

Prairie Heritage Center is located on the Glacial Trail Scenic Byway.

E Lime Creek Nature Center

Nine miles of trails will take you to an old brewery built in 1873; a bird blind that looks out over the wetland area, a stopover point for many migrating waterfowl; floodplain forests along the Winnebago River; an old quarry-turned-lake; and several prairie restorations. The Easy Access Trail is paved; the rest of the trails are mowed footpaths.

Start: Lime Creek Nature Center
Elevation gain: Variable; all of the trails are level and have minimal elevation change
Distance: 9 miles of trails
Difficulty: Easy
Hiking time: Variable; more than 3 hours if you hike the entire trail system
Seasons/schedule: Trails are open daily, year-round from 6 a.m. to 10:30 p.m.
Fees and permits: None
Trail contact: Lime Creek Nature Center, 3501 Lime Creek Rd., Mason City 50401; (641) 423-5309; cgcounty.org/departments/conservation/lime-creek
Dog-friendly: Yes, on leash
Trail surface: Natural (dirt) and gravel

Land status: Lime Creek Nature Center (Cerro Gordo Conservation)
Nearest town: Mason City, 2.5 miles to the south
Maps: USGS Mason City, IA; trail map available online and posted outside the nature center
Other trail users: Equestrians and mountain bikers
Special considerations: None
Amenities available: Restrooms and water in the nature center when open (check website for hours)
Maximum grade: Variable; all of the trails are level and have minimal elevation change
Cell service: Adequate

Finding the trailhead: From Mason City, head north on N Federal Avenue/US 65. After 1.4 miles, turn east onto Nature Center Road, then east again after one-half mile onto Lime Creek Road. Reach Lime Creek Nature Center after 0.4 miles. GPS: N43° 11.036' W93° 11.571'

Trail conditions: The trails are well maintained and easy to navigate. There are numerous trails, so take a trail map with you or just wander the trails at your leisure. The trails receive heavy traffic.

F Grimes Farm and Conservation Center

Leonard and Mildred Grimes purchased a farm near Marshalltown in 1964, and over the subsequent decades, they implemented conservation practices that turned 700 acres of marginal land into models of prairie and forest restoration. In 1992, the Grimes donated 162 acres of land to the Marshall County Conservation Board, creating Grimes Farm. In 2003, the Grimes Farm and Conservation Center was constructed on the land. Hiking trails provide access to the forests, wetlands, prairies, and crop fields. A nature playscape, amphitheater, and observation tower have been added over the years.

Start: Picnic shelter east of the nature center
Elevation gain: Variable; 902 (lowest) to 1,024 feet (highest) on Tower Loop
Distance: 3.91 miles of trails
Difficulty: Easy
Hiking time: Variable; 1 hour on Tower Loop to 2 hours for all the trails
Seasons/schedule: Open year-round from 5:30 a.m. to 10 p.m.
Fees and permits: None
Trail contact: Grimes Farm and Conservation Center, 2359 233rd St., Marshalltown 50158; www.grimesfarm.org
Dog-friendly: Yes, on leash
Trail surface: Natural (grass and dirt)

Land status: Grimes Farm and Conservation Center (Marshall County Conservation)
Nearest town: Marshalltown
Maps: USGS Marshalltown, IA; trail brochure available online
Other trail users: None
Special considerations: For your safety, headphones are discouraged.
Amenities available: Restrooms in the nature center
Maximum grade: 9%; if you hike Tower Loop clockwise, there is a 100-foot climb over one-half mile
Cell service: Adequate

Finding the trailhead: From US 30 south of Marshalltown, head north on Highland Acres Road. After 1 mile, turn west on 233rd Street, then after one-half mile turn north into Grimes Farm and Conservation Center. GPS: N42° 1.346' W92° 58.279'

Trail conditions: The mowed grass trails are well maintained. There are many trail options, so either consult the trail brochure or wander at your leisure. The trails receive light to moderate traffic.

Southern Iowa Drift Plain

As you cruise across the Southern Iowa Drift Plain on I-80, you'll observe what many consider to be the quintessential Iowa landscape: pastoral scenes painted onto a canvas of billowy hills. Artist Grant Wood captured the essence of these southern Iowa hills in his paintings Fall Plowing, Near Sundown, Spring Corn, and Stone City.

The ancient plain was composed of glacial till deposited by Pre-Illinoian ice sheets more than a half million years ago. Today, the Southern Iowa Drift Plain, the largest landform region in the state, bears the mark of its age. Drainage networks have carved out the once-level glacial plateau, forming the rills, streams, creeks, and major rivers that now define the landscape. The only remains of the plain are today's hill summits, which reveal the parts of the plain that have not been carried away by water. Standing atop these ancient hills brings perspective on change in landscape and form.

During the Pennsylvanian period, 290 to 365 million years ago, a vast shallow sea covered the bulk of the continent, with Iowa sitting near the equator. Tropical swamps fringed the coastline, which migrated with the rising and falling ocean levels. The swamps flooded periodically, and the organic matter decomposed and was covered by sand and mud. South-central Iowa's coal deposits, interbedded with Pennsylvanian sandstones and shales, are reminders of these swamps.

From 1874 to 1900, Iowa produced more coal than any other state west of the Mississippi. For a brief time Iowa was the last place that westward-bound coal-burning trains could stock up before their trip over the Great Plains. Thriving during the 1870s, Buxton, in Monroe County, was the largest unincorporated town ever in Iowa. Buxton once housed nearly 8,000 coal miners and their families, the majority of whom were African Americans recruited from the South to man the mines. The need for higher grade coal and discoveries of deposits elsewhere put an end to boom times, and Buxton was a ghost town by 1925. Many other towns in the southern hills survived the coal bust, but as much quieter reflections of their coal boom heyday.

Although the hills of southern Iowa seem to be uniformly curved, they are anything but homogenous. For the most part, loess deposits sit atop various layers of ancient soils, or paleosols. These clayey strata have been leached of nutrients and covered by windblown loess. The clay nature of the hills allowed for most of Iowa's man-made lakes to be created in southern Iowa. Farm ponds are found throughout, and the bulk of state parks and wildlife management areas are situated around the

Bur oak savanna at Whiterock Conservancy

larger lakes: Ahquabi, Bobwhite, Icaria, Little River, Nine Eagles, Rathbun, Three Fires, Twelve Mile, and Wapello, to name a few. As elsewhere in the state, the endless prairies of the region have been converted to agriculture and have undergone a succession into forests and shrubs due to overgrazing and the suppression of fire.

16 Long Creek Trail

The historic Garst Farm developed hybrid seed corn, hosted Soviet Premier Nikita Khrushchev during the Cold War, and continues to innovate today as Whiterock Conservancy in Guthrie County. The 5,500-acre nonprofit property was one of the largest land gifts in Iowa history; the Garst family's goal was to protect and restore their land for future generations to cultivate, conserve, and enjoy. More than 40 miles of trails are open to walkers, hikers, runners, mountain bikers, equestrians, and provides guided tours for visitors to explore the varied terrain on utility terrain vehicles (UTVs).

Start: Riverside Trailhead on Fig Avenue west of the Middle Raccoon River
Elevation gain: 584 feet total gain; 1,113 (lowest) to 1,288 feet (highest)
Distance: 6.05-mile loop
Difficulty: Moderate to difficult due to distance and uneven trail surface
Hiking time: 2.5–3 hours
Seasons/schedule: Weather permitting, trails are open year-round.
Fees and permits: There is no fee for hikers but a suggested user donation of $5 per person can be made at any trailhead/kiosk.
Trail contact: Whiterock Conservancy, 1436 IA 141, Coon Rapids 50058; (712) 790-8221; whiterockconservancy.org
Dog-friendly: Dogs do not need to be on a leash if they are well behaved and stay in close proximity to you while hiking. However, during burn season and hunting season, all pets must be kept on a leash for their safety.
Trail surface: Natural (dirt, grass, some sandy parts)
Land status: Whiterock Conservancy (private nonprofit)

Nearest town: Coon Rapids, 5 miles to the north
Maps: USGS Coon Rapids South, IA; trail map available online and at River Campground
Other trail users: Mountain bikers (there are also equestrian trails in the park)
Special considerations: Hikers are advised to use the rocked "double track" town loop trail if other trails are wet and muddy. Stop by a kiosk or the Bur Oak Visitor's Center to pick up a trail map. Trail updates can be found at whiterockconservancy/singletrack on Facebook or on the website.
Amenities available: Portable toilets, water, showers at River Campground
Maximum grade: 10%; completing the loop clockwise, there are two climbs of approximately 100 feet, the first one-quarter of a mile from the trailhead. Going counterclockwise, there are two steep climbs of 150 feet.
Cell service: Cell coverage is spotty in the lower sections of the valley (along the river). Verizon provides the best cell coverage throughout the conservancy, followed by US Cellular, AT&T, and T-Mobile.

Finding the trailhead: From Coon Rapids, head east on IA 141. After 2.2 miles, turn south on CR N56/Fig Avenue and continue for 2.3 miles. Pass the Whiterock Conservancy River Campground and cross the bridge over the Middle Raccoon River. The trailhead is on the west bank of the river on the north side of the road. GPS: N41° 49.016' W94° 38.875'

Trail conditions: The trails are in excellent condition. Trails can be muddy after rain, so if your activity leaves marks, turn around. Each junction has trail markers with navigational and distance information. Trees may be hazardous in high winds or after storms. The trails receive moderate traffic.

Middle Raccoon River

The Hike

Whiterock Conservancy is new to the second edition of *Hiking Iowa*, as it was created the year before the first edition was published in 2005. Its creation was the culmination of a 5,500-acre gift from the Garst family, one of the largest land gifts in Iowa history. In 1959, long before the land transfer, Soviet Premier Nikita Khrushchev visited the farmstead at his request. Khrushchev had befriended Roswell Garst on the latter's trips to the Soviet Union to sell hybrid corn. Garst's farm was comparable to Soviet collective farms, and its use of hybrid seed and other agricultural innovations was appealing to the Soviet leader.

Visitors can book overnight stays at the historic, six-bedroom Garst farmhouse, which is listed on the National Register of Historic Places. There is also a guest farmhouse, log house, several other farmhouses and cottages, and a rustic river cabin that are available to rent. In addition to multiuse trails, the 8-mile Middle Raccoon Water Trail connects River Campground at Whiterock with Riverside Park in Coon Rapids. An annual Star Party is held under the darkest skies in Iowa at the Star Field Campground. If you can't hike the trails, you can request a guided tour on a UTV to explore the double-track trail system that connects different areas of the conservancy.

805 Cabin

The trails at the conservancy make one of the best history hikes in Iowa not only for its Cold War history, but also as a piece of living history in the 21st century. Whiterock is a working ranch that balances sustainable agriculture with conservation practices and recreational opportunities. The nonprofit has always had a three-part mission: conservation, recreation and education, and sustainable agriculture, so it's only fitting that the property continues to innovate in conservation.

One of the many recreation opportunities at Whiterock Conservancy is at the River Campground, where the nonprofit organization gets its name. Whiterock is named after a sandstone outcropping at the top of a bluff along the Middle Raccoon River south of the River Campground. Across the road from the campground is the River House Barn and Woodland Carriage House. Cross the bridge west over Long Creek to reach foot access to the eponymous trail, one of several excellent trails at Whiterock Conservancy.

Long Creek Trail heads north along the west side of the creek. After one-quarter mile, you will reach the junction of Long Creek and Riverside Trails. If you are not up for the 6-mile loop, continue north on Riverside Trail to the 805 Cabin, then turn around and hike back to Fig Avenue for a 2-mile out-and-back hike. If you have the energy, Long Creek Trail is worth the extra distance as it meanders through oak

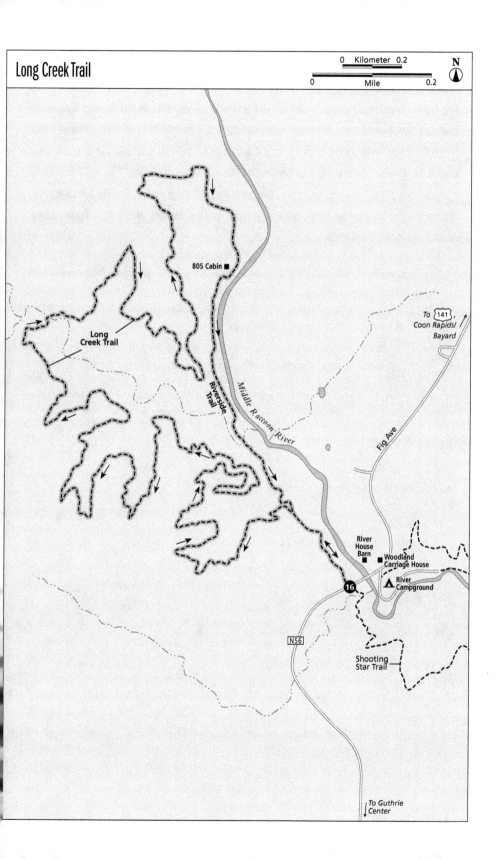

0   Kilometer   0.2

0   Mile   0.2

N

805 Cabin ■

To 141,
Coon Rapids/
Bayard

Long
Creek Trail

Riverside
Trail

Middle Raccoon River

Fig Ave

River
House
Barn

Woodland
Carriage House

16

River
Campground

N56

Shooting
Star Trail

To Guthrie
Center

KUEHN CONSERVATION AREA

The Kuehn Conservation Area is the largest property managed by Dallas County Conservation. The 1,000-acre tract includes hardwood forest, restored prairie, and access to the South Raccoon River. There is more than 4 miles of hiking-only trails in the eastern section of the conservation area, with parking at the end of Houston Trail. The wildlife refuge includes two primitive camping areas. Kuehn is home to the annual Prairie Awakenings/Prairie Awoke Celebration, with music, dances, stories, drums, and songs from native Iowans to today's landscape.

savanna, hardwood forest, and upland prairie. After a 100-foot climb, Long Creek Trail turns into an undulating trail following the rim of the creek valley as it wanders north with several wayward diversions. There are no intersecting trails, so don't be tempted to shortcut a section by walking off-trail, which can disturb fragile plants and vulnerable animals.

After crossing a drainage, the landscape begins to turn to an oak savanna as you reach the northern reach of Long Creek Trail. Head south on Riverside Trail. The hike will be flat, easy, and pleasant as you follow the creek back to Fig Avenue. Along the way, pass the 805 Cabin, a rustic riverside cabin without electricity or water.

Miles and Directions

0.00 Head north at the bicycle and pedestrian access toward 805 Cabin.

0.24 Turn left (southwest) onto Long Creek Trail.

2.62 Footbridge.

3.43 Footbridge.

4.89 Turn right (east) onto Riverside Trail.

5.23 805 Cabin.

5.26 Footbridge/boardwalk.

5.61 Water crossing.

5.81 Continue straight (south).

6.05 Arrive back at the trailhead on Fig Avenue.

17 Ahren's Access Loop

When Jacob Krumm bequeathed his farm to the Jasper County Conservation Board, he did so with the express intention that it become a wildlife refuge. The board followed through, and reconstruction efforts have jump-started the improving health of prairie, wetland, savanna, and forest. Today, muskrats build dens on the site of a former hog lot, and fish use junked cars at the bottom of ponds as breeding habitat. Seven miles of trails offer excellent bird watching and exploration of native habitat.

Start: Ahren's Access (14892 Jacob Ave., Grinnell, IA 50112)
Elevation gain: 611 feet total gain
Distance: 5.25-mile double loop
Difficulty: Easy to moderate
Hiking time: 2–2.5 hours
Seasons/schedule: Trails open daily, year-round
Fees and permits: None
Trail contact: Jasper County Conservation, 1030 W 2nd St. S, Newton 50208; (641) 792-9780; conservation@jasperia.org; co.jasper.ia.us/facilities/facility/details/Jacob-Krumm-Nature-Preserve-2
Dog-friendly: Yes, on leash

Trail surface: Natural (dirt and grass)
Land status: Jacob Krumm Prairie (Jasper County Conservation)
Nearest town: Grinnell, 6 miles to the northeast
Maps: USGS Oakland Acres, IA; trail map available online
Other trail users: None
Special considerations: Ticks and poison ivy are potential hazards.
Amenities available: None
Maximum grade: 13%; there are two climbs of 100 feet and two climbs of 75 feet
Cell service: Adequate

Finding the trailhead: From I-80, take exit 179 heading north on CR T38 N. After one-third of a mile, turn east onto Jacob Avenue. The turn west into Ahren's Access in three-quarters of a mile down the road. GPS: N41° 42.313′ W92° 47.188′

Trail conditions: The trails are well maintained. There is little shade on large sections of the trails, so bring plenty of water and dress accordingly. The trails will be muddy after rain, so consider turning around if your activity leaves a mark. The trails receive light to moderate traffic.

The Hike

Following the death of Jacob Krumm in 1976, his will provided for the transfer of his 300-acre farm to the Jasper County Conservation Board "to be retained as a wildlife refuge." A bachelor-farmer who was more a steward of the land than its owner, Krumm shunned destructive agricultural practices. However, he did allow townspeople to junk nearly 300 cars on his land. During the park's development, gas tanks were removed from the cars and the frames bulldozed together. The mass of metal now functions as a fish habitat at the bottom of the three ponds on Sugar Creek.

A double-loop hike from Ahren's Access takes hikers past all three ponds. It may be hard to believe, but the area now covered by the 25-acre lake at Ahren's Access

Waldo Walker Memorial Bird Blind KATIE CANTU

was once described by a director of the Jasper County Conservation Board as "one of the most disgusting hog lots you've ever smelled." In 1996 local businessman Claude Ahrens bought the 80-acre hog lot and generously donated the land to the board. Several rat-infested buildings were disassembled, the manure-choked lagoon was dredged, and its contents were spread out to compost into soil. The dam was built—and a former environmental disaster zone is now a place where Canada geese raise their young.

After hiking along the west bank of the pond for nearly 1 mile, the woods thin out and give way to prairie on the south side of the train tracks. Because more than 99.9 percent of Iowa's native prairie is gone, the hunt for prairie remnants usually takes you to places you least expect. Railroad rights-of-way—the unplowed swaths on the sides of train tracks—have long served as refuges for prairie plants. The adjacent land along the rail tracks has visibly benefited from the right-of-way seedbank and is the best prairie remnant in the park. Sparks flying from the coal engines of passing trains probably started small fires that helped rejuvenate the prairie. In 1977, several other areas within the park were seeded to native prairie grasses. Try to discern the difference between the seeded tracts throughout the preserve and the prairie south of the train tracks by assessing the plant diversity. You'll find big and little

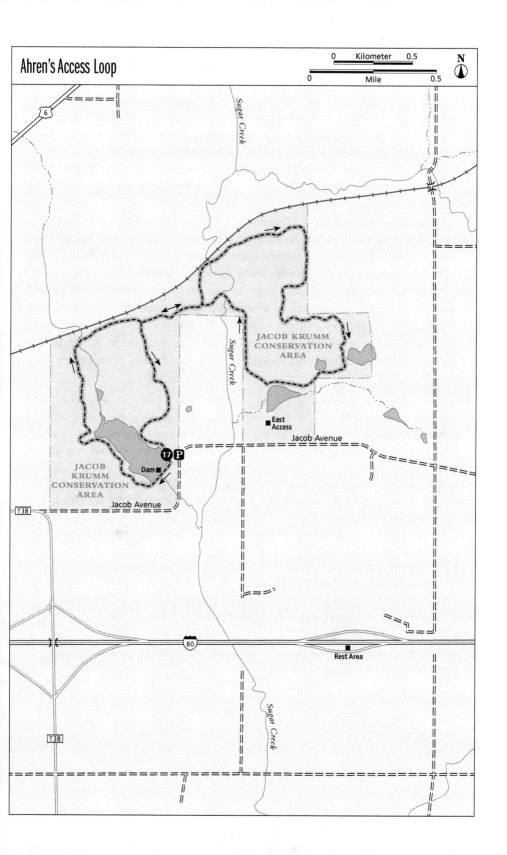

Ahren's Access Loop

0   Kilometer   0.5

0   Mile   0.5

N

Sugar Creek

6

JACOB KRUMM
CONSERVATION
AREA

Sugar Creek

East
Access

Jacob Avenue

17 P

JACOB
KRUMM
CONSERVATION
AREA

Dam

Jacob Avenue

T38

80

Rest Area

T38

Sugar Creek

bluestem, Indian grass, Canada wild rye, and switchgrass throughout, but wildflowers such as pale purple coneflower, wild rose, cream gentian, butterfly milkweed, compass plant, and several species of goldenrod usually can be found only south of the railroad.

Hike northeast along the railroad tracks for 1 mile, then head south. The eastern boundary of the preserve is more wooded, but the proximity of prairie to the west provides ample opportunities to view both woodland and grassland bird species as you hike south toward the two other preserve ponds and the east access trailhead and parking area. Follow the trail back north toward the rail tracks to catch the trail across Sugar Creek to return to Ahren's Access.

North of the train tracks is Uhlenhopp Arboretum, opened in 2021 and also managed by Jasper County Conservation. Originally scheduled to open in 2020, the August 2020 derecho delayed the opening for one year. The land was willed to Jasper County by a Grinnell College professor who planted thousands of trees at the property, dubbing it "The Arb." A 3-mile loop will take you by seven ponds, each named after a day of the week. Adjacent to Uhlenhopp to the north is the Sugar Creek Audubon Nature Sanctuary. It has several trails through woodland and prairie remnants along Sugar Creek. Additionally, Rock Creek State Park lies to the northwest of the previously mentioned preserves and has more than 8 miles of multiuse trails.

Miles and Directions

0.00 Start by walking west across the dam; the trail fringes the west side of the lake.

1.20 After looping around the north side of the lake, you'll be walking next to the train tracks. (FYI: During the growing season, you're going to want to spend a little time here checking out prairie plants.)

1.40 At the fork go straight (east) to continue into the eastern portion of the park. **Bailout:** If you're close to being done walking, take a right (south) and head back the 0.6 miles to the trailhead.

1.70 At the fork turn left (northeast) to explore the savanna area in the northeast corner of the park.

3.70 At the fork you'll be able to see the east parking area directly to the south. Take a right (north) to get back to the other trailhead.

4.00 After the trail has gone due north and just as it begins to curve to the west, check out the newly created wetland described above; amazing stuff.

4.30 At the fork turn left (southwest).

4.50 At the fork at the top of the hill, turn left to cruise down to the lake.

5.25 Arrive back at the trailhead.

18 Brown's Woods Loop

Brown's Woods is the largest urban forest in Iowa. Despite the din of highway traffic, the 4 miles of trails that loop through the stand of timber along the Des Moines River are peaceful and rejuvenating. The canopy of oak and hickory trees stretches from Brown's Woods Drive to the Raccoon River.

Start: Northeast corner of the parking loop
Elevation gain: 220 feet total gain; 809 (lowest) to 945 feet (highest)
Distance: 3.31-mile loop
Difficulty: Easy
Hiking time: 1.5–2 hours
Seasons/schedule: Park open 6:30 a.m. to 10:30 p.m., Apr 1 through Oct 31; sunrise to sunset, Nov 1 through Mar 31
Fees and permits: None
Trail contact: Polk County Conservation, 465 SE Brown's Woods Dr., West Des Moines 50265; (515) 323-5300; polkcountyiowa.gov/conservation/parks-trails/brown-s-woods/
Dog-friendly: Dogs must be kept on a 6-foot leash; please remember to pick up after your pets.
Trail surface: Natural and crushed rock

Land status: Brown's Woods
Nearest town: Des Moines
Maps: USGS Des Moines SW, IA; trail map available online
Other trail users: None
Special considerations: Visitors may collect nuts, fruit, and edible mushrooms for non-commercial use if the plant is not harmed. If you hike the loop counterclockwise, there are two spur trails that you can hike if you do not want to hike the full loop.
Amenities available: Restrooms and water at the parking area
Maximum grade: 10%; the biggest climb is from the Raccoon River on the north end of the loop, gaining 150 feet over one-half mile
Cell service: Above average reception throughout the loop

Finding the trailhead: Brown's Woods is located north of IA 5 and just west of IA 28. From IA 5, take exit 101 and head northeast on Veterans Parkway. After 1.4 miles, turn west onto Brown's Woods Drive, then turn east after 0.2 miles to reach the trailhead. GPS: N41° 32.480' W93° 42.235'

Trail conditions: The trails are well maintained and there are trail markers with navigational information at each junction. The trails will get soft and muddy after rains, so if your activity leaves a mark, consider turning around. The trails receive heavy traffic.

The Hike

Brown's Woods is named after Tallmadge E. Brown, a successful Des Moines lawyer who acquired large tracts of land around Des Moines in the late 1800s. One of the tracts of land was this beautiful forest, acquired by the Polk County Conservation Board in 1972. The property was formerly known as Brown's Woods Forest Preserve, but a recently developed land management plan dropped the preserve label. You might still see signage that carries the former name.

The parking area and trailhead are in the southeastern corner of the property. There are restrooms and water in the parking lot, as well as picnic tables and an

Brown's Woods

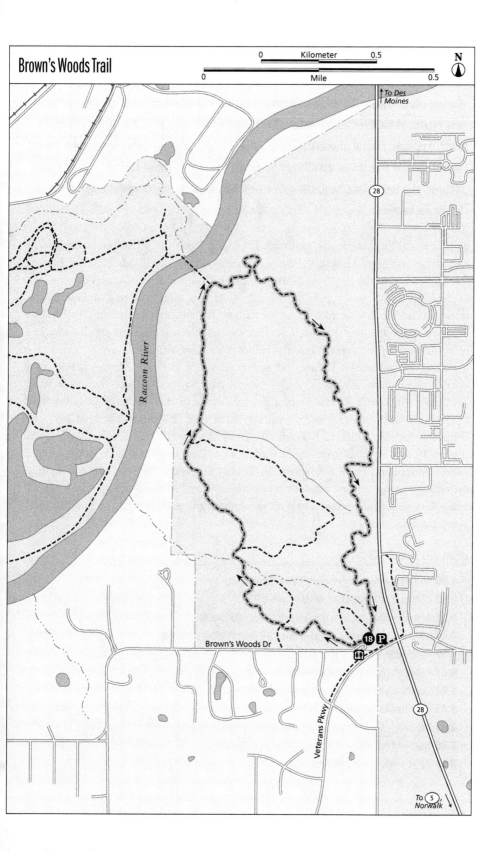

Brown's Woods Trail

0 — Kilometer — 0.5

0 — Mile — 0.5

N

Raccoon River

To Des Moines

28

Brown's Woods Dr

18 P

Veterans Pkwy

28

To 5 Norwalk

BRENTON ARBORETUM

Explore approximately 2,500 plants representing more than 500 different species, cultivars, and hybrids at the Brenton Arboretum. The 140-acre arboretum in Dallas Center has a lake, pond, wetlands, several streams, walking paths, bridges, prairies, wildflowers, and a small library. Natural prairie was established to restore the land to native habitat. Signature collections of trees include Kentucky coffee tree, oak, hickory, elm, Osage orange, and large landscape conifers.

informational kiosk near the trailhead. There is a half-mile accessible interior loop trail at the trailhead. Hiking the loop clockwise allows you to shorten the hike at three locations on the west side of the large loop around the woodland. The west side of the loop is also the farthest from IA 28, so if you want a more complete escape from the Des Moines metro, stick to the trails on the west side of Brown's Woods. The full loop totals just over 3 miles. There are no notable landmarks along the way, just beautiful bottomland forest along the banks of the Des Moines River.

There are numerous hiking and walking trails in the Des Moines metro; two notable public parks are north of Des Moines near Saylorville Lake. Sycamore Trails has 6 miles of hike/bike trails along the west bank of the Des Moines River. The Sycamore Trail North (3.5 miles) and Top Shelf Trail (2.7 miles) north of I-80 can connect two trails south of I-80 via the Trestle-to-Trestle Trail. The trails are open from 6:30 a.m. to 10:30 p.m. daily. Farther north, on the west shore of Saylorville Lake, is Jester Park. The 1,600-acre Polk County property includes various amenities, including a nature center, outdoor recreation and wellness center, equestrian center, and golf course. There are nature trails throughout the park, as well as a multiuse trail along the lakeshore.

Miles and Directions

0.00 At the trailhead, take the left fork to head west.

0.03 Continue straight (west) at trail marker #2.

0.29 At trail marker #3, take the left fork to continue west.

0.48 Keep left (northwest) at trail marker #4 onto Wilderness Loop.

0.59 Footbridge.

0.63 Keep left (north) at trail marker #5.

1.02 Continue straight (north) at trail marker #6.

1.49 Spur trail to the Raccoon River.

2.65 Bench.

3.25 Keep left (south).

3.31 Arrive back at the trailhead.

19 Tallgrass Trail

Less than 0.1 percent of the original native tallgrass prairie that once covered Iowa remains today. That's why the reconstruction of 4,000 acres of tallgrass prairie at Neal Smith National Wildlife Refuge is truly inspirational. Take the ½ mile Overlook Trail and the 2 mile Tallgrass Trail loops to experience the tallgrass prairie grasses, wild-flowers, and wildlife. You can view the bison and elk enclosure from the trails. The Prairie Learning Center, which serves as a visitor center, features in-depth exhibits and is a base for the restoration and ongoing research, The half-mile Overlook trail is wheelchair accessible.

Start: Prairie Learning Center

Elevation gain: 197 feet total gain; 814 (lowest) to 902 feet (highest)

Distance: Overlook Trail is a ½ mile loop, concrete surface, wheelchair accessible Tallgrass Trail is 2 mile loop, asphalt surface

Difficulty: Easy

Hiking time: 1–1.5 hours

Seasons/schedule: Refuge lands are open from dawn to dusk daily.

Fees and permits: None

Trail contact: Neal Smith National Wildlife Refuge, PO Box 399, 9981 Pacific St., Prairie City 50228; (515) 994-3400; nealsmith@fws.gov; fws.gov/refuge/neal-smith

Dog-friendly: Yes, on leash

Trail surface: Paved

Land status: Neal Smith National Wildlife Refuge (US Fish and Wildlife Service)

Nearest town: Prairie City, 5 miles to the north

Maps: USGS Runnells, IA; refuge map available online and at the Prairie Learning Center

Other trail users: None

Special considerations: Please note that GPS units and online mapping services do not always give accurate directions to the refuge. Ticks are abundant in warmer months.

Amenities available: Restrooms are available inside the visitor center, outside the visitor center parking lot, and at the Oak Savanna Trail parking lot.

Maximum grade: 5%; there is a 75-foot climb from the creek bottom to the Prairie Learning Center

Cell service: Average

Finding the trailhead: From Des Moines, take IA 163 to the Prairie City exit. Go straight from the off-ramp and follow the paved 4.5-mile entry road to the visitor center. From I-80, take the Colfax exit and turn south on IA 117. Drive 6 miles following IA 117; turn right in Prairie City to continue on IA 117. Cross IA 163, and turn right on the paved entry road. GPS: N41° 33.532' W93° 16.789'

Trail conditions: The Overlook Trail is accessible, and while Tallgrass Trail is paved, cracks and other impairments would make wheelchair access difficult. Weeds and other vegetation may be present along sections of the trail. The trails receive moderate traffic.

The Hike

Created by an act of Congress in 1990, the refuge staff and volunteers work to reconstruct large tracts of tallgrass prairie and restore the oak savanna ecosystem. After plans for a nuclear power generating station fell through in the late 1970s, the US Fish and

The refuge has a small herd of bison in an 800-acre enclosure. SALLY ORTGIES

Wildlife Service purchased 3,622 acres in the Walnut Creek watershed from Redlands Corporation, a subsidiary of Iowa Power. Neal Smith, a longtime congressman from Iowa, supported the tallgrass reconstruction project and helped obtain federal funding. Formerly known as Walnut Creek National Wildlife Refuge, it was renamed to honor Smith's dedication and service.

Bison were introduced in 1996 and elk in 1997, and they can be seen happily munching on prairie grasses and forbs. Although it will take time before all the floral and faunal components of the prairie return, and ultimately they may not, the infancy

Tallgrass Trail

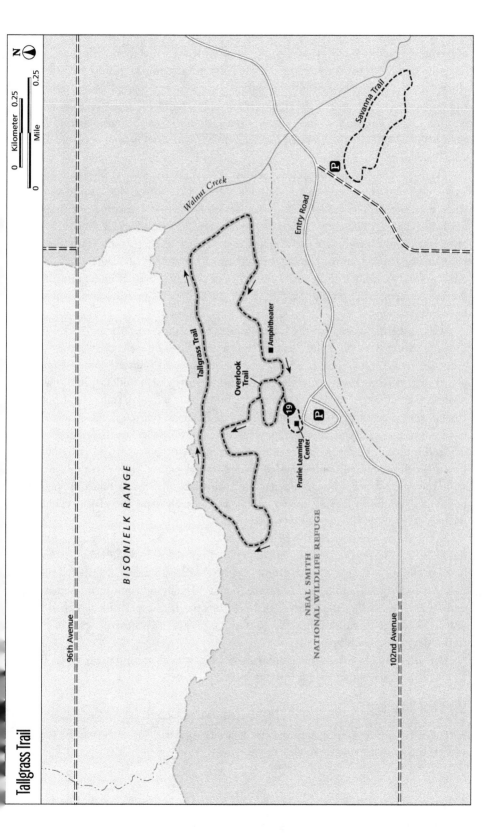

of the refuge prairie is a spectacular thing all the same. In Sand County Almanac, Aldo Leopold wrote: "What a thousand acres of Silphiums [compass plants] looked like when they tickled the bellies of the buffalo is a question never again to be answered, and perhaps not even asked." We don't yet know, but Leopold's question may yet be worth asking. The creation and ongoing management of the refuge wouldn't have been possible without the work of many committed volunteers who accepted Leopold's challenge.

There are four short hiking trails within the refuge (Basswood, Savanna, Overlook, and Tallgrass), as well as a 6-mile hike along a fire break that can be walked when it's mowed. (The 0.5-mile Basswood Trail is far from the learning center and is not covered here.) The auto tour takes you through the bison and elk enclosure and gives you a landscape view of the Walnut Creek watershed. Stop at the Prairie Learning Center, which features exhibits on prehistoric cultures that inhabited the area, pre-settlement natural history, various ecosystems currently present in the refuge, and the prairie reconstruction process. Check out the under-the-prairie maze—but look out for the badger!

Walk out the east side of the learning center and onto the half-mile Overlook Trail, following signs onto the Tallgrass Trail, a paved 2-mile walkway with benches every one-third mile. Here is where you'll really start to immerse yourself in the prairie: big and little bluestem, Indian grass, and sideoats grama undulate in the wind. Scores of wildflowers, including cup plants, butterfly milkweed, yellow and purple coneflowers, tick trefoil, Culver's root, and bee balm, among countless others, add vivid colors to the scene. Black swallowtails, clouded sulphurs, great spangled fritillary, and monarch butterflies are seen flitting from flower to flower, gathering nectar. Listen for the flight calls and songs of several typical prairie birds that flush as you walk: the American goldfinch's descending ti-di-di-di, dickcissel's buzzy fpppt, and bobolink's soft bink. During spring, you'll undoubtedly hear the classic wichety-wichety-wichety of the common yellowthroat.

At the three-quarter mile the trail makes a 180-degree turn and begins to follow the fence that separates the bison and elk range from the rest of the refuge. If you're lucky, some of the animals may be down by the creek for a drink or foraging in the lush vegetation surrounding it. It's estimated that 30 million bison once roamed the prairies of Iowa, while their extermination from the landscape took less than 150 years. The reintroduction of these beacons of the prairie has restored a sense of hope to this devastated landscape.

On your way to or from the learning center, take a stroll around the Savanna Trail. The half-mile gravel path winds through burr oaks.

Miles and Directions

The half-mile Overlook Trail is a loop inside the 2-mile Tallgrass Trail loop. Both trails are easy to navigate and have interpretive signs to guide you.

20 Coal Miner's Daughter Trail

The trails at Banner Lakes at Summerset State Park are popular with mountain bikers, but the multiuse trails also offer a fun and different experience for hikers. The narrow single-track trails zig and zag through forest around two lakes created by a former coal mining operation.

Start: Coal Miner's Daughter Trailhead located in the northwest corner of the state park
Elevation gain: 72 feet total gain; 790 (lowest) to 819 feet (highest)
Distance: 2.61-mile loop
Difficulty: Easy
Hiking time: 1–1.5 hours
Seasons/schedule: Open daily, year-round from 4 a.m. to 10:30 p.m.
Fees and permits: None
Trail contact: Banner Lakes at Summerset State Park, 13084 Elk Horn St., Carlisle, IA 50047; (515) 961-7101; Lake Ahquabi State Park, 16510 118th Ave., Indianola 50125; (515) 961-7101; Summerset@dnr.iowa.gov; iowadnr.gov/

Places-to-Go/State-Parks/Iowa-State-Parks/Banner-Lakes-at-Summerset-State-Park
Dog-friendly: Yes, on leash
Trail surface: Natural (dirt and grass) and paved roads
Land status: Banner Lakes at Summerset State Park (Iowa DNR)
Nearest town: Indianola, 6 miles to the south
Maps: USGS Scotch Ridge, IA; park map available online
Other trail users: Mountain bikers
Special considerations: No storm shelters are available at the park.
Amenities available: Restrooms
Maximum grade: 5%; there are no substantial inclines but numerous ups and downs
Cell service: Adequate reception

Finding the trailhead: From the intersection of US 69 and IA 92 in Indianola, head north on US 69 for 6 miles. Turn east onto Elk Horn Street, then take the next right (south) to enter the state park. The parking area is on the left (southwest) of the park road; the trailhead is opposite the parking area. GPS: N41° 26.695' W93° 33.366'

Trail conditions: The trails are designed for mountain bikers but also welcome hikers. The winding trail system can be confusing, so it's best to put the map away and just wander. Coal Miner's Daughter Trail is a narrow dirt single-track, while Missing Link is a wider grassy path. It is recommended to not hike with earbuds/headphones so you can hear approaching bikers. The trails receive moderate traffic.

The Hike

The two large lakes and multiple small ponds that attract anglers to their water and bikers and hikers to their shores are the remnants of mining operations in the 1930s. Known as Banner Pits to locals, lakes and ponds were created by the Banner Coal Company operating a strip mine. The open-pit methods left the lakes and ponds that are populated with channel catfish, largemouth bass, bluegill, and crappie.

The trails at Summerset State Park are popular with mountain bikers.

The Banner Shooting Range is adjacent to the park on its eastern boundary. Gunshots from target practice will likely accompany your entire hike. Don't drown out the noise with headphones or earbuds, however, as mountain biking is very popular at Summerset. The trails are narrow and have blind curves, so you need to be aware of your surroundings and hear approaching bikers.

At the beginning, Coal Miner's Daughter begins like many other mountain bike trails: confusing, chaotic, and ultimately, frustrating. However, keep pushing through on the trail and hikers will encounter an extremely fun hiking roller-coaster. There are plenty of twists, turns, ups, and downs on the dirt single-track trails around the Banner Lakes at Summerset State Park. Once you get past the first three-quarter mile section—a web of trails that almost touch water in sections—the trails follow right along the edge of the northern lake. There are fun boardwalks built for bikes but equally enjoyable on foot. Children would love this trail, but with the presence of mountain bikers they shouldn't be allowed to run freely along the trail as a collision would be a possibility. Missing Link is a wider trail that runs between the two Banner Lakes. If you want a challenge at the end of the loop, take Extra Credit and see if you can make it back to the park road without retracing your steps.

Coal Miner's Daughter Trail

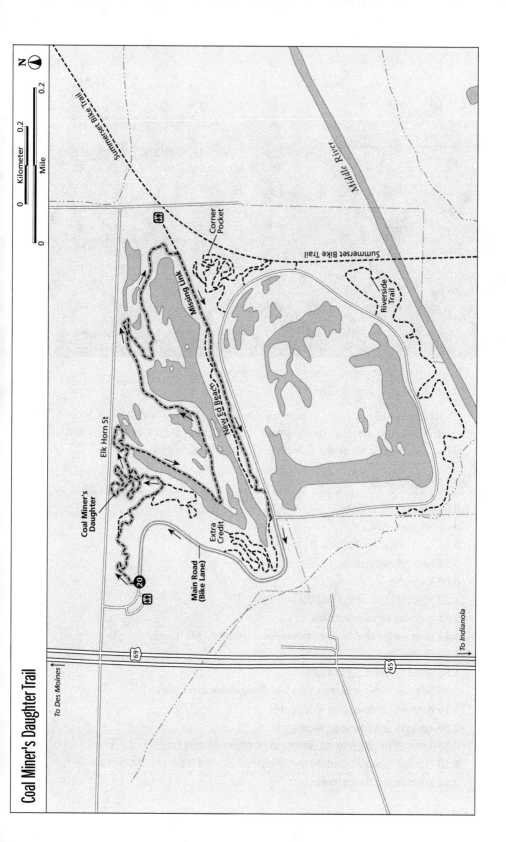

The state park was originally a coal mining operation.

Visit in late July or early August for the famous Indianola Balloon Classic. While there are no campgrounds, the state park is also 6 miles from Des Moines and would make a quiet retreat from the crowds during the Iowa State Fair.

Miles and Directions

0.00 Begin at the trailhead.

0.16 Petroleum pipeline.

0.25 Keep left (southeast) onto the bypass trail.

0.28 Keep left (northeast).

0.80 Footbridge.

1.20 Keep right (northeast) onto the blue trail.

1.33 Short but very steep decline.

1.52 Keep left (east) at the fork marked by the "Problem Child" post.

1.60 Footbridge.

1.66 At the fork, keep right (south).

1.70 Turn left (south) at the mountain bike obstacle next to the lake.

1.75 Keep left (southwest) on Missing Link.

1.85 Keep left (southwest) on Missing Link.

1.90 Turn right (north), then left (southwest) to stay on Missing Link.

2.15 Turn right (south) toward the park road, then turn right (west) onto the park road.

2.61 Arrive back at the trailhead.

21 Woodland Mounds Trail

A group of six burial mounds built 900 to 1,600 years ago are perched atop a bluff overlooking the South River, on the north end of Woodland Mounds State Preserve. Footpaths lead through forested uplands to the native burial mounds, then through the adjacent Woodland Mounds Wildlife Area. Two words: mushrooms and woodland wildflowers!

Start: Service road entrance on west end of the parking area
Elevation gain: 190 feet total gain; 816 (lowest) to 928 feet (highest)
Distance: 3.12-mile loop
Difficulty: Easy
Hiking time: About 1.5 hours
Seasons/schedule: Park hours are 6:30 a.m. to 10 p.m.
Fees and permits: None
Trail contact: Warren County Conservation, 15565 118th Ave., Indianola 50125; (515) 961-6169; wccb@warrenccb.org; mycounty parks.com/county/warren/Park/Woodland -Mounds-Preserve.aspx
Dog-friendly: Yes, on leash

Trail surface: Natural (dirt and grass)
Land status: Woodland Mounds State Preserve (Warren County Conservation)
Nearest town: Indianola, 8 miles to the west
Maps: USGS Milo, IA; trail map displayed at trailhead; park map available online
Other trail users: None
Special considerations: Hunting is allowed on the west half of the property, so check season dates and dress accordingly.
Amenities available: Restrooms were closed as of Oct 2023.
Maximum grade: 8%; the trail descends 100 feet over one-half mile at the trailhead, then climbs 75 feet over one-quarter mile

Finding the trailhead: From Indianola, head east on IA 92. After 3.5 miles, turn south onto 165th Avenue/CR S23. After approximately 1 mile, turn east onto Kennedy Street. Continue east for 1.2 miles, and after crossing the South River, turn east onto Keokuk Street. Keokuk Street becomes 193rd Avenue as it bends south, then Kirkwood Street as it bends to head east again. Turn north into the entrance to Woodland Mounds Preserve. The parking area and trailhead are at the end of the gravel road. GPS: N41° 20.698' W93° 25.906'

Trail conditions: The trails are well maintained and there are trail markers at the junctions providing trail and navigational information. The natural surface trails get soft and muddy after rains, so avoid hiking after heavy rains to prevent trail degradation. The trails receive moderate traffic.

The Hike

Woodland Mounds State Preserve is a 185-acre area featuring a group of six conical burial mounds dating from the years 400 to 1100. The Woodland culture that built the mounds gives its name to a preserve located in Warren County east of Indianola. The indigenous Woodland culture lived in villages along the forested rivers 3,000 to 800 years ago.

There is an informational kiosk in the parking lot, but there is no officially marked trailhead. You can begin right at the kiosk, or the most logical starting

Foragers will find the trails fruitful.

point is on the eastern end of the parking lot at the service road entrance. The pit toilets in the opposite corner of the recreation area were closed as of September 2023. Woodland Mounds State Preserve is one of the few state preserves in Iowa with officially established hiking trails. From the service road entrance, head north along a wide, natural surface trail into one of the largest continuous stands of timber remaining in Warren County. Hunting is permitted in the western half of Woodland Mounds (the eastern half is a refuge with no hunting allowed), so check hunting season dates and dress accordingly.

After more than one-half mile, the trail reaches Gilbert's Grove. Take a break here to enjoy this beautiful section of the forest, then continue north on Woodland Mounds Trail. There is a connector trail at Gilbert's Grove and another at the halfway point of the full 3-mile loop. The first burial mounds you will encounter are after 1.25 miles of hiking from the trailhead.

The group of conical burial mounds are located on a ridge near the northern boundary of the preserve. The Woodland Indian culture was widespread throughout the eastern United States and was more common in the eastern portion of the state. Woodland Indians were hunters, gatherers, and farmers, and mound building was part of their culture. Mounds were often raised on the highest point of a ridge overlooking

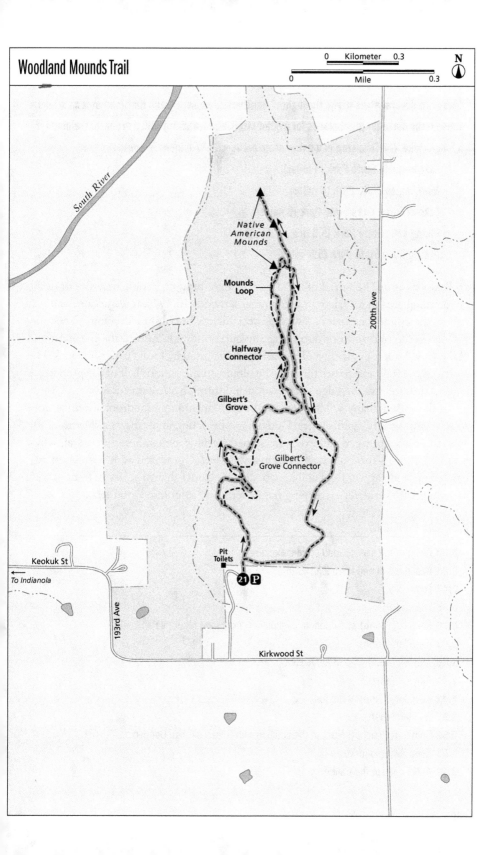

Woodland Mounds Trail

0   Kilometer   0.3

0   Mile   0.3

N

South River

*Native
American
Mounds*

Mounds
Loop

Halfway
Connector

Gilbert's
Grove

Gilbert's
Grove Connector

200th Ave

Pit
Toilets

21 P

Keokuk St

To Indianola

193rd Ave

Kirkwood St

LAKE LOOPS

There are several state parks throughout southern Iowa with trails that loop around a lake. These trails make for great places for a quiet stroll, bird watching with a group, or training for a longer hike. The following is a list of state parks with lake loops in southern Iowa:

Lake Ahquabi State Park (4 miles)

Nine Eagles State Park (6 miles)

Lake of Three Fires State Park (6 miles)

Viking Lake State Park (5.5 miles)

Prairie Rose State Park (5.5 miles)

a village or camp. The burial of the dead may have brought people together from the surrounding area in a variety of ceremonial activities. In 1976, Iowa became the first state in the country to enact a law to protect ancient burial sites. Pay your respects by staying on the trail and not disturbing any burial mounds. Also in the northern end of the park, look for evidence of a quarry that was used by local farmers for rock. The return to the trailhead passes through the refuge on the eastern half of the property. A long section follows the edge of the woodland through a hay meadow.

In the spring, many wildflowers can be seen, including bloodroot, Virginia bluebells, spring beauty, wild ginger, Dutchman's breeches, and false rue anemone. By May, the early spring wildflowers are joined by blue phlox, Solomon's seal, white trout-lily, jack-in-the-pulpit, and Virginia waterleaf. Goldenrod adds a touch of yellow to the landscape in the fall. The woodland includes many species of ferns as well, including rattlesnake fern, creeping fragile fern, and spinulose wood fern.

Miles and Directions

0.00 Begin at the service road entrance and head north.

0.05 Reach a fork and keep left (north).

0.47 Footbridge.

0.49 Footbridge.

0.70 Keep left (north) at the fork to continue on Woodland Mounds Trail.

1.02 Keep left (north).

1.25 Turn left (west) onto Mounds Loop.

1.41 Turn left (east).

1.42 Keep left (north) at the fork.

1.97 Turn left (east).

2.52 Continue straight (south) at the junction with Gilbert's Grove Connector.

2.87 Keep right (southwest).

3.12 Arrive back at the trailhead.

22 Woodburn Unit Backpack Trail

Stephens State Forest is the largest state forest in Iowa, with seven separate units total-ing more than 15,500 acres in five counties. The Woodburn Unit is designated as the backpacking unit and contains 2,011 acres of rolling hills dissected by Sand and Blue-bird Creeks. A gravel road divides the unit into two parts, allowing hikers to follow the two 3-mile loop trails in a figure-eight fashion to maximize trail length. There are five "backcountry" campsites in the unit, making Woodburn a great place for novice backpackers or those training for a longer trek.

Start: Stephens State Forest Woodburn Trailhead
Elevation gain: 702 feet total gain; 924 (low-est) to 1,089 feet (highest)
Distance: 6.85-mile double loop
Difficulty: Moderate to difficult, due to dis-tance and multiple steep inclines
Hiking time: About 3 hours
Seasons/schedule: Trails open daily year-round
Fees and permits: None
Trail contact: Stephens State Forest, 1111 N 8th St., Chariton 50049; (641) 774-4559; stephens_forest@dnr.iowa.gov; iowadnr.gov/places-to-go/state-forests/stephens-state-forest
Dog-friendly: Yes, on leash
Trail surface: Natural (dirt and grass)

Land status: Stephens State Forest, Woodburn Unit (Iowa DNR)
Nearest town: Osceola, 14.5 miles to the northwest
Maps: USGS Le Roy, IA; trail map available online and posted at the trailhead
Other trail users: None
Special considerations: Hunting is allowed in the state forest, so check season dates and dress accordingly.
Amenities available: Water pump at the trailhead
Maximum grade: 17%; there are four sub-stantial climbs, two each on both loops, between 100 to 150 feet of gain over less than one-half mile
Cell service: Average to weak

Finding the trailhead: From the intersection of US 34 and US 69 in Osceola, head east on US 34. Low crossings may have varying levels of water in them. In non-drought times, hikers may have to be more aware of possible stream crossings. Then, keep slight right to stay on 330th Avenue and continue for 2.3 miles until reaching the trailheads for the west and east loops. GPS: N40° 57.842' W93° 34.610'

Trail conditions: The trails are maintained, although they can get overgrown in summer. Some low-lying sections can be wet, so proper footwear is recommended. The campsites and trails are marked and there are no intersecting trails (with the exception of game trails), so navigation is simple. The trails receive light traffic.

The Hike

The primary function of Stephens State Forest is to provide an example of forest management for Iowa woodland species. The forest was created in the 1930s through

White Oak Camp is one of five hike-in campsites.

an effort by the Civilian Conservation Corps to expand hardwood and conifer forest in the region. When the lands were purchased in the 1930s by the Forest Service, the plan was to create a national forest. However, the lands, then referred to as the Lucas-Monroe Forest Area, were sold to the state of Iowa in the 1950s. The forest was then named after T. C. Stephens, a prominent educator, ornithologist, and conservationist from Morningside College in Sioux City. The original CCC plantings can still be seen today when you visit the seven units.

The Woodburn Unit (the designated hiking trail unit) is a mosaic of native upland and bottomland forests, nonnative hardwood and softwood plantings, and leased agricultural land. The unit's dynamic ecological communities make it home to diverse plant and animal species. There have been several mountain lion sightings over the years in the Stephens State Forest vicinity. Though you're unlikely to glimpse a cougar, if you camp out you will hear coyotes at dusk. In the early morning you may catch a red fox slipping through the underbrush.

During warm seasons, brown thrashers, red-winged blackbirds, and eastern towhees will greet you noisily in the parking area and can be found on the forest-grassland edges throughout the unit during late spring and summer. Stephens State Forest was designated as a Bird Conservation Area (BCA) in 2008, while a second

Stream crossings were dry in early fall.

BCA with core habitat in Stephens State Forest was designated in 2014. The Iowa DNR designates BCAs as areas of more than 10,000 acres with approximately 25 percent of the area established as key bird habitat. Stephens is one of the largest tracts of contiguous forest in the state, making it prime habitat for bird conservation.

The double loops in the Woodburn Unit are simple but challenging hikes. There are no intersecting trails, with the exception of game trails, and the trails are well marked, so navigation is easy. The parking area and self-registration kiosk is located on the west side of the gravel road that bisects the unit, so the logical loop to begin is the western loop. If you hike the loop counterclockwise, the climb back to the trail-head is a greater distance than if you hike clockwise. North Slope Trail will lead you to Bottom Oak Camp, tucked into the bottomland hardwood timber. Bottom Oak is the lowest of the five campsites, so expect bugs and more humid conditions. Buck Stop Camp is on the southwestern end of the western loop, perched at the end of Pine Ridge. Pine Ridge Trail is named after the CCC conifer plantings that populate this section of the forest unit.

After completing the western loop, cross the road heading west to follow Twin Oaks Trail through the upland oak/hickory-dominated forests, where typical spring wildflowers abound. Scattered amid the uplands, several large black oaks form huge

Woodburn Unit Backpack Trail

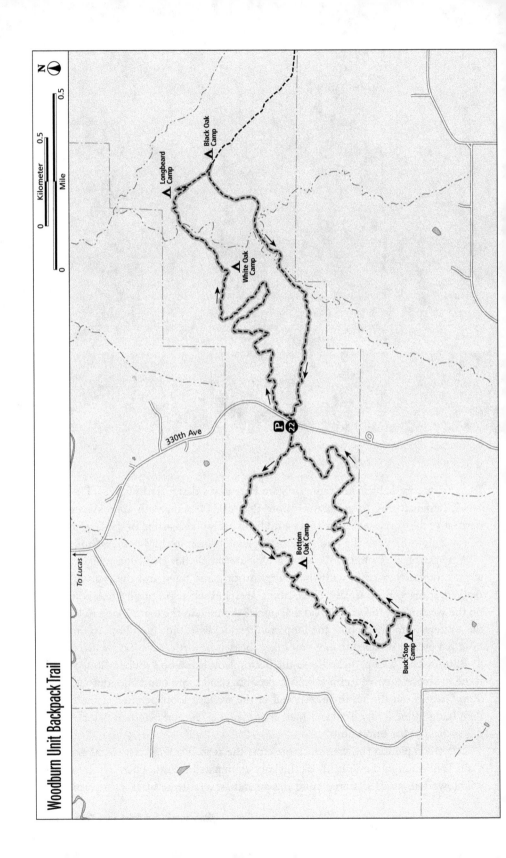

To Lucas

330th Ave

Longbeard Camp

Black Oak Camp

White Oak Camp

Bottom Oak Camp

Buck Stop Camp

P 22

N

Kilometer
0   0.5

Mile
0   0.5

canopies that provide ample shade for a midafternoon picnic or nap. The only discernible difference between hiking the eastern loop clockwise or counterclockwise is that the latter has the two 100-foot climbs on the first half of the loop. All three campsites on this loop—White Oak, Longbeard, and Black Oak—are set in beautiful upland hardwood forest. The section of Turkey Foot Trail closest to the gravel road passes by agricultural fields to the south. Look for chipping, field, and white-throated sparrows, which forage on barren or broken ground but find solace in the thick rose, sumac, and chokecherry shrubs at the edge of the forest. Here you'll also see many wild turkeys, once eradicated from the state because of habitat destruction and excessive hunting. After the DNR released the birds in Stephens State Forest, their population grew rapidly; turkey hunting has been allowed in the park since 1971.

Miles and Directions

0.00 Head west from the parking area.

0.06 Keep right (northwest) onto North Slope Trail.

0.53 Big Bend Crossing.

0.83 Turn left (southeast) for Bottom Oak Camp.

0.89 Bottom Oak Camp.

1.23 At the "DNR Access Lane Only" sign, turn left (southeast).

1.71 Turn right (south) toward Buck Stop Camp.

2.42 Cottonwood Crossing.

3.20 Turn right (east).

3.27 West trailhead; cross the road to access the east trails.

3.34 Continue north on Twin Oaks Trail.

4.65 Turn right (southeast) for White Oak Camp.

4.70 White Oak Camp.

4.98 Broken Bone Crossing.

5.20 Turn left (north) to Longbeard Camp.

5.25 Longbeard Camp.

5.41 Continue straight (southeast) to Black Oak Camp.

5.45 Black Oak Camp.

5.91 Unnamed crossing.

6.08 Unnamed crossing.

6.14 Unnamed crossing.

6.74 Turn right (south).

6.85 Arrive back at the parking area.

Honorable Mentions

G Nishnabotna Rock Cut Trail

A quiet, 1.5-mile forest trail on the northern edge of Cold Springs Park leads to one of the most underrated and fascinating geology sites in Iowa. The limestone outcrop and, when the water level is low, flat rock shelf on the East Nishnabotna River are wonderful places to explore and relax on a beautiful fall day.

Start: Trailhead one-tenth of a mile north of the main entrance to Cold Springs Park

Elevation gain: 13 feet total gain; 1,109 (lowest) to 1,129 feet (highest)

Distance: 1.5-mile out-and-back (not including exploring the East Nishnabotna River)

Difficulty: Easy

Hiking time: 1–1.5 hours

Seasons/schedule: Park is open daily until 10 p.m.

Fees and permits: None

Trail contact: Cass County Conservation, 57744 Lewis Rd., Lewis 51544; (712) 769-2372; mycountyparks.com/County/Cass/Park/Cold-Springs-Park.aspx

Dog-friendly: Yes, on leash

Trail surface: Natural (grass)

Land status: Cold Springs Park (Cass County Conservation)

Nearest town: Atlantic, 9 miles to the northeast

Maps: USGS Lewis, IA

Other trail users: None

Special considerations: The river level changes seasonally; currents can be strong, so use caution if you descend to the river

Amenities available: Restrooms at Cold Springs Park

Maximum grade: 1%; the trail is level the entire hike

Cell service: Above average

Finding the trailhead: From Atlantic, head southwest on US 6 for 7.5 miles. Turn south onto CR M56 toward Lewis. Once reaching Lewis, continue south on Lewis Road, then turn west after one-half mile. The trailhead is located at a gate at the end of the parking area on the northeast corner of Cold Springs Lake. GPS: N41° 17.600' W95° 5.099'

Trail conditions: The trail is wide and easy to follow. There are no trail markers, but there are no intersecting trails. Once you reach the East Nishnabotna River, there are several trails leading to the river. The footpath on the north of the loop at the end of the trail leads to an access point requiring a short scramble down to the river. The trail receives light traffic.

East Nishnabotna River

⊢ Clanton Creek Natural Resource Area

Clanton Creek Natural Resource Area is one of Madison County's largest remaining remnants of land-locked wilderness. The 1,115-acre property spans four units (Deer Creek, Turkey Ridge, Clanton, and Sawyer) with more than 5 miles of trails and two hike-in campsites (one each in Sawyer and Turkey Ridge). There are four access points, but the campsites are most easily accessed from the Sawyer Unit Trailhead.

Start: Sawyer Unit Trailhead
Elevation gain: Variable
Distance: More than 5 miles of trails
Difficulty: Moderate due to rugged terrain and remoteness
Hiking time: Variable
Seasons/schedule: Open daily, year-round
Fees and permits: None
Trail contact: Madison County Conservation, PO Box 129, Winterset 50273; (515) 462-3536; spearson@madisoncounty.iowa .gov; madisoncountyparks.org/parks/ clanton-creek-natural-resource-area/
Dog-friendly: Yes, on leash

Trail surface: Natural (grass and dirt)
Land status: Clanton Creek Natural Resource Area (Madison County Conservation)
Nearest town: Winterset, 13 miles to the north
Maps: USGS East Peru, IA; trail map available online
Other trail users: None
Special considerations: Hunting is permitted, so check season dates and dress accordingly.
Amenities available: 4 hike-in campsites
Maximum grade: The trail traverses a multitude of gradients, and would require a hearty traveler approximately 2 to 3 hours to complete.
Cell service: Average to weak

Sawyer Unit Trailhead

Finding the trailhead: From Winterset, head south on CR P71/Clark Tower Road. After 6.3 miles, turn east onto Peru Road, then turn south onto Millstream Avenue. After 4.5 miles, turn east onto Clanton Creek Road. After 1 mile, turn north into the parking area for Sawyer Unit. GPS: N41° 10.711' W93° 58.483'

Trail conditions: Trail markers are set every one-quarter mile. Ticks are prevalent during the summer. The trails receive light traffic.

| Chichaqua Bottoms Greenbelt

Woodland and prairie hikes are common around Des Moines, so the 8,000-plus acres of wetlands, marshes, and oxbow lakes, along with the most diverse prairies in Polk County, making a hike at Chichaqua Bottoms a unique experience. The pony truss bridge that crosses the old Skunk River is one of the only seventeen remaining bridges in Iowa of this design. Hike nearly 5 miles of trails through prime waterfowl habitat. Campsites provide a weekend escape from Iowa's capital.

Start: 8700 NE 126th Ave., Maxwell, IA 50161

Elevation gain: The trails have minimal to no elevation gain.

Distance: 4.55 miles of trails

Difficulty: Easy

Hiking time: Variable; 2 hours if you hike all the trails

Seasons/schedule: Apr 1 through Oct 31, 6:30 a.m. to 10:30 p.m.; Nov 1 through Mar 31, sunrise to sunset

Fees and permits: None

Trail contact: Polk County Conservation Natural Resources Headquarters, 11204 NE 118th Ave., Maxwell 50161; (515) 967-2596; polkcountyiowa.gov/conservation/parks-trails/chichaqua-bottoms-greenbelt/

Dog-friendly: Yes, on leash

Trail surface: Natural (grass)

Land status: Chichaqua Bottoms Greenbelt (Polk County Conservation)

Nearest town: Ankeny, 14 miles to the southeast

Maps: USGS Loring, IA; trail map available online

Other trail users: None

Special considerations: Hunting is permitted, so check season dates and dress accordingly.

Amenities available: Restrooms, campground, water

Maximum grade: 0%; the trails are nearly level

Cell service: Adequate

Finding the trailhead: From I-35, take exit 96 and head east on NE 126th Avenue through Elkhart. At the T-intersection, turn north onto NE 72nd Street, and turn south onto NE 80th Street, which turns into NE 126th Avenue after it curves to head east. GPS: N41° 47.628' W93° 25.774'

Trail conditions: The mowed trails are mostly easy to follow, although some trails disappear or are thin in places. Due to the wetland habitat, trails can be muddy or even partially or completely flooded. The trails receive moderate traffic.

Driftless Area

I n her book *Landforms of Iowa*, geologist Jean Prior observed that, "if you had to divide Iowa into two different regions, one would be the extreme northeast corner and the other would be the rest of the state." The Driftless Area, also known as the Paleozoic Plateau, is bound by the Minnesota state line to the north, the Mississippi River to the east, and a landform called the Silurian escarpment to the west and south. Whereas most of Iowa is covered by a thick blanket of loess and glacial till, northeast Iowa's bedrock is much closer to the surface, dominating the landscape. Spring-fed streams meander through narrow canyons framed by the towering blocky cliffs of Paleozoic strata—the limestones, dolomites, sandstones, and shales deposited 300 to 550 million years ago. Sinkholes, ice caves, and algific (cold-air) slopes can be found, characteristic of the karst topography of the area. This is a truly rugged part of the state and the most densely forested. It's home to many boreal plant species on their southernmost margin and the only place in the state to find native populations of brook trout.

Until quite recently, the eastern part of Iowa's Driftless Area was once lumped with parts of southwestern Wisconsin, southeast Minnesota, and northwest Illinois known as the "Driftless Area." This name represents the area's position as a supposedly unglaciated island within the ice-scoured Midwest. Indeed, Iowa's section of the island was bypassed by the glaciers of recent times. However, 500,000-year-old Pre-Illinoian glacial drift has been found on isolated ridgetops. Although missed by recent glaciers, the Paleozoic Plateau was affected by their proximity. Ancient streams slowly eroded the narrow canyons, and glacial meltwater thundered through drainages, carving its way to the Mississippi River. Today the entrenched valleys of the Volga, Turkey, Yellow, and Upper Iowa Rivers are some of the most scenic and heavily canoed waterways in Iowa.

Almost all the parks in the Driftless Area are located within the labyrinth of hidden valleys. Pikes Peak State Park is located on the tallest bluff overlooking the entire length of the Mississippi River. Driving north on the Great River Road, you'll find Effigy Mounds National Monument, which harbors the largest congregation of bird- and bear-shaped mounds in Iowa, sculpted 1,400 to 750 years ago by hunter-gatherer peoples who lived along the Mississippi River and its major tributaries. The Paint Creek Unit of the Yellow River State Forest is home to 25 miles of loop trails that wind through the valleys and bluffs overlooking the Big and Little Paint Creeks. The Maquoketa River's wanderings have carved a narrow quarter-mile ridge from which

Pikes Peak State Park

Backbone State Park got its name. The dense forests and wide floodplains of Frog Hollow Creek and the Volga River are protected in the Volga River State Recreation Area. Maquoketa Caves State Park encompasses the most concentrated cave system in Iowa, a treat for spelunkers and a home to the endangered Indiana bat. Mines of Spain State Recreation Area, just south of Dubuque, encompasses the first white settlement in Iowa and the grave of Julien Dubuque, for whom the town was named. Bellevue State Park is located on bluffs overlooking the Mississippi and has the largest planted butterfly garden in the state.

Besides hiking the bluffs and canoeing the rivers, driving on the scenic byways of northeast Iowa is another great way to meet the landscape. The Great River Road, part of a ten-state scenic byway, follows the Mississippi River. The River Bluffs Scenic Byway traverses Clayton and Fayette Counties, and the Driftless Area Scenic Byway passes through Alamakee County. Due to the topography of the Driftless Area, dead zones exist throughout the region, although trails located along the bluff tops usually have service.

23 Yellow River Backpack Trail

When you tell Iowa outdoor enthusiasts that you're going backpacking in the state, most assume your destination is Yellow River State Forest. With 25 miles of trails that wind through deep river valleys, over huge bluffs to scenic overlooks with stunning vistas, and four backcountry campsites, it's truly the place for a wilderness experience in Iowa.

Start: Forester's Trail parking area (there are multiple parking areas with access to the backpack trail)

Elevation gain: 1,653 feet total gain; 630 (lowest) to 1,085 feet (highest)

Distance: 13.5-mile loop

Difficulty: Difficult

Hiking time: Variable; 5.5–6 hours if hiked in 1 day

Seasons/schedule: Trails open year-round

Fees and permits: Free

Trail contact: Yellow River State Forest, 729 State Forest Rd., Harpers Ferry 52146; (563) 586-2254; YellowRiverForest@dnr.iowa.gov; iowadnr.gov/places-to-go/state-forests/yellow-river-state-forest

Trail surface: Natural and gravel roads

Land status: Yellow River State Forest, Paint Creek Unit (Iowa DNR)

Nearest town: Harpers Ferry, 7 miles to the northeast

Maps: USGS Waterville, IA and USGS Harpers Ferry, IA, WI; backpack trail map available online

Other trail users: Mix of hiking-only and multi-use trails (equestrian and bikers)

Special considerations: Hikers using the backpacking campsites must sign in at the forest headquarters prior to camping. Water may not be available at the campsites, so fill up at the registration station.

Amenities available: Drinking water is available near the office complex; vault toilets at the campgrounds (no toilets at the backpacking campsites)

Maximum grade: 28%; there are three big climbs over 200 feet

Cell service: No service on most of the trails

Finding the trailhead: From Harpers Ferry, head west on CR B25/Lansing Harpers Road for 2.4 miles. Turn west onto State Forest Road and continue for 4 miles until reaching Forester's Trail parking area, which is after Big Paint Campground. GPS: N43° 10.291' W91° 15.517'

Trail conditions: The trail is well maintained and marked as "BP Loop." The trails can be extremely buggy in summer and there is a lot of poison ivy. The trails receive moderate traffic.

The Hike

The general view of Iowa is that it's a flat expanse of cornfield stretching as far as the eye can see. While agriculture does encompass many millions of acres of land in the state, Yellow River State Forest doesn't fit the stereotypical Iowan landscape. The Paint Creek Unit, where the Backpack Trail is located, is dominated by rugged forest-covered bluffs that you can satisfyingly walk up, over, and around for days on end.

There are four backpack campsites at Paint Creek Unit. SALLY ORTGIES

Yellow River SALLY ORTGIES

State forest staff get a lot of comments from users saying that they love coming to Yellow River State Forest because it provides the closest thing to a wilderness experience in the area short of driving many miles further north.

In 1932, Civilian Conservation Corps (CCC) funds were used to purchase land at the mouth of the Yellow River on the Mississippi. In 1949, the land was transferred to the National Park Service to create Effigy Mounds National Monument. Land was bought along trout-bearing Big and Little Paint Creeks, and the CCC began planting and harvesting native and nonnative softwoods on the previously cultivated land in order to control soil erosion and provide lumber for projects on other state lands.

Though many plantations exist, native upland forests are anything but row crops: Dry south- and west-facing slopes are dominated by red, white, and bur oaks as well as shagbark hickory. North/east-facing slopes consist of sugar maple, basswood, white ash, and elm, with cottonwoods and willows surrounding the marshes and creeks. On the overlooks and rock outcrops, you'll find prairie plants like big and little bluestem, leadplant, Indian grass, and jeweled shooting star, an endangered species in Iowa.

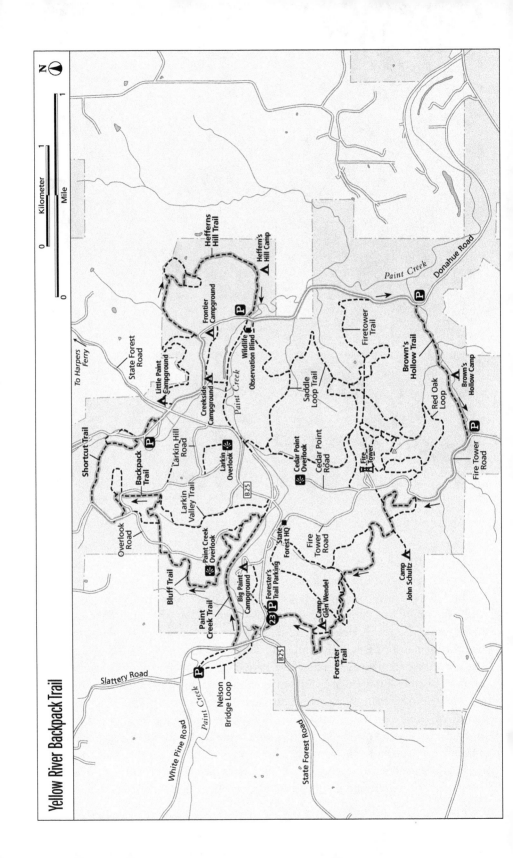

Yellow River Backpack Trail

Today, DNR staff maintain 51.3 total miles of trails. In recent years, they have added new trail sections to the Paint Creek, Paint Rock, and Luster Heights Units. In total, 29.8 miles are classified as multi-use, 17.5 miles hiking only, and 4 miles of snowmobile only trails. If you plan to spend several days at Yellow River, be prepared to do a little road-hiking—it'll be necessary to complete a full loop around the park. The quality of trails is varied because of their history and multiuse status. They've evolved from fire breaks built by the CCC in the 1930s and 1940s, and many have severe erosion problems caused by heavy horse and bicycle traffic. There are several steep sections, and some people gripe about the lack of switchbacks.

Yellow River has four primitive campsites: Glen Wendell, John Shultz, Brown's Hollow, and Heffern's Hill (a fifth backcountry campsite, called Camp Terry Hennessy, has been added in the Paint Rock Unit). Each site is set in a spacious opening in the forest with at least one firepit. The backpack camps are no longer supplied with firewood for burning; DNR staff ask campers to use anything that is already down, and not to fell any standing tree. There are creeks near Heffern's Hill and Brown's Hollow and a pond at Glen Wendell, but unless you have a pump filter, it's important to carry all the water you'll need for the trip. Fill up at the spigot behind the state forest headquarters before your hike.

If you are planning a multiday trip within the forest, stop by the forest headquarters on the west side of the unit before leaving. You'll be able to chat with the seasoned head forester and look at a larger map (or pick up one of their color-coded topographic maps). Printed maps can be found in every kiosk throughout the forest. The maps are provided courtesy of Friends of Yellow River State Forest. All people camping overnight in the backcountry are asked to register at the Forestry Building kiosk. There is also plenty of trail head parking and water at this location. Day hikes at Yellow River State Forest are also quite satisfying, and the trail-running can be great as long as you avoid the heavily used equestrian trails. Ramble here for a few hours or a few days to fit your mood and your stamina.

Miles and Directions

0.00 Begin at Forester's Trail parking area.

2.30 Paint Creek Overlook.

5.50 Little Paint Campground.

5.80 Creekside Campground.

6.10 Frontier Campground.

7.60 Heffern's Hill Camp.

9.80 Brown's Hollow Camp.

11.60 Junction to Camp John Schultz.

12.80 Camp Glen Wendel.

13.50 Arrive back at Forester's Trail parking area.

24 Hanging Rock Trail

Traversing the bluffs that overlook the confluence of the Mississippi and Yellow Rivers provides one of the best cultural history lessons to be found in Iowa. After a day spent wandering among the earthen sculptures of bird and bear, you'll undoubtedly return. Of 10,000 mounds thought once to have existed in northeastern Iowa, 191 known mounds lie within the monument, twenty-nine of which are shaped like animals. Two units include 13 miles of trails that navigate the forested bluffs, pass through prairie remnants and reconstructions, and pause at the overlooks where the remarkable mounds rest.

Start: North side of the visitor center

Elevation gain: 1,040 feet total gain; 650 (lowest) to 953 feet (highest)

Distance: 7-mile out-and-back (options include 2-, 3-, and 4-mile out-and-back)

Difficulty: Difficult (shorter options are easier but all have steep climb at the beginning)

Hiking time: About 3 hours

Seasons/schedule: Park trails are open daily from dawn to dusk.

Fees and permits: No entrance fee or pass is required.

Trail contact: Effigy Mounds National Monument, 151 IA 76, Harpers Ferry 52146; (563) 873-3491 ext. 123; nps.gov/efmo/index.htm

Dog-friendly: Yes, on leash (only service animals permitted in the visitor center)

Trail surface: Natural

Land status: Effigy Mounds National Monument (National Park Service)

Nearest town: Marquette, 3 miles to the south

Maps: USGS Prairie du Chien, WI, IA; trail map available at the visitor center and online (nps.gov/subjects/gisandmapping/nps-maps.htm)

Other trail users: None

Special considerations: Seek shelter in the visitor center during any weather event; there are no shelters on the bluff trails.

Amenities available: Restrooms, water at the visitor center (closed federal holidays)

Maximum grade: 16%; the biggest climb is nearly 300 feet over the first one-half mile of the trail

Cell service: Depending on your service provider, your cell service can be normal, spotty or nonexistent.

Finding the trailhead: From Marquette, head north on Great River Road. After nearly 3 miles, cross the Yellow River, then turn north into the parking lot at the Effigy Mounds National Monument Visitor Center. There are trailheads in the northeast corner of the parking lot and on the north side of the visitor center. GPS: N43° 5.341' W91° 11.136'

Trail conditions: The trails are in excellent condition and well marked. Please stay on the trails to respect this sacred space. The North Unit and South Unit trails are very steep as they lead you up the bluff. There are very few railings along the trail system, and the ones in place are not safety rated, so be aware of your footing and keep children and pets away from the edges of overlooks. Stay on the trails to limit exposure to ticks and make sure to check your clothes after hiking. The trails receive heavy traffic.

Fire Point

The Hike

The Effigy Mound Builders inhabited the Upper Mississippi River Valley in Iowa, Illinois, Minnesota, and much of Wisconsin 750 to 1,400 years ago. This complex culture lived in campsites along river valleys in summer and in rock shelters on uplands during the harsh winters. They made lightweight, cord-impressed pottery, harvested a bounty of wild edibles, and hunted with bows and arrows. What they're best known for, however, are their complex religious ceremonies and burial traditions, expressed through the earthen effigy mounds they sculpted.

The first recorded evidence of the mounds was produced by Major Stephen Long's expedition to the Upper Mississippi River in 1817. Excavation of the mounds began in 1817, and many ideas surfaced as to their origin. A popular myth was that they had been built by the Lost Tribe of Israel, whose early, civilized society had been annihilated by migrating Indians. During Iowa's settlement, that belief was used to justify extermination of the Indians, theft of their ceremonial objects, and destruction of the mounds.

Present-day understanding of Effigy Moundbuilder culture developed from the work of archaeologists and surveyors during the late 1800s and early 1900s. It is

Eagle Rock

now believed that the effigy mounds were constructed to honor the land's sustaining benevolence, as well as to venerate the Moundbuilders' relation to the cycles of life.

In 1949, in accordance with the American Antiquities Act of 1906, President Harry S. Truman declared Iowa's Effigy Mounds a national monument. Because they constitute an ancient burial ground and are considered sacred by many, these lands must be treated with utmost respect and honor. It is a federal criminal offense to alter a mound or to take any organic material from within the boundaries of the monument.

In the North Unit, the Hanging Rock Trail departs from behind the visitor center, passes three 2,000-year-old conical mounds at the base of the bluff, and ascends in a series of switchbacks. After reaching the top of the bluff, keep left (north) toward the Little Bear Mound Group. Park staff recommend this approach to Fire Point, as you will pass several mounds as you approach the viewpoint. If you plan to hike 2 miles, head toward Fire Point and Eagle Rock before returning to the visitor center. Otherwise, continue straight, leaving Fire Point and Eagle Rock for the return leg for a longer out-and-back hike to Twin Views and Hanging Rock.

On the way to Hanging Rock, you'll pass the 80-foot-long Little Bear Mound and 137-foot-long Great Bear Mound, the monument's largest. As you continue northeast

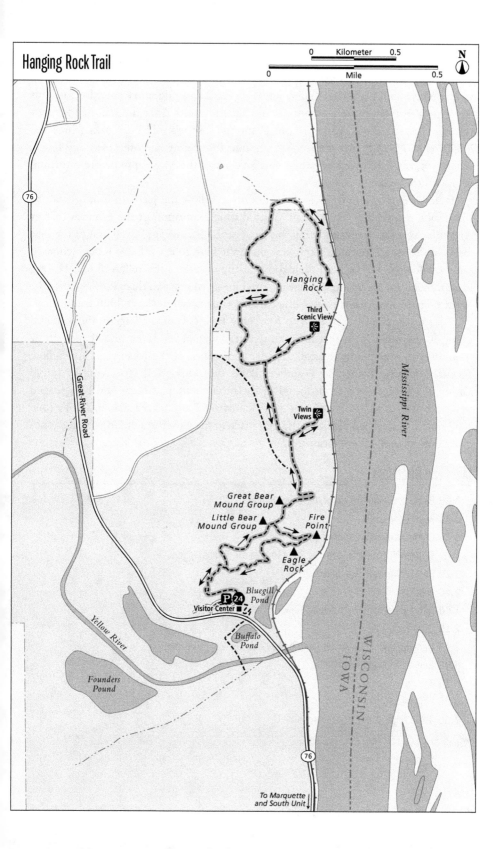

Hanging Rock Trail

0   Kilometer   0.5

0   Mile   0.5

N

76

Mississippi River

Great River Road

Hanging Rock

Third Scenic View

Twin Views

Great Bear Mound Group

Little Bear Mound Group

Fire Point

Eagle Rock

Bluegill Pond

P 24

Visitor Center

Buffalo Pond

Yellow River

Founders Pound

IOWA

WISCONSIN

76

To Marquette and South Unit

along the edge of woodland and prairie, take the two eastbound trails leading to Twin Views and Third Scenic View. These overlook the backwaters of the 260-mile-long Upper Mississippi National Wildlife and Fish Refuge, a migratory corridor for birds and crucial habitat for fish, mammals, and aquatic plants. After the trail bends south toward Hanging Rock, pass six conical mounds. Several old burr oaks fringe the bluff's edge, a perfect spot for lunch. Continue 400 feet up and onto Hanging Rock, where you can catch your breath as you gaze across the Mississippi before returning to the visitor center.

Returning to the Little Bear Mound Group, follow the series of mounds east to Fire Point, named for charred clay found during excavation of the mounds that sit atop this overlook. Stop and enjoy the view of the Mississippi River, one of the best views in the state. Continue southwest along the bluff to reach Eagle Rock, where in winter bald eagles fly around their roosts at the mouth of the Yellow River. During summer look for leadplant, spiderwort, and blue-eyed grass on this sunny opening, or "goat prairie." The visitor center is less than 1 mile down the steep bluff trail.

Hike to the South Unit trails to Marching Bear Group, the largest effigy mound group in the monument that includes ten bear-shaped and three bird-shaped effigy mounds; two viewpoints overlooking the confluence of the Mississippi and Yellow Rivers, Nezekaw Point and Founders Pond Overlooks; and Compound Mound Group, the longest earthwork found in the monument, past bear- and bird-shaped effigy mounds as well. The Yellow River Boardwalk Trail, an accessible half-mile (one way) trail over recycled planks, is the best place in the park for wildlife viewing, especially during seasonal migrations.

Miles and Directions

0.00 Begin at the north side of the visitor center.

0.40 Keep left (north).

0.70 Continue straight (northeast).

　　　Option: Turn east toward Fire Point to hike the 2-mile option.

1.20 Turn east toward Twin Views.

1.40 Twin Views.

1.80 Turn east toward Third Scenic View.

2.10 Third Scenic View.

3.70 Hanging Rock; turn around and head back the way you came.

5.90 Turn east toward Fire Point.

6.10 Fire Point.

6.20 Eagle Rock.

7.00 Arrive back at the visitor center.

25 Pikes Peak to Point Ann

Though Iowa's Pikes Peak shares its name with the better known 14,110-foot peak in Colorado, Lieutenant Zebulon Pike encountered the grand bluffs rising above the Mississippi River long before he came to know the Rocky Mountains. In comparison, Iowa's Pikes Peak rises a meager 500 feet above the floodplain. However, the view of the Upper Mississippi River National Wildlife and Fish Refuge and the mouth of the Wisconsin River is almost as majestic as its western counterpart. Trails begin at Pikes Peak and travel up and down several forested ravines to Point Ann at the park's northern tip.

Start: Overlook parking area
Elevation gain: 1,033 feet total gain; 633 (lowest) to 1,116 feet (highest)
Distance: 10.1-mile out-and-back (options for shorter hikes)
Difficulty: Difficult
Hiking time: 4 or more hours
Seasons/schedule: The state park is open daily, year-round
Fees and permits: None
Trail contact: Pikes Peak State Park, 32264 Pikes Peak Rd., McGregor 52157; (563) 873-2341; Pikes_Peak@dnr.iowa.gov; iowadnr.gov/Places-to-Go/State-Parks/Iowa-State-Parks/Pikes-Peak-State-Park

Dog-friendly: Yes, on leash
Trail surface: Boardwalk and natural
Land status: Pikes Peak State Park (Iowa DNR)
Nearest town: McGregor, 3 miles to the north
Maps: USGS Clayton, IA, WI and USGS Prairie du Chien, WI, IA; park map available online and posted at the overlook parking area
Other trail users: Point Ann Trail is multiuse, while the other trails are hiking-only.
Special considerations: Be aware of poison ivy, ticks, and steep bluff faces.
Amenities available: Modern restrooms, water
Maximum grade: 12%; there is a 250-foot climb one more than one-half mile
Cell service: Average to weak under tree cover

Finding the trailhead: From the junction of US 18 and 52 west of McGregor, take US 18 east. Turn east onto IA 76 toward McGregor and then south onto IA 340 (which becomes CR X56 and is also known as the Great River Road). Look for signs to Pikes Peak State Park and turn east toward the campground and overlook parking area. GPS: N42° 59.669' W91° 9.844'

Trail conditions: The trails are well maintained and well marked. Use caution around steep bluffs. The trails receive heavy traffic.

The Hike

In 1673, Jacques Marquette and Louis Joliet left northern Michigan on an expedition in search of the "big river in the hidden valley," which they hoped might flow into the Pacific Ocean. From Green Bay, Wisconsin, they came up the Fox River, portaged overland to the Wisconsin River, and floated down to its mouth on the Mississippi at present-day Prairie du Chien. Astounded by the sight of the tall bluffs (present-day Pikes Peak State Park) over the Mississippi, Marquette referred to them as mountains in his journal.

One of several viewpoints overlooking the Mississippi River

Zebulon Pike explored the Upper Mississippi River in 1805, recommending to the US Army that a fort be built at the top of Pikes Peak. Luckily, one was built in Prairie du Chien instead, and Iowa's bluffs were left undeveloped. In 1837 Alexander McGregor established a ferry across the Mississippi and used the bluffs above the ferry landing as a family picnic ground. The land was passed down through his family until 1928, when it was donated to the federal government and then to the State of Iowa to serve as Point Ann and Pikes Peak State Parks.

Begin the hike at the main overlook platform above the massive girth of the Mississippi where the Wisconsin River enters from the northeast. As you follow the boardwalk toward Crow's Nest, stop at the Bear Mound, an effigy built by people of the Late Woodland culture between AD 600 and 1100, one of many mounds within the park.

The boardwalk takes you past Crow's Nest, a semi open ridge that's home to prairie grasses and wildflowers nestled between old eastern red cedars and chinquapin oaks. Signs lead toward Bridal Veil Falls, where an unnamed creek tumbles over a dolomite shelf on its way down to the Mississippi several hundred feet below. An extremely precipitous trail leads down the creek to Sand Cave, one of the most beautiful sandstone outcrops in Iowa. Striking red, yellow, brown, and orange bands

The boardwalk descending to Bridal Veil Falls

formed by iron oxide precipitates appear in the creamy St. Peter sandstone. The small footpath is slippery, steep, and fragile and should not be attempted unless you are a very strong hiker.

The boardwalk ends at Bridal Veil Falls, and the rest of the trails in the park are wide paths that can get quite muddy when wet. Heading north toward Point Ann, you'll hike in and out of the park's three major ravines, all steeply dissected by small spring-fed streams. There are several ways to loop around to shorten or lengthen your trip. (The westernmost trail in the park, from Homestead parking to McGregor parking via Point Ann, is the only trail in the park open to mountain bikers.) The oldest exposed bedrock in the area, Jordan sandstone is exposed at Point Ann and was deposited near the end of the Cambrian period, about 505 million years ago. This sandstone is a very important aquifer for southeast Iowa and provides water to wells for surrounding communities, as well as the state park itself.

General Land Office surveys taken between 1837 and 1849 deemed Clayton County the most forested county in Iowa, with 70 percent "timber" coverage. Since those surveys, extensive logging has taken place surrounding the park, but the island of Pikes Peak remained relatively untouched because of previous owners' insight and its transfer to public land status in the early 1900s.

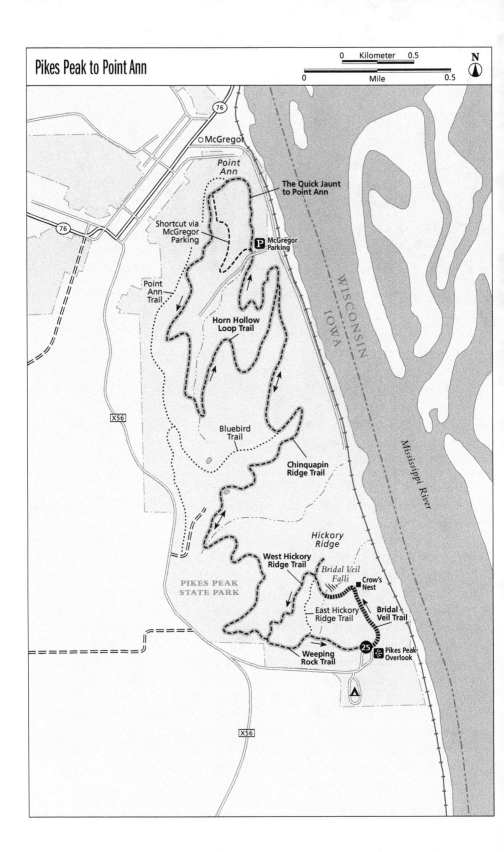

Pikes Peak to Point Ann

0   Kilometer   0.5

0   Mile   0.5

N

76

McGregor

Point Ann

The Quick Jaunt to Point Ann

Shortcut via McGregor Parking

76

P McGregor Parking

Point Ann Trail

Horn Hollow Loop Trail

X56

Bluebird Trail

Chinquapin Ridge Trail

Hickory Ridge

West Hickory Ridge Trail

Bridal Veil Falls

Crow's Nest

WISCONSIN

IOWA

Mississippi River

PIKES PEAK STATE PARK

East Hickory Ridge Trail

Bridal Veil Trail

25 Pikes Peak Overlook

Weeping Rock Trail

X56

The mature upland forests are dominated by white and red oaks, shagbark hickory, sugar maple, and basswood, with small stands of eastern white pine scattered throughout. Because the Mississippi functions as a major flyway for migratory birds, forests in Pikes Peak along this corridor serve as perfect breeding areas for nesters or stopover sites for birds headed farther north to raise families. Look for cerulean, Kentucky, and blue-winged warblers; Bell's vireos; yellow-billed cuckoos; and scarlet tanagers, among many others.

The most special features of this place are the many spring-fed streams that tumble down steep gullies toward the Mississippi, many of them forming waterfalls. The water is somewhat cold, and although it's definitely not suitable for drinking, a splash on the face or back of the head will do you well on a hot day.

Miles and Directions

0.0 Start at the Overlook parking area.

0.2 Pikes Peak Overlook; continue north on the boardwalk past the Crow's Nest toward Bridal Veil Falls.

0.5 Arrive at Bridal Veil Falls; continue toward Hickory Ridge.

0.6 Atop Hickory Ridge you will see burial mounds extending toward the river.

2.0 At the fork, turn right (east). Going the other way will take you to the Homestead parking area and the shortcut to Point Ann.

3.3 At the fork, go right (north).

4.5 Arrive at McGregor parking area. Turn left (west) on the road to connect to the Point Ann Trail.

5.3 At both forks, turn right (east) for a quick jaunt out to Point Ann. When you return, take the first right fork for a shortcut or the second right fork for the long return. The mileage from here on out is via the long route.

7.0 Arrive back at the main trail, and take a right (south). At each of the two successive forks, stay left for the best route to the trailhead. At the third fork, go right to return to the parking lot or left to revisit Bridal Veil Falls and the Crow's Nest.

10.1 Arrive back at the trailhead.

26 Lima Trail and Frog Hollow Trail

In the 1960s, the Iowa Department of Natural Resources bought land around Frog Hollow Creek, a tributary of the Volga River, to create a large lake for recreational purposes. Because of cracks in the underlying bedrock, the lake never came to be. Instead the Volga River State Recreation Area was established, offering 25 miles of multiuse trails and canoe access to the Volga River. Trails take you through weathered bluffs, along the floodplains of the creek and river, and past several recovering grasslands and savannas. With room to roam and loop trails to choose among, the area offers hikes of varying length and difficulty.

Start: Upper Lime Trailhead south of Lakeview Campground on I Avenue
Elevation gain: 922 feet total gain; 948 (lowest) to 1,165 feet (highest)
Distance: 10-mile loop
Difficulty: Difficult due to distance
Hiking time: 4–6 hours
Seasons/schedule: Park open daily, year-round
Fees and permits: None
Trail contact: Volga River State Recreation Area, 10255 Ivy Rd., Fayette 52142; (563) 425-4161; Volga_River@dnr.iowa.gov; iowadnr .gov/Places-to-Go/State-Parks/Iowa-State -Parks/Volga-River-State-Recreation-Area
Dog-friendly: Yes, on leash
Trail surface: Natural
Land status: Volga River State Recreation Area (Iowa DNR)

Nearest town: Fayette, 6 miles to the south
Maps: USGS West Union, IA; park map available online
Other trail users: Equestrians and bikers
Special considerations: Park staff plan to remove the overlook on the Frog Hollow Trail as trees have grown in front of it. Lima and Lower Lima Trails have their own trailheads off Ivy Road. The Depot Trail no longer starts out of the Albany Campground; the trailhead is now past the campground and up the road on the hill and can also be accessed by the Day Use Area.
Amenities available: Modern restrooms, campgrounds located throughout the recreation area
Maximum grade: 19%; there are two 150-foot plus climbs on the second half of the loop
Cell service: Reception will vary depending on provider; average to weak

Finding the trailhead: From the junction of US 18 and IA 150 in West Union, drive south on IA 150. North of Fayette turn left (east) onto Ivy Road. Within the park, at the T-intersection turn left (north) onto I Avenue; follow to Frog Hollow Lake and the trailhead. GPS: N42° 53.581' W91° 45.885'

Trail conditions: Some sections of the trail are sandy. There are a handful of natural water crossings on the route. Some can be regularly stepped over, but some can be knee deep or deeper in the right conditions. The trails receive light traffic.

The Hike

The State Conservation Commission (now the Iowa Department of Natural Resources) selected the then Big Rock Wildlife Area for part of its 1960s–era new "large lakes program." With rugged bluffs overlooking the picturesque Volga River Canyon, it seemed a perfect place. However, the idea for a large lake was dropped after discovery that the underlying bedrock was fractured and wouldn't hold water. The state had already acquired more than 5,000 acres of highly cultivated, grazed, and logged land. In the end, a recreation area was created, complete with 135-acre Frog Hollow Lake, food plots, brome fields, forested bluffs, and a number of multiuse trails. In its northern two-thirds, there are 25 miles of trails consisting of old gravel and dirt farm roads and large mowed firebreaks.

The area is split down the middle by the floodplains of Frog Hollow Creek and the Volga River; hills and bluffs are mainly located in the western and southern portions. The prairie and savanna ecosystems that probably once dominated the area are all but gone. Several small prairie glades along the creeks and a wet meadow near the eastern entrance are the only places where native grasses and prairie wildflowers still can be found. The DNR is carrying out an extensive management plan to use fire, logging, and planting to rehabilitate the native forest, prairie, and savanna.

The Lima Trail traverses the eastern half of the park, following a small creek toward the northeast corner and then heading south up and over several ridges. Though rarely seen, the two species of shrews that live in the area both like wet forests, characteristic of the habitat along the Lima Trail. Masked shrews consume their weight in food each day, and the northern short-tailed shrew produces a poison in its saliva that can paralyze small prey and leave humans with a nasty wound.

The Albany, Ridge, and Frog Hollow Trails ascend the bluffs on the west side of the park, following steep gravel roads and mowed paths through dense forests. The woodlands consist of bur, red, and white oaks, shagbark and bitternut hickories, white ash, basswood, elm, and sugar maple. You'll stumble upon several old homestead sites, evident because of the nonnative evergreen trees planted years ago as windbreaks. Though most homesites are situated on the floodplains, you'll find corn and alfalfa plantings scattered throughout the uplands, which now serve as food plots for wildlife.

Because of the area's fragmented landscape, it's a good place to observe birds that prefer woodland edge habitat. The usually secretive American woodcock puts on a marvelous early spring territorial display, described eloquently in Sand County Almanac by native Iowan and naturalist Aldo Leopold. Populations of northern bobwhite, also known as quail, have fluctuated dramatically because of habitat change and harsh weather, but the birds enjoy the hedgerows, food plots, and forest cover of the area. Look for the white belly, black cap, and gray wings of the eastern kingbird, which you'll see sitting on a fencepost and then swooping up to catch an insect.

Just north of Volga River State Recreation lies Echo Valley State Park. The 100-acre park preserves many historical structures hand-built by the Civilian Conservation Corps in the 1930s. Hike the 2-mile Echo Valley Environmental Nature Trail along Otter Creek.

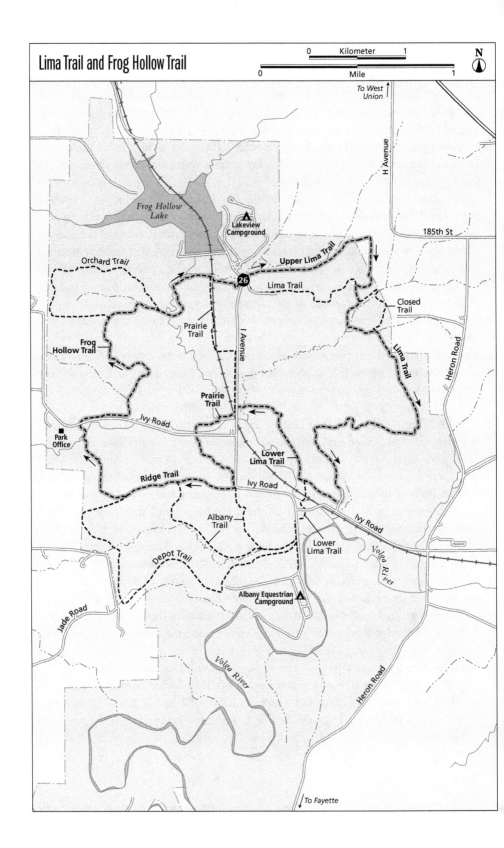

Lima Trail and Frog Hollow Trail

Kilometer
Mile
N

To West Union

H Avenue

185th St

Frog Hollow Lake

Lakeview Campground

Orchard Trail

Upper Lima Trail

26

Lima Trail

Closed Trail

Prairie Trail

Frog Hollow Trail

I Avenue

Lima Trail

Heron Road

Prairie Trail

Ivy Road

Park Office

Lower Lima Trail

Ridge Trail

Ivy Road

Albany Trail

Lower Lima Trail

Ivy Road

Volga River

Depot Trail

Jade Road

Albany Equestrian Campground

Volga River

Heron Road

To Fayette

Miles and Directions

0.00 Start at the trailhead and head east on Upper Lima Trail.

1.30 Turn south onto Lima Trail.

3.90 Turn northwest onto Lower Lima Trail.

5.00 Cross I Avenue and continue west on Prairie Trail.

5.30 Turn south onto Ridge Trail

5.90 Continue west on Ridge Trail.

6.80 Head north to continue on Ridge Trail.

7.40 Cross Ivy Road, then head east on Frog Hollow Trail.

7.80 Continue north on Frog Hollow Trail.

8.70 Continue east on Frog Hollow Trail.

10.00 Arrive back at I Avenue.

27 Backbone, East Lake, and West Lake Trails

When E. R. Harlan spoke during the 1920 ceremonies dedicating Iowa's first state park, he quoted Shakespeare to convey the importance of the sanctuary: "those who 'find tongues in trees, books in the running brooks, sermons in stones, and good in everything' will find here an exalted interest." Indeed, the Backbone, a narrow ridge sculpted by the Maquoketa River, towers above Backbone Lake and offers a breathtaking view of the gorge below. In the park's large tract of forest—untouched for the past one hundred years—you'll find diverse migratory bird visitors and more than 600 species of plants.

Start: Six Pine Campground
Elevation gain: 132 feet total gain; 984 (lowest) to 1,141 feet (highest)
Distance: 8.0-mile loop
Difficulty: Difficult
Hiking time: 3–5 hours
Seasons/schedule: Park open year-round from 4 a.m. to 10:30 p.m. daily
Fees and permits: None
Trail contact: Backbone State Park, 1347 129th St., Dundee 52038; (563) 924-2527; Backbone@dnr.iowa.gov; iowadnr.gov/Places-to-Go/State-Parks/Iowa-State-Parks/Backbone-State-Park
Dog-friendly: Yes, on leash
Trail surface: Mowed footpaths, some road hiking; Backbone Trail is a narrow ridge trail
Land status: Backbone State Park (Iowa DNR)

Nearest town: Strawberry Point, 6 miles to the north
Maps: USGS Dundee, IA; park map available online
Other trail users: Mountain bikers on West Lake–East Lake Loop; snowmobiles in winter on West Lake Trail; Hikers only on Backbone Trail
Special considerations: West Lake–East Lake Loop can be very wet and muddy in spring. The park's roads close during winter and are open for cross-country skiing and snowmobiling. Hazards to be aware of are poison ivy, ticks, very steep rock faces.
Amenities available: Water, modern and non-modern restrooms, campground, shelters, picnic areas throughout the state park
Maximum grade: 20%
Cell service: Adequate

Finding the trailhead: From the junction of IA 13 and IA 3 in Strawberry Point, take IA 13 south. After 1 mile, instead of following the big curve to the east, go straight (south) and then right (west) onto IA 410. This will take you in through the north side of the park, past Richmond Springs and the cave, until you get to the Backbone. GPS: N42° 36.690' W91° 34.043'

The Hike

Iowa's first Board of Conservation was appointed in 1918. The same year, locals from Manchester, Strawberry Point, and Lamont formed the Travel Club and met several members of the board at the Backbone in an attempt to persuade them to preserve the area. It took several years to purchase the land, but at the dedication of Iowa's first state park on May 28, 1920, the statewide vision of a park system became a reality.

Backbone Trail traverses rugged dolomite limestone cliffs. Nate Detrich

To fully appreciate the sculpted terrain of Backbone State Park, hike the 8-mile West Lake–East Lake Loop around Backbone Lake, formed by damming the Maquoketa River. In 1996, the lake was drained and dredged to remove 200,000 tons of silt, which had clogged the lake. Start by following the West Lake Trail, which winds through forested ravines dominated by red, black, and white oaks as well as basswood, sugar maple, shagbark hickory, and a scattering of eastern white pine. The understory is quite diverse here in the upland forest, with wild geranium, mayapple, Virginia creeper, tick-trefoil, and several species of ferns (lady, maidenhair, and interrupted). The large continuous tract of forest offers habitat for red fox, gray squirrel, skunk, and white-tailed deer, as well as diverse avifauna. In spring and summer, look for American redstart, black- and yellow-billed cuckoos, great crested flycatcher, scarlet tanager, and eastern wood pewee. Winter residents include ruffed grouse, black-capped chickadee, northern cardinal, and tufted titmouse.

Once you cross the dam you'll have to navigate the more heavily developed area of the park, but the easily found East Lake Trail will lead you along the base of 30-to-50-foot bluffs. Diverge east off the main trail to walk the Bluebird Trail (forks after you've passed the last of the cabins) or to stand atop the Overlook Platform, which you'll see 0.2 miles before you reach the Backbone Trailhead. Return to the trailhead

The picturesque East Lake and West Lake Trails loop around Backbone Lake. NATE DETRICH

by road hiking and catching a connector trail from the picnic area southwest of the Backbone.

The Backbone, for which the park is named, is a narrow ridge of bedrock carved by the meandering Maquoketa River. The entrenchment of the river, or downcutting into the valley walls, has formed the steep-sided canyon framed by Silurian dolomite cliffs, deposited as lime roughly 430 million years ago. The tallest section of the Backbone rises almost 200 feet above the water and then tapers to as narrow as several yards across. The ridge then descends to the floodplain in a series of slump blocks.

Traverse the Backbone via the 1-mile loop trail. The ridge is an inhospitable place for most woodland plant species because of its sun exposure and thin soils. Here you'll find eastern red cedar, chinquapin oak, and quaking aspen overstory with an interestingly diverse understory of prairie and cliff species. Look for bastard toadflax, columbine, golden Alexander, porcupine grass, little bluestem, lousewort, Indian paintbrush, smooth cliff brake, and creeping fragile fern. Check the sky above for turkey vultures and red-tailed hawks riding the wind currents or for the occasional flyover by a pileated woodpecker or great blue heron.

Many small trails diverge from the main path, following crevices down to the water's edge. With so many hidden spots to find, you could spend an entire day exploring the various gullies formed by blocks of the Backbone splitting away. The trails that follow the cliff base wind through riparian wetlands, willow groves, and tall cottonwoods and can be impassable if the river is high.

Although they are not along hiking trails, there are several other pretty cool features within the park. The Backbone Cave necessitates some serious spelunking, crawling, etc., to navigate to its end. Balanced Rock, a massive boulder, is supported

Backbone, East Lake, and West Lake Trails

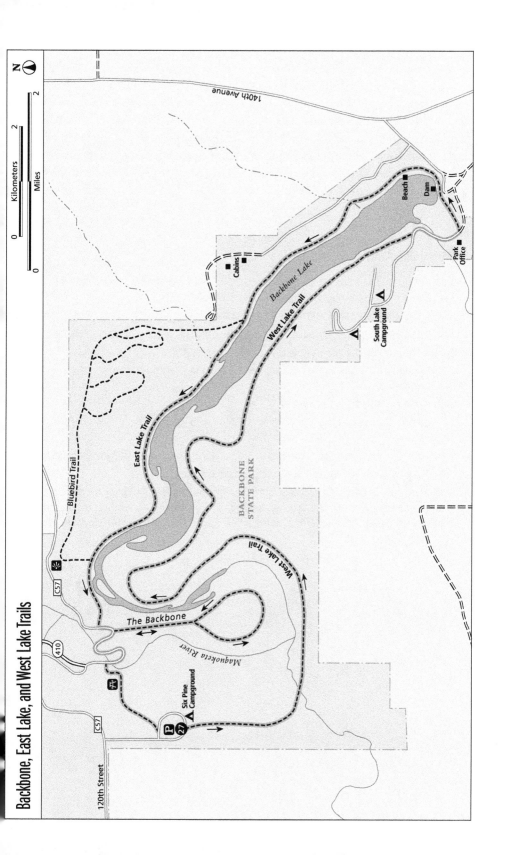

by a very small base. Richmond Springs, on the north end of the park, flows 2,000 gallons per minute, bubbling up through the porous limestone. It flows into the Maquoketa River within the park and is stocked with native trout, a place to do a little fishing or just cool your feet in the 48-degree water. Refreshing watercress grows along the edges of the spring. Backbone State Forest, just to the north of the park, contains several equestrian trails through the eastern white pine plantation. A Civilian Conservation Corps (CCC) museum is located just before you exit through the west gate of the park. Here you can view pictures of various projects in Iowa that were completed by the CCC, including all the structures in Backbone except the park office and residence.

Miles and Directions

0.00 Start at Six Pines Campground; the West Lake Trailhead is on the southwest side of the loop around the campground.

3.30 Arrive at the boat ramp, and follow the trail to the dam.

4.40 Walk past the beach, continuing along the side of the lake onto the East Lake Trail.

4.90 At the fork take the left (west) trail.

Option: The Bluebird Trail will add another 1.5 miles to your total and explores the uplands.

5.80 At the fork take the left (west) trail.

Option: The Bluebird Trail will add another 1.5 miles to your total and explores the uplands.

6.00 Arrive at CR C57; turn left (west) and walk around the curve to get to the Backbone Trail.

6.10 Arrive at Backbone Trailhead; walk south along the ridge.

7.20 Arrive back at Backbone Trailhead. Turn left (west) onto the road and follow the curve down to the picnic area. Just after you pass the huge rock outcrop on the west side of the road, turn left (west) onto a small trail leading up the gully. This will take you back toward Six Pines Campground.

8.00 Arrive back at the north side of Six Pines Campground.

28 Horseshoe Bluff Trail via Mesquakie Foot Trail

Mines of Spain State Recreation Area, located on the bluffs overlooking Catfish Creek and the Mississippi River, encompasses Catfish Creek State Preserve and the Julien Dubuque Monument (on the National Register of Historic Places). Steeped in cultural history, Mines of Spain is situated in an area that has been inhabited for at least the past 8,000 years. It was also the site of the first Euro–American settlement in Iowa and the beginning of river town Dubuque. A short jaunt around the E. B. Lyons Interpretive Center's trails or a 15-mile day, over bluff and down valley, can be enjoyed within the gorgeous park.

Start: Pine Chapel Foot Trail
Elevation gain: 696 feet total gain; 594 (lowest) to 768 feet (highest)
Distance: 6.77-mile out-and-back
Difficulty: Moderate to difficult, due to distance and a few steep climbs
Hiking time: 3 hours
Seasons/schedule: Park open daily from 4:30 a.m. to 10:30 p.m.
Fees and permits: None
Trail contact: Mines of Spain State Recreation Area and E. B. Lyons Interpretive Center, 8991 Bellevue Heights Rd., Dubuque 52003; (563) 556-0620; Mines_of_Spain@dnr.iowa.gov; iowadnr.gov/Places-to-Go/State-Parks/Iowa-State-Parks/Mines-of-Spain-State-Rec-Area
Dog-friendly: Yes, on leash
Trail surface: Grass, crushed rock, and pavement
Land status: Mines of Spain State Recreation Area

Nearest town: Dubuque, 4 miles to the north
Maps: USGS Dubuque South, IA, IL; park map available online
Other trail users: None
Special considerations: The parks have no designated storm shelters. Although the park does not have a severe weather siren, sirens from Dubuque and East Dubuque can normally be heard. Limited deer hunting is allowed in portions of the recreation area. Rock climbing and rappelling are not permitted.
Amenities available: Nonmodern restrooms at the parking lots at E. B. Lyons Interpretive Center and Horseshoe Bluff Trailhead
Maximum grade: 18%; the biggest climbs are from Catfish Creek to Julien Dubuque Monument (150 feet over 0.2 miles), Horseshoe Bluff Trailhead to the overlook (75 feet over 0.1 miles), and back to E. B. Lyons Interpretive Center (150 feet over 0.4 miles)
Cell service: Average reception throughout the trail

Finding the trailhead: From Dubuque, head south on US 151/US 61. After 3 miles, turn east onto US 52, then immediately turn north onto Bellevue Heights Road. Continue for one-half mile, then turn north into the parking lot for E. B. Lyons Interpretive Center. Pine Chapel Foot Trail is south of the center next to a gazebo. GPS: N42° 27.547' W90° 39.836'

    Trail conditions: The trails are well maintained and marked. There are trail markers at junctions and trailheads listing trail names and distances. The trails are wide and clean, but there may be poison ivy off-trail. The stone steps from the overlook down into Horseshoe Bluff will be slippery if wet. The trails receive heavy traffic.

Horseshoe Bluff

The Hike

Julien Dubuque, a French fur trader, was one of the first Europeans to settle in Iowa, and his namesake city lies just north of where he first settled. In 1788, the Mesquakie, who had controlled the nearby lead mines since the mid-1700s, permitted Dubuque to begin mining. Near their village at the mouth of Catfish Creek, he built a small settlement with a trading post, sawmill, blacksmith shop, forge, and smelting furnace. It's said he became very close with the tribe and that he married Potosa, daughter of chief Peosta. In 1796, Dubuque petitioned the governor of Louisiana, Baron Hector de Carondelet, to cede him a tract of land surrounding the mines 3 by 7 leagues (or 9 by 21 miles), which he named the "Mines of Spain," apparently to oblige the Spanish government. When Dubuque died in 1810, he was buried on a bluff overlooking the Mississippi River where the Julien Dubuque Monument, built in 1897, stands today.

South of the nature center, find the Pine Chapel Foot Trailhead near a gazebo and head east downhill through hardwood forest. Cross a prairie glade and continue east to climb the hill to Pine Chapel. Trails wind around the chapel and old homestead built by the Junkermann family in the 1860s; two cellars excavated from rock outcrops for storage of wine and food; a sinkhole formed by a mine-shaft collapse; and small depressions of the pit mines from earlier days.

Head north to join Mesquakie Trail. After one-half mile, the trail reaches Catfish Creek and follows it until reaching the state park road. Cross the bridge over the creek and turn north into the parking lot to access the Julien Dubuque Trailhead. Climb up the fifty steps and follow the trail to the monument's parking lot. There is a paved trail leading to the monument honoring the founder of the city of Dubuque. The 25-foot-tall tower was built with limestone quarried from the hill on which it stands. From the blufftop overlook, look south for the mouth of Catfish Creek below, with Horseshoe Bluff rising in the distance. To the north is the city of Dubuque; across the river in Wisconsin rises Sinsinawa Mound, an erosional outlier of the Silurian escarpment.

Retrace your steps to the bridge over Catfish Creek. After you cross the creek bridge heading east, take the footpath on the north side of the park road. This section of the Calcite Trail parallels railroad tracks and is rather mundane. Cross the park road again and continue on the footpath as it makes its way through a picnic area along the edge of the woods. When you reach the parking lot at the Horseshoe Bluff Trailhead, take either path as the trail loops back to the parking lot. Hiking the loop clockwise gets the climbing done first, while approaching Horseshoe Bluff hiking counterclockwise gives a different perspective of the canyon.

Horseshoe Bluff was once a hill overlooking the Mississippi, but intensive quarrying carved out its center, forming the U-shaped canyon. The trail through the canyon has interpretive signs describing the rock exposures and the quarrying that took place and a prime example of "stream piracy" where you're standing. Both Catfish and Granger Creeks once occupied different streambeds, and Horseshoe Bluff was once an island in the Mississippi. Large amounts of glacial meltwater surging down the river and the two creeks repositioned the channels and the mouths of the creeks, leaving several valleys in Mines of Spain without the waterways they once housed.

Time your hike to visit the E. B. Lyons Nature Center. Exhibits include bird and mammal mounts, projectile points and pottery shards found on-site, tools once used by miners, and several pieces of the lead ore they searched for. In the southern half of the park, the Prairie Ridge, Cedar Ridge, Eagle Scout, and Catesse Hollow Trails traverse upland prairie reconstructions and dive into heavily forested, cool ravines. These trails are wide, mowed swaths used mainly for cross-country skiing, but they're worth the energy if you're looking for a long hike.

Miles and Directions

0.00 Start at Pine Chapel Foot Trail.

0.13 Continue straight (east) toward the interpretive sign and benches.

0.18 Keep right (southeast) toward the Pine Chapel.

0.25 Pine Chapel; take the trail by the stone bench and interpretive sign heading northwest.

0.37 Turn right (northwest), then continue straight (north) at the next junction.

0.42 Continue straight (north).

Option: Turn right (east) to view the root and wine cellars.

Horseshoe Bluff Trail via Mesquakie Foot Trail

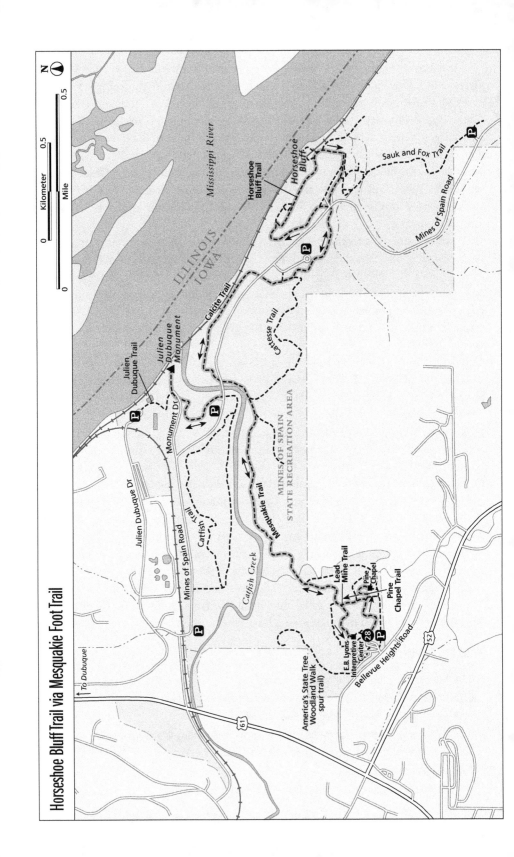

0.48 Continue straight (north) on Lead Mine Trail.

0.50 Keep right (east) onto Mesquakie Foot Trail.

1.30 Continue straight (east).

1.43 Keep left (northeast) toward Julien Dubuque Monument on Calcite Foot Trail.

1.57 Turn left (west) onto the road, cross the bridge, and then turn right (north) into the parking area.

1.90 Turn right (north) onto the road and head toward Julien Dubuque Monument.

2.03 Julien Dubuque Monument.

2.51 Turn left (northeast) onto Calcite Foot Trail.

2.58 Turn right (east).

3.04 Cross the road and continue on Calcite Foot Trail.

3.19 At the rock, continue southeast through the picnic area toward the parking area and road.

3.52 Parking area and Horseshoe Bluff Trailhead; head up the stairs.

3.55 Turn left (northwest) toward the overlook.

3.76 Overlook.

3.89 Continue southeast toward the wetland, parking lot, and lower level.

3.98 Continue straight (southeast).

4.28 Wetland viewing deck.

4.34 Keep left (northwest).

4.49 Turn left (west) and cross the road.

4.85 Keep left (north).

4.95 Cross the road and continue on Calcite Foot Trail.

5.40 Turn right (southwest).

5.46 Cross the road and head south toward Mesquakie Foot Trail.

5.61 Keep right (west) onto Mesquakie Foot Trail.

6.54 Continue straight (south).

6.56 Turn left (west).

6.77 Arrive at E. B. Lyons Interpretive Center.

29 Lost Canyon and Stream Bottom Trails

Whitewater Canyon Wildlife Area, one of the jewels of Dubuque and Jones County Conservation Departments, contains one of only three true canyons in the state of Iowa. A trail leads from the trailhead down into the canyon, then through beautiful prairie. Stream Bottom Trail leads to a breathtaking view overlooking Whitewater Creek, then down to the creek itself. Combined, the two trails offer one of the best hikes in the Hawkeye State.

Start: Lost Canyon Trailhead
Elevation gain: 499 feet total gain; 800 (lowest) to 1,027 feet (highest)
Distance: 4.08-mile double loop
Difficulty: Moderate
Hiking time: 1.5–2 hours
Seasons/schedule: Open daily from 4:30 a.m. to 10:30 p.m.
Fees and permits: None
Trail contact: Dubuque County Conservation, 13606 Swiss Valley Rd., Peosta 52068; (563) 556-6745; mycountyparks.com/county/Jones/Park/Whitewater-Canyon.aspx. Jones County Conservation, 12515 Central Park Road, Center Junction, Iowa 52212, (563) 487-3541; https://www.jonescountyiowa.gov/conservation/parks/whitewater_canyon/
Dog-friendly: Pets must be kept on a leash no longer than 6 feet.
Trail surface: Natural (mowed grass trails with some rock and gravel)

Land status: Whitewater Canyon Wildlife Management Area (Dubuque and Jones County Conservation Departments)
Nearest town: Cascade, 5 miles east
Maps: USGS Fillmore, IA; trail map available online and posted at the parking area
Other trail users: None
Special considerations: Public hunting is allowed; check hunting seasons before you arrive and dress accordingly. No plants except mushrooms, asparagus, nuts and fruits of hardwood trees, raspberries, blackberries, and gooseberries can be removed or harvested.
Amenities available: None.
Maximum grade: 19%; the climb out of Lost Canyon is 200 feet over nearly 1 mile; the scenic overlook requires a steep but short descent to reach; Stream Bottom Trail descends almost 200 feet over just 0.2 miles, while the ascent out climbs 200 feet over nearly 1 mile
Cell service: Weak coverage at the parking area and in open prairie; no coverage in the canyon or at the stream bottom

Finding the trailhead: Located 5 miles east of Cascade. Take US 151 east and turn south onto Curoe Road. Follow the brown county conservation board arrowhead signs. Keep traveling south on Curoe Road until it turns to gravel (do not follow the curve on the highway). Turn right into the driveway that leads to the parking lot. GPS: N42° 17.677' W90° 53.995'

   Trail conditions: The mowed grass trails are well maintained. There are trail markers at major junctions that provide navigational information. The south slope to reach Whitewater Creek is steeper than the north slope and may be difficult if muddy. The trail receives moderate traffic.

Scenic overlook on Stream Bottom Trail

The Hike

Wildlife management areas owned and managed by the Iowa DNR must not have established trails, but since Whitewater Canyon is property of Dubuque and Jones County Conservation Departments, hikers can use an excellent trail system to explore the eponymous creek and one of only three true canyons in Iowa. This hike traverses two loops, so if your time or energy isn't enough for this full 4-mile hike, pick one but remember to return to hike the other loop as both are worth exploring.

Whitewater and Lost Canyons are thought to be remnants of an ancient cave system that collapsed around 20,000 years ago. Slabs of dolomite can be found along the floor of Lost Canyon, as well as small caves, concaves, and other interesting formations along the limestone canyon walls. The forest understory blooms with woodland wildflowers from March to May, while autumn is a beautiful time to hike.

Head southeast at the Lost Canyon Trailhead in the parking area. The trail descends nearly 200 feet over 1 mile to the bottom of the canyon. The canyon begins about one-third mile into the hike, then passes a picturesque rocky cliff after four-tenths of a mile. There are some interesting outcrops, caves, and other rock formations near the trail. If you venture off-trail, watch where you step to avoid poison ivy, dead timber, and uneven terrain. After one-half mile, follow the trail east toward Henneberry Stone Dam.

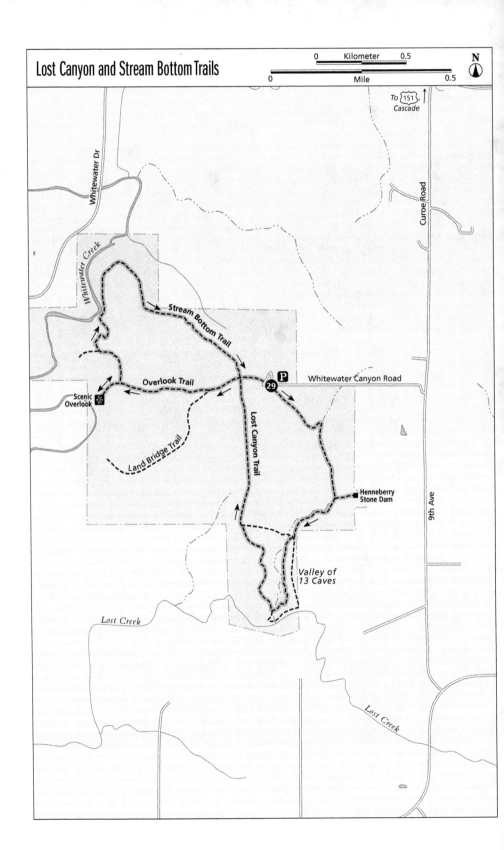

Lost Canyon and Stream Bottom Trails

To 151 Cascade

Curoe Road

Whitewater Dr

Whitewater Creek

Stream Bottom Trail

Overlook Trail

P
29

Whitewater Canyon Road

Scenic Overlook

Land Bridge Trail

Lost Canyon Trail

Henneberry Stone Dam

9th Ave

Valley of 13 Caves

Lost Creek

Lost Creek

Kilometer 0 0.5

Mile 0 0.5

N

Hennebery Dam was built by the Civilian Conservation Corps in 1935 with limestone quarried from the Hennebery farm. The Henneberry family were early practitioners of soil conservation practices. The dam drained excess water from fields to the east via two tile outlets at the bottom of the dam. Hike back to Lost Canyon Trail and continue south for three-quarter miles. The trail heads west, then north as it climbs through beautiful prairie. After 1.65 miles, continue north through first a woodland, then again prairie as you reach the junction with Stream Bottom Trail.

Follow Overlook Trail west for one-half mile, then keep left to reach the overlook above Whitewater Creek. The viewpoint overlooks two hairpin bends in the creek. There are no benches, but sit down on the clifftop and take time to enjoy the incredible view. There is a descent to the overlook and the subsequent climb back to the main trail, however, that is good preparation for the steepest part of the hike.

Soon after rejoining Stream Bottom Trail from the overlook, the trail plunges 175 feet over less than one-quarter mile to the creek bottom. Whitewater Creek is mere yards from the trail. The trail heads north parallel to the creek for a short distance, then climbs east through restored upland prairie to return to the parking lot.

Southwest of Whitewater Canyon, near the town of Monticello, Pictured Rocks County Park offers hiking trails through hardwood forest and Indian Bluffs State Preserve. Rock climbing is permitted, but spelunking Pictured Rocks County Park requires written approval from Jones County Conservation in order to protect bats from white nose syndrome.

Miles and Directions

0.00 Begin at the Lost Canyon Trailhead and head southeast.

0.55 Turn left (east) toward Henneberry Stone Dam.

0.64 Henneberry Stone Dam.

0.72 Continue west on Lost Canyon Trail.

0.94 Continue straight (south).

1.21 Keep right (west).

1.65 Continue straight (north).

2.17 Keep left (north), then turn left (west) onto Overlook Trail.

2.30 Keep right (west) on Overlook Trail.

2.63 Keep left (west) toward the overlook.

2.74 Scenic overlook.

2.85 Turn left (north) onto Stream Bottom.

3.01 Keep right (north) on Stream Bottom.

3.15 Whitewater Creek.

4.02 Turn left (southeast) toward the parking area.

4.08 Arrive back at the trailhead and parking area.

30 Meadow and Quarry Trails

Located on 300-foot bluffs overlooking the Mississippi River, Bellevue State Park was named for the town on the Mississippi to its north. The park is divided into two tracts: Nelson Unit to the north and Dyas Unit to the south. The park is a perfect place to camp out and explore with children. Several short trails, a butterfly garden, and three Woodland Period Indian mounds offer valuable glimpses into the area's natural history.

Start: South Bluff Nature Center
Elevation gain: 240 feet total gain; 630 (lowest) to 873 feet (highest)
Distance: 2.0-mile lollipop
Difficulty: Easy
Hiking time: About 1 hour
Seasons/schedule: Park open daily from 4 a.m. to 10:30 p.m., year-round
Fees and permits: None
Trail contact: Bellevue State Park, 24668 US 52, Bellevue 52031; Bellevue@dnr.iowa .gov; (563) 872-4019; iowadnr.gov/Places -to-Go/State-Parks/Iowa-State-Parks/ Bellevue-State-Park
Dog-friendly: Yes, on leash

Trail surface: Paved and natural
Land status: Bellevue State Park (Iowa DNR)
Nearest town: Bellevue
Maps: USGS Springbrook, IA, IL; park map available online
Other trail users: None
Special considerations: The Nelson Unit storm shelter is in the basement of the South Bluff Nature Center.
Amenities available: Modern and nonmodern restrooms, water, campground, picnic area
Maximum grade: 21%; the climb from Mill Creek back uphill on Quarry Trail gains 200 feet over one-half mile
Cell service: Average to below average

Finding the trailhead: From the junction of US 52 and IA 62 in Bellevue, drive south on US 52. The Nelson Unit's entrance is just south of town. GPS: N42° 14.731' W90° 25.408'
   Trail conditions: Meadow Trail is paved and accessible to wheelchairs and strollers. The trails are easy to follow. The Dyas Unit trails have been reported as overgrown and difficult to follow. The trails receive moderate traffic.

The Hike

Within the Nelson Unit, four named trails offer a total of more than 2 miles of walking paths. The Overlook Trail is a short jaunt down to an overlook from which you can view the town of Bellevue and a wide swath of the Mississippi River. During winter, congregations of bald eagles in the open waters below Lock and Dam #12 scavenge fish that have gone through the turbines.

   The Meadow, Quarry, and Nature Trails all start at South Bluff Nature Center. Follow the Meadow Trail 0.15 mile through reconstructed prairie and into the Garden Sanctuary for Butterflies. Volunteers from neighboring towns first helped create the garden in 1985 and now donate time and money to plant, weed, and water

The town of Bellevue on the Mississippi River

individual plots. Cottonwood, wild cherry, willow, and hackberry trees enclose the garden, which is planted with flowering trees and plants that serve as hosts and food for butterflies.

Sixty species of Lepidoptera have been sighted feeding on black-eyed Susan, borage, cosmos, coneflower, dianthus, heliotrope, lupine, oxeye daisy, phlox, zinnia, and countless other native and nonnative plants, many of which are labeled. On a hot summer day, look for such butterflies as tiger and giant swallowtails, clouded and fiery skippers, large wood nymph, red admiral, eastern tailed blue, red-spotted purple, and tawny emperor, among many others. During the fall migration, you might see larger numbers of monarchs as well. Interpretive signs in the garden include pictures of many butterflies and an explanation of their life cycle.

Continuing onto Quarry Trail to complete a 1.2-mile loop, passing the quarry from which stone was taken to build the park's shelters in the 1920s. The forest here is early successional, recovering from extensive logging that probably took place when the quarry was active. Garlic mustard, an invasive species, is prevalent throughout, forming almost uniform stands in some areas and displacing the native woodland wildflowers.

Meadow and Quarry Trails

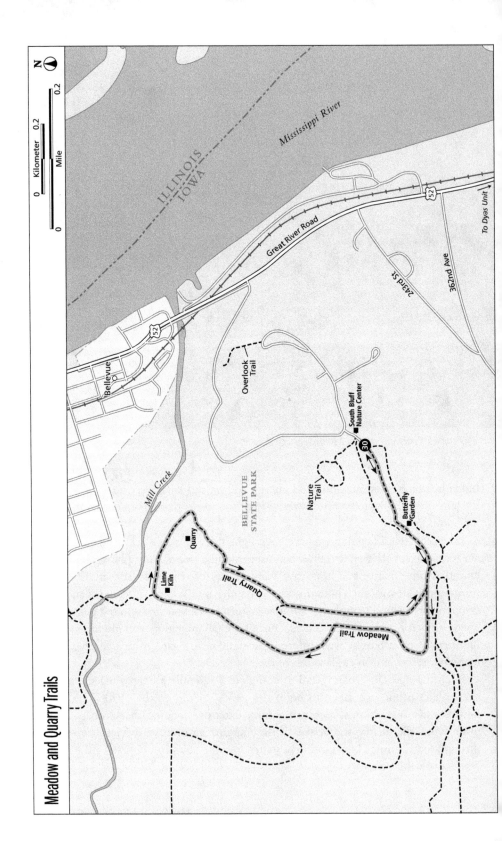

The Nature Trail is a short loop through native forest where spring wildflowers bloom in profusion. If you spend the afternoon in the Nelson Unit, head down to camp in the Dyas Unit. You can explore the Bluff, Duck Creek, Deer, and Bluff Trails. Willow thickets and stinging nettles surround the trails, which can get quite muddy and buggy during the rainy season.

Miles and Directions

0.00 Start at the trailhead, located at the South Bluff Nature Center parking lot.

0.15 Arrive at the Butterfly Garden; continue southwest on Meadow Trail.

0.30 At the fork, keep left (west) onto Quarry Trail.

0.60 At the fork, turn left (west) onto Quarry Trail.

1.70 At the fork, turn left (south) back onto the Meadow Trail.

1.80 Arrive back at the Butterfly Garden; follow the main trail back toward the trailhead.

2.00 Arrive back at the South Bluff Nature Center.

31 Maquoketa Caves Loop

The 370-acre Maquoketa Caves State Park offers 6 miles of hiking trails and spelunking for varying levels of curiosity and ability. Situated in the Raccoon Creek Valley and one of the most geologically interesting sites in the state, the park is home to Iowa's largest cavern system, a 50-foot natural bridge spanning Raccoon Creek, and a 17-ton balanced rock.

Start: Lower parking area
Elevation gain: Variable
Distance: 6 miles of trails
Difficulty: Moderate due to rugged terrain
Hiking time: 2-4 hours, including cave exploration
Seasons/schedule: Park open from 4 a.m. to 10:30 p.m. daily, year-round; visitor center open Sat and Sun from Memorial Day to Labor Day
Fees and permits: None
Trail contact: Maquoketa Caves State Park, 9688 Caves Rd., Maquoketa 52060; (563) 652-5833; Maquoketa@dnr.iowa.gov; iowadnr .gov/Places-to-Go/State-Parks/Iowa-State -Parks/Maquoketa-Caves-State-Park
Dog-friendly: Yes, on leash
Trail surface: Natural, boardwalk, and paved road
Land status: Maquoketa Caves State Park (Iowa DNR)

Nearest town: Maquoketa, 8 miles to the southeast
Maps: USGS Baldwin, IA; park map available online and posted at the lower parking area
Other trail users: None
Special considerations: Always travel in pairs and take extra flashlights or headlamps. Be ready to get muddy and wet and possibly a little scraped up if you explore the caves. Explorations of Bat and Steel Gate Passages should not be attempted without headlamps and water. Also, claustrophobia must be conquered or at least dealt with if hikers are going to make it to the back of most caves. Be extremely careful of the stalactites and other speleothems, since even a small amount of oil from human skin can halt their growth.
Amenities available: Restrooms at the lower parking area and group campsite
Maximum grade: Variable
Cell service: Below average to weak

Finding the trailhead: From the west end of Maquoketa and the junction of US 61 and IA 64, head north on US 61 for 1.5 miles. Turn west (left) onto Caves Road and drive until state park signs point west into the park. Follow the road past the visitor center to the two parking lots. GPS: N42° 7.148' W90° 46.385'

Trail conditions: The trails are well maintained. There are numerous trails throughout the cave complex; trail markers help provide navigational information to points of interest. The trails receive heavy traffic.

The Hike

The Cave Trail begins at the lower of the two parking lots. Wooden staircases lead to the upper and middle entrances of the 1,100-foot-long Dancehall Cave, the most awe-inspiring and accessible cave in the park because of its sheer enormity and the

Lower Dance Hall Cave

electrically lit, paved walkway through its entirety. The park's two most complex caverns to explore, Steel Gate Passage and Bat Passage, are accessed from between the upper and middle entrances to Dancehall Cave. Exiting from the lower entrance of Dancehall Cave, look upslope for a glimpse of 17-ton Balanced Rock.

Walking south into Rainy Day Cave, pass through the first room and into the second, where you'll find the source of Raccoon Creek, which enters the Maquoketa River several miles south of the park. Here the lowlands are dominated by cottonwood, elm, and ash trees. Wild geranium, Virginia waterleaf, and woodland phlox form a dense undergrowth. Keep an eye out for white-breasted nuthatch, red-eyed vireo, common yellowthroat, American redstart, northern oriole, and indigo bunting.

Follow the trails to the bluff-top overlooks on either side of the valley to see tree, northern rough-winged, barn, bank, and cliff swallows perched in the upper canopy or foraging above. Eastern red cedar, Canada yew, columbine, and walking fern all grow precariously from the upper rock ledges, while Virginia creeper vines hang down almost to the valley floor. Along the edge of the bluffs, small prairie openings, or "glades," support big bluestem, sideoats grama, and bastard toadflax. More than 350 plant species have been counted throughout the small park, a high diversity reflecting numerous habitats.

To access the natural bridge and eight caves north of Dancehall Cave, retrace your steps through the large cavern. Photographs taken in 1920 of Dancehall Cave's interior show a scene much different from today's: Milky white stalactites and flowstones once covered the walls and ceiling. However, a century of thievery has left us to wait another several thousand years to replace the geologic wonders once housed inside this cave.

The Maquoketa Caves are a prime example of the karst topography typical of northeast Iowa. This configuration is characterized by shallow carbonate bedrock (such as the park's limestone and dolomite) dissected by fissures, sinkholes, and cavern systems. All but two of the caves are "dissolution caves," formed when surface water drained into the soil and combined with carbonic acid to dissolve the limestone bedrock.

Many historic cultures used the caves as dwellings and meeting places and for ceremonies. Explorers and archaeologists have discovered thousands of artifacts from the past 6,500 years. The name "Maquoketa" is derived from the Mesquakie words "maqua" (medicine) and "keto" (place). A second meaning from the Fox words "mako" (bear) and "keta" (river) refers to the historically high density of bears along the Maquoketa River.

Although no bears remain, another, although much smaller, mammal still inhabits the caves. Each fall, up to 700 Iowa bat species fly into the cave housing their hibernaculum; months later, they emerge together as a group. When they aren't hibernating, the bats spend their days roosting in the trees throughout the park and coming out at dusk to forage for insects.

Miles and Directions

There are numerous trails and caves to explore; recommending a specific route would extinguish the spontaneity that the park's landscape encourages. Hikers should read about the various caves and decide how intense a spelunking experience they want.

1. Wide Mouth Cave: A large gash in the bluff that leads back 100 feet to three rooms.
2. Dug Out Cave: Little more than a shelter dug out of the natural bridge, accessed by climbing up the rocks. A little difficult to get to if you're afraid of heights, this is a nice spot for lunch nonetheless.
3. Twin Arch Cave: A rock shelter within the limestone bluff that looks like a huge nose with two flaring nostrils coming out of the hillside. Crinoid and brachiopod fossils can be seen in the 20-foot-diameter domed roof; seating is provided by large boulders within the cave.
4. Hernando's Hideaway: A fairly good climb from the path to the entrance; belly crawling and slithering necessary to get to the back.
5. Up-N-Down Cave: A gnarled opening several feet off the ground that's tough to get up into, after which you will head down into the 27-foot-long cave.
6. Window Cave: A small crevice in the limestone bluff.
7. Match Cave: Good for beginners. Two passages lie within the cave; the largest is about 30 feet long. Belly crawling is necessary, but the cave is dry.
8. Barbell Cave: Two visible openings; however, the left entrance is impassable. Boost yourself inside the hole on the right and shimmy to the back of the cave, where it opens up to offer enough room for two persons to lie down. Excellent speleothems.

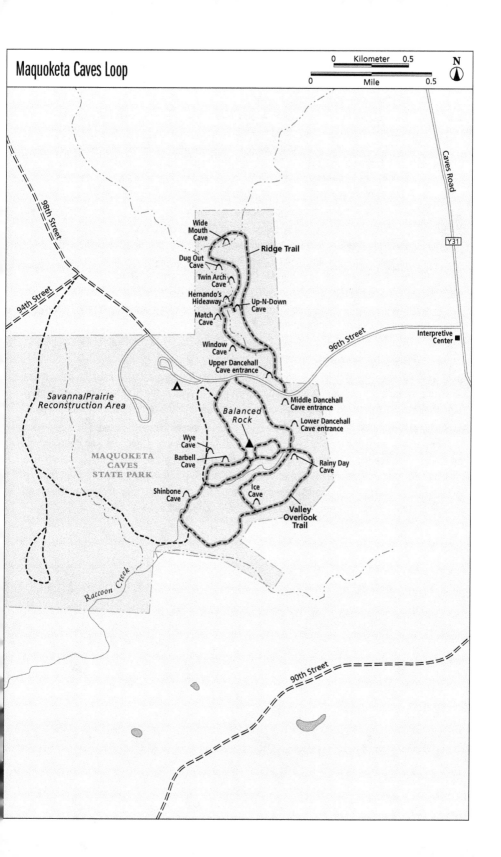

Maquoketa Caves Loop

0   Kilometer   0.5
0   Mile   0.5

N

Caves Road

98th Street

94th Street

Wide Mouth Cave

Ridge Trail

Dug Out Cave

Twin Arch Cave

Hernando's Hideaway

Up-N-Down Cave

Match Cave

Window Cave

96th Street

Interpretive Center

Upper Dancehall Cave entrance

Savanna/Prairie Reconstruction Area

Balanced Rock

Middle Dancehall Cave entrance

Lower Dancehall Cave entrance

Wye Cave

Barbell Cave

MAQUOKETA CAVES STATE PARK

Rainy Day Cave

Shinbone Cave

Ice Cave

Valley Overlook Trail

Raccoon Creek

90th Street

Y31

9. Shinbone Cave: From a distance, the apparent opening is quite visible; however, the actual access lies to the right of the big hole. Crawl 75 feet back into the interconnected space between boulders—and watch your shins.

10. Wye Cave: Begins in the debris of an enormous sinkhole, much higher in the park than other caves. Enter by dropping down 6 feet into the small hole in the right corner of its cavern face. The route plummets in depth and divides, with the left passage becoming the main one. Farther along, there is more passage to explore, but it's very tight and easy to get stuck in. One of the most interesting caves in the park, Wye is nearly 500 feet long. Don't enter unless you are very sure of your athletic capability!

11. Balanced Rock: A 17-ton boulder balances precariously on a small rock platform.

12–14. Dancehall Cave: The biggest, most developed of the Maquoketa Caves is 1,100 feet long. Raccoon Creek flows through its entirety. Other than a short distance at the north entrance, you can walk upright throughout the cave on a lighted concrete walkway. Because Raccoon Creek flows through the cave, it's always wet and muddy.

15. Rainy Day Cave: One of its two rooms is enormous and easy to find. Listen for gurgling, and find the source of Raccoon Creek in the dark depths of the cave's other room. Nearly constant 55-degree F temperature.

16. Ice Cave: Two rooms approximately 20 feet above the stream, with cold air being funneled down into them; perfect on a hot day.

Steel Gate Passage: Accessible from upper Dancehall Cave, it's the most difficult of the Maquoketa Caves to explore. It will take about 45 minutes to an hour to explore the 800 feet of tunnel. Jagged stones will cut up your knees and elbows, but you'll see some of the best speleothems in the park.

Bat Passage: Located inside Dancehall Cave close to the upper entrance. The access hole is several feet above the ground, and the first several yards are cut by a channel a foot wide and deep. Stooping and crawling are occasionally required. As you reach the end of the cave, through a large hole you'll be able to see the paved walkway of Dancehall Cave below. However, unless you want to jump 10 feet down, retrace your steps and leave the way you came. If you're claustrophobic or have broad shoulders, think twice before entering Bat Passage. You don't want to get stuck.

Honorable Mentions

J Decorah Area Trails

The trail system surrounding the town of Decorah is one of the most extensive in the state and traverses an area dense with natural wonders. Twenty miles of multiuse and single-track trails on the north side of town connect Dunning's Spring, Ice Cave Hill, Barbara Barnhart Van Peenen Memorial, and Palisades Parks. You'll find huge waterfalls, densely forested bluffs, and the biggest ice cave in the state.

Start: Variable
Elevation gain: Variable
Distance: Variable
Difficulty: Variable
Hiking time: Variable
Seasons/schedule: Variable
Fees and permits: None
Trail contact: Decorah Parks and Recreation, PO Box 513, 400 Claiborne Dr., Decorah 52101; (563) 382-4158; parkrec@decorahia .org; parks.decorahia.org

Dog-friendly: Check specific park regulations
Trail surface: Natural or paved
Land status: Decorah Parks and Recreation
Nearest town: Decorah
Maps: Trail maps available online
Other trail users: Bikers
Special considerations: None
Amenities available: Variable
Maximum grade: Variable
Cell service: Average at most parks

K Gilbertson Conservation Education Area

Ten miles of wooded trails leave from an access road behind the Gilbertson Nature Center. Walk through forests of oak, shagbark hickory, and black walnut. Brome grass dominates here, and you will most likely see white tailed deer following the browsing line. Other trails lead down through wetland and around several buildings filled with home and farm antiques. The nature center has numerous animal mounts and live turtles and snakes.

Start: Gilbertson Nature Center
Elevation gain: Variable
Distance: 10 miles of trails
Difficulty: Easy to moderate
Hiking time: Variable; 4 hours or more if you hike the entire trail system
Seasons/schedule: Open daily year-round
Fees and permits: None
Trail contact: Gilbertson Nature Center; 22580 A Ave., Elgin 52141; (563) 426-5740;

director@fayettecountyconservation .org; fayettecountyconservation.org/ gilbertson-conservation-education-a
Dog-friendly: Yes, on leash
Trail surface: Natural (grass and dirt) and paved
Land status: Gilbertson Conservation Education Area (Fayette County Conservation)
Nearest town: Elgin

Maps: USGS Gunder, IA; trail map available online

Other trail users: Equestrians (there are also biking trails)

Special considerations: None

Amenities available: Nature center, restrooms, water, modern and backpacking campsites

Maximum grade: Variable

Cell service: Average to below average

Finding the trailhead: From Elgin, head east on Center Street, which becomes CR B64/Agate Road after crossing the Turkey River. Turn north onto A Avenue toward the Gilbertson Nature Center. GPS: N42° 57.469' W91° 36.693'

∟ Swiss Valley Nature Preserve

Named after Swiss settlers, the verdant valley is missing the Swiss Alps but is still a hiking destination in Dubuque County. Ten miles of trails through forest, prairie, and wetland converge on the Swiss Valley Nature Center. The trails are groomed for cross-country skiing in the winter, and the nature center has snowshoes available to rent.

Start: Swiss Valley Nature Center

Elevation gain: Generally ranges from 775 to 1,050 feet

Distance: More than 10 miles of hiking trails

Difficulty: Moderate

Swiss Valley Nature Center in October

Hiking time: Variable; 4 hours or more if you hike the entire trail system

Seasons/schedule: Preserve hours are from sunrise to sunset.

Fees and permits: None

Trail contact: Swiss Valley Nature Preserve and Nature Center, 13606 Swiss Valley Rd., Peosta 52068; (563) 556-6745; mycountyparks.com/county/ubuque/Park/Swiss-Valley-Nature-Preserve-and-Nature-Center.aspx

Dog-friendly: Yes, on leash

Trail surface: Natural (dirt and grass) and wood chips

Land status: Swiss Valley Nature Preserve and Nature Center (Dubuque County Conservation)

Nearest town: Dubuque, 9 miles to the northeast

Maps: USGS Peosta, IA; trail map available online

Other trail users: None

Special considerations: In winter, many of the trails convert to groomed cross-country ski trails. The nature center also has snowshoes for visitors to use, free of charge.

Amenities available: Restrooms, water

Maximum grade: 30%; each climb from the valley bottom to the ridges on either side of the valley is approximately 250 feet over less than one-half mile

Cell service: Adequate

Finding the trailhead: From Dubuque, head south on US 61 and continue southwest on US 61 past the junction with US 52. One-half mile after the junction, turn west onto Maquoketa Drive, then immediately southwest onto Key West Drive. Continue for 3 miles, then turn west onto Swiss Valley Road and continue for 2 miles before reaching the turn into Swiss Valley Nature Preserve. GPS: N42° 25.379' W90° 45.545'

Trail conditions: The trails are well maintained and well marked. There are a lot of forks and turns, so take a map with you if you want to follow a specific set of trails. The trails receive moderate traffic.

Bluffs over Rivers

I owa is known as "The Land Between Two Rivers," and its eastern and western boundaries—the Mississippi and Missouri Rivers—usually receive the most notice. Little attention is paid to their countless tributaries, from which these mighty waterways draw their size and power. The undulating hills that sweep across the southeast Iowa landscape were created and are defined by the rills, creeks, streams, and rivers that drain them. And the Mississippi River doesn't just absorb its tributaries, it swallows them.

Though each of southeast Iowa's rivers is distinct, as the waterways near their short-term destination (a mouth into the Mississippi River), they share several common traits. They all possess wide and deep valleys and, in some places, exposed bedrock in the form of bluffs, or Palisades, for which the state park on the Cedar River was named. A short 11,000 years ago, the Cedar, Iowa, and Skunk Rivers all had glaciers in their headwaters, and as the vast Des Moines Lobe ice sheet eroded, meltwater found various paths to the sea. Valley walls were eroded down to the underlying bedrock and widened considerably. The bluffs that now preside over and frame our rivers are a testament to the sheer velocity of erosion caused by waters melting off glaciers.

The first people in Iowa lived along the floodplains of streams and rivers, hunting and gathering and later growing corn, squash, beans, tobacco, sunflowers, and goose-foot. They used the rivers as trade routes and quarried flint and chert from banks and bluffs for tools. Euro-American steamships brought the first loads up the Cedar and Iowa Rivers in the 1830s and 1840s. Saw and grist mills stood along the bulk of the larger streams and rivers, providing energy to mill the forests that were being logged and process the grain that was being grown, fueling the infant Iowan economy.

Southeast Iowa houses a plethora of river towns. The biggest are the Quad Cities (Bettendorf and Davenport in Iowa and in Moline and Rock Island in Illinois) sitting alongside the Mississippi River. Iowa City and Cedar Rapids (their names indicating the associated rivers) are two cities rapidly sprawling into one megalopolis. The corridor for development is broken only by the Coralville Reservoir and Lake MacBride, two lakes created by damming the Iowa River and several small tributaries, respectively. During the 1993 floods, the Devonian Fossil Gorge, located next to Coralville Dam, was scoured out by water flowing over the spillway, exposing 375-million-year-old coral, brachiopod, crinoid, and armored fish fossils.

Wildcat Den State Park, located east of the Mississippi River town of Muscatine, boasts an entrenched, sandstone-framed canyon just upstream of Pine Creek's

Wildcat Den State Park

mouth. In his book *Life on the Mississippi*, river-rat-turned-author Mark Twain wrote, "I remember Muscatine—still more pleasantly—for its summer sunsets. I have never seen any, on either side of the ocean, that equaled them. They used the broad smooth river as a canvas, and painted on it every imaginable dream of color."

The Mark Twain National Wildlife and Fish Refuge encompasses 45,000 acres divided between units spanning 345 river miles along the Mississippi, as well as the Iowa River Corridor, a 10,000-acre greenbelt located in Tama, Benton, and Iowa Counties. Iowa's portion of the Mark Twain NWRF, Port Louisa National Wildlife Refuge (and adjacent state-owned Lake Odessa Wildlife Management Area), is located just south of Muscatine. Between the bluffs and the levee along the river are nearly 4 square miles of wetlands and floodplain forests teeming with wildlife.

Between hikes at Geode State Park and Starr's Cave Park and Preserve, you can check out Snake Alley in Burlington, known as the "crookedest street in the world." Aldo Leopold, a seasoned conservationist, forester, wildlife biologist, and writer of several books, including *A Sand County Almanac*, was born and raised in Burlington, and his legacy lives on through the work of many. From Geode State Park, if you travel up the Skunk River, you'll pass the town of Mount Pleasant on your way to Brinton Timber, a park in Washington County just next door to Lake Darling State Park.

Standing atop a bluff and peering down onto any of our rivers, you can't help but look to the water for reflection. Rivers that course through our Iowa valleys are monuments to change. Harbingers of transformation, they bring the promise of a healthy crop of corn, a new family of wood ducks, or a hatch of russet-tipped clubtail dragonflies. Our rivers do not always reflect such beauty as Mark Twain wrote of; instead, their health is evidence of grave injury. The Cedar, Iowa, Mississippi, and Skunk Rivers, as well as Lake MacBride and the Coraville Reservoir, are all on the Environmental Protection Agency's "Impaired Waters List" due to high levels of nitrates, siltation, fecal matter, and pesticides. Restoration and cleanup work that state and federal agency staff, local volunteers, and organizations like Living Lands & Waters do each year is crucial to the health of our rivers—and help is always welcomed.

32 Cedar Cliff Trail

"The valley of the red cedar is in eastern Iowa, a long strip of fertile land sprawling out besides the river whose name it bears." So said native Iowan Bess Streeter Aldrich of the Cedar River Valley in her book *Song of Years*. The palisades for which the park was named are sheer 60-foot-high cliffs that loom over the valley of the red cedar. Hiking trails traverse the palisade crests and the forested hills of the park, which doubles as a rock-climber's paradise.

Start: North end of Kepler Drive along the Cedar River

Elevation gain: 190 feet total gain; 669 (lowest) to 785 feet (highest)

Distance: 2.03-mile out-and-back

Difficulty: Moderate due to rugged trails and steep cliffs

Hiking time: 1–1.5 hours

Seasons/schedule: Park open daily from 4 a.m. to 10:30 p.m., year-round

Fees and permits: None

Trail contact: Palisades-Kepler State Park, 700 Kepler Dr., Mount Vernon 52314; (319) 895-6039; Palisades_Kepler@dnr.iowa.gov; iowadnr.gov/Places-to-Go/State-Parks/Iowa -State-Parks/Palisades-Kepler-State-Park

Dog-friendly: Yes, on leash

Trail surface: Natural (dirt)

Land status: Palisades-Kepler State Park (Iowa DNR)

Nearest town: Mount Vernon, 5 miles to the east

Maps: USGS Bertram, IA; park map available online

Other trail users: None

Special considerations: The park does not have a designated storm shelter. The shower building can be used for an emergency shelter during storms. Swimming is allowed in the Cedar River, but dangerous currents warrant using extreme caution.

Amenities available: Campground, restrooms, and water available in the state park.

Maximum grade: 16%; there are three steep climbs between 75 to 100 feet over one-quarter mile each

Cell service: Adequate

Finding the trailhead: From Mount Vernon, head west on US 30. After 3.2 miles, turn southwest onto Kepler Drive. Continue on Kepler Drive for 1.4 miles, then turn left to head northwest. The trailhead is located at the end of the road. GPS: N41° 54.388' W91° 30.731'

Trail conditions: The trails have numerous exposed rocks and tree roots, so watch your step as you hike. The trails also follow along the top of steep cliffs above the river, so hike with caution. The trails receive heavy traffic.

The Hike

To stand above an eastern Iowa river, whose downward action has cut a wide chasm in the surrounding forested hills, is to see that river not only for what it is but for what it once was. The resistant dolomite cliffs towering above the Cedar River at Palisades-Kepler were deposited 420 to 440 million years ago, when they were muddy tropical reef-like masses on the Silurian sea floor. Colonial coral, crinoid beds,

Viewpoint overlooking the Cedar River

and brachiopod fossils found in the mounds of the exposed Scotch Grove and Gower Formations paint a picture of a sea that was very different from those of today. Organisms that once inhabited shallow marine shelves are now deepwater dwelling, their old niches having been commandeered during the last 400-plus million years. Also, the coral reefs of today are composed mainly of piled-up coral cemented together by calcifying algae, whereas the carbonate "mounds" of the Silurian age were made of various fossils held in a carbonate mud matrix. Because of the resistance to erosion of the dolomite bedrock, the ridgelike Silurian Escarpment is a major landscape feature in northeast Iowa and can also be seen at Backbone, Maquoketa Caves, and Bellevue State Parks.

Also found within Palisades-Kepler's bluffs are nodules of chert, a hard rock composed of silicon dioxide. Because of its sharp, glasslike edges, many native peoples used chert to make tools. Archaeological excavations from rock shelters in Palisades-Dows State Preserve across the river have yielded extensive caches of animal bones and pottery shards, evidence of occupation over the past 2,500 years.

From the parking lot walk north onto the Cedar Cliff Trail, which passes along the river and then climbs up on the ridge overlooking it. The sugar maple–basswood forest is quite dense, but as you ascend the rocks to the blufftop, the world opens up. Oak-hickory forest covers the dry uplands, while prairie glades command the exposed ridgetops. The oldest known tree in Iowa, an eastern red cedar approaching 500 years old, lives here on the bluffs, hanging fast to its rock base over the river that bears its name.

Continue up the trail and you'll ascend stairs to the overlook gazebo, built by the Civilian Conservation Corps (CCC) in the 1930s and recently restored. Eastern Iowa rock climbers flock to the palisades below for some of the best top-roping and traditional routes around. The climbing is free, but climbers can register on paper at the park office, and because of the fast-flowing river below, don't attempt anything if you're unsure of yourself. Always have a climbing spotter and never climb alone. Whether you're climbing or just exploring, be careful not to disturb the diverse communities of moss, liverwort, lichen, and fern growing on the rocks.

The Cedar Cliff Trail continues to the northern boundary of the park, where you'll have to turn around and hike back to the trailhead. The trail follows just below

INDIAN CREEK NATURE CENTER

Indian Creek Nature Center's mission is to promote a more sustainable future by nurturing individuals through environmental education, providing leadership in land protection and restoration, and encouraging responsible interactions with nature. The center's new building, opened in 2016, fulfills its mission with high quality environmental education, restoration of important habitat, and outdoor recreation opportunities like 5 miles of groomed trails. The center is located on the east side of Cedar Rapids.

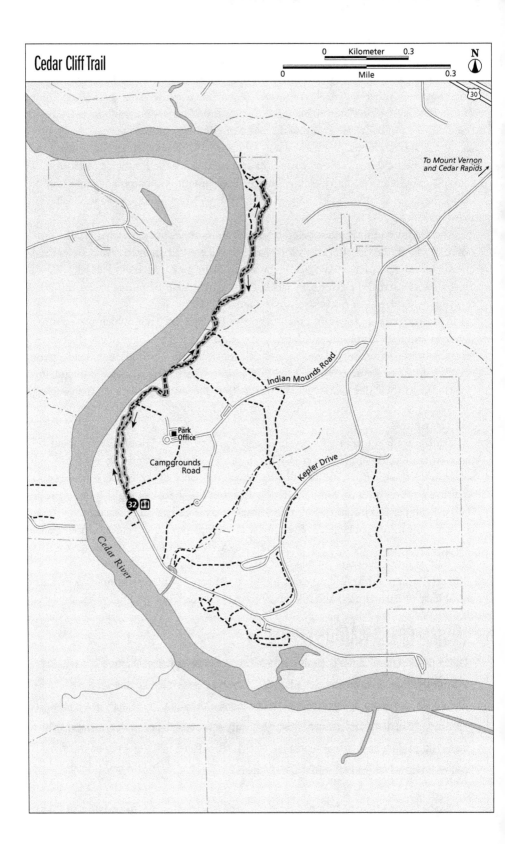

Cedar Cliff Trail

0   Kilometer   0.3

0   Mile   0.3

N

30

To Mount Vernon
and Cedar Rapids

Indian Mounds Road

Park
Office

Campgrounds
Road

Kepler Drive

32

Cedar River

Cedar River

the ridge, above several steep ravines. You'll find yourself at the canopy height of the trees growing on the sides of the steep drainages, the perfect place to look for birds. Look for scarlet tanager and American redstart flitting along.

Miles and Directions

0.00 Begin at the trailhead.

0.23 Keep left (north).

0.25 Shelter.

1.01 End of Cedar Cliff Trail; turn around.

1.78 Keep left (south).

2.03 Arrive back at the trailhead.

33 Woodpecker Trail and Squire Point

One of the many developed trail systems around the Coralville Reservoir–Lake Mac-Bride complex, the connecting loops of Linder and Squire Points Trails have long served as a haven for dog walkers and trail runners. A few loops on the trails here combined with a nice bike ride around the reservoir make for a great day.

Start: Linder Point Recreation Area on West Overlook Road
Elevation gain: 364 feet total gain; 700 (lowest) to 810 feet (highest)
Distance: 4.4 miles of connecting loops
Difficulty: Moderate
Hiking time: 1–3 hours
Seasons/schedule: Open year-round, dawn to dusk
Fees and permits: None
Trail contact: Coralville Lake Project Office, 2850 Prairie Du Chien Rd. NE, Iowa City 52240-7820; (319) 338-3543; coralville .lake@usace.army.mil; mvr.usace.army.mil/ Missions/Recreation/Coralville-Lake/
Dog-friendly: Dogs permitted while on leash

Trail surface: Forested footpath, connecting trails
Land status: Coralville Lake (US Army Corps of Engineers)
Nearest town: Iowa City, 5.5 miles to the south
Maps: USGS Iowa City West, IA; trail map available online
Other trail users: Cross-country skiers in winter
Special considerations: Poison ivy and ticks are common.
Amenities available: Restrooms and campground at Linder Point
Maximum grade: 14%
Cell service: Adequate

Finding the trailhead: From I-80, take exit 244, and follow Dubuque Street north 2.6 miles. Turn right (east) onto West Overlook Road; you'll see a sign for Linder Point and Woodpecker Trail parking area. GPS: N41° 43.495' W91° 32.548'

Trail conditions: The trails are well marked. Sections of the trail system may have downed trees or be overgrown. The trails receive heavy traffic.

The Hike

Floods in the 1930s prompted Congress to establish the Flood Control Act of 1938, which authorized the US Army Corps of Engineers (USACE) to build dams on tributaries of the Mississippi. The Iowa River was one of the first to be dammed. The Coralville Dam, 100 feet high and 1,400 feet long, was completed in 1958. Land bordering the newly created Coralville Reservoir was left fallow after decades of agricultural use had decimated the native flora. The Woodpecker Trail interpretive loop connects the Squire and Linder Point Trail networks on the southern end of the Coralville Reservoir. Loops of various lengths and elevation gains allow hikers to choose desired distances and difficulty. Deep ravines cut the hilly terrain, and limestone outcrops offer picturesque views of the lake as well as visual lessons in the geologic history of the area.

LITERARY IOWA

In honor of the University of Iowa's Iowa Writers' Workshop, here is a selection of books about Iowa:

The Indians of Iowa by Lance Foster

Landforms of Iowa by Jean Prior

Wildflowers of the Tallgrass Prairie by Sylvan Runkel

Tending Iowa's Land: Pathways to a Sustainable Future edited by Cornelia Mutel

Iowa's Remarkable Soils: The Story of Our Most Vital Resource and How We Can Save It by Kathleen Woida

Fragile Giants: A Natural History of the Loess Hills by Cornelia Mutel

The Wapsipinicon Almanac: Selections from Thirty Years edited by Timothy Fay

Both Linder and Squire Point trailheads begin where upland forest trees dominate: shagbark hickory, white and red oaks, silver maple, honey locust, and hop hornbeam. Easily distinguished amid the neighboring deciduous trees are the interspersed eastern red cedars. The eastern red cedar, a coniferous tree, normally colonizes open, sunny places, such as the pastureland this area was used as after it was logged during the early 1800s. When the Corps bought the land, domesticated animals and fences were removed, and a more typical upland forest grew around the eastern red cedars.

In the oak-hickory forest covering the hills, you'll find wildflowers blooming throughout spring and summer. Look for anemone, bloodroot, mayapple, black snakeroot, bellwort, jack-in-the-pulpit, and lobelia. You will most likely encounter white-tailed deer nibbling on greens, as the wooded areas around the lake provide a sanctuary for deer driven from their historic range by intense agricultural cultivation in much of Johnson County.

The trail follows a contour about 50 feet above the water's edge, depending on fluctuating lake levels. On the disturbed banks next to the trail, look for moss and lichen groundcover: hair cap moss, tree moss, and fairy cups. The crossing of two bridges provides overhead views of the flood-prone sites surrounding the lake, as well as a small creek's entrance to the lake, fringed by willow thickets.

Many songbirds can be observed in the upland forest during breeding and migration times. If you're lucky you'll see prothonotary and cerulean warblers, red-eyed vireo, American redstart, blue-gray gnatcatcher, and ovenbird. While focusing on the birds, try to tell the difference between two common and extremely similar-looking woodpeckers, the downy and hairy. These are the only woodpeckers with entirely white backs, although they have the black-and-white checkers and spots common to other woodpecker species. The males have a distinguishing small patch of red on the backs of their heads. The hairy woodpecker is approximately 3 inches longer than

Woodpecker Trail and Squire Point

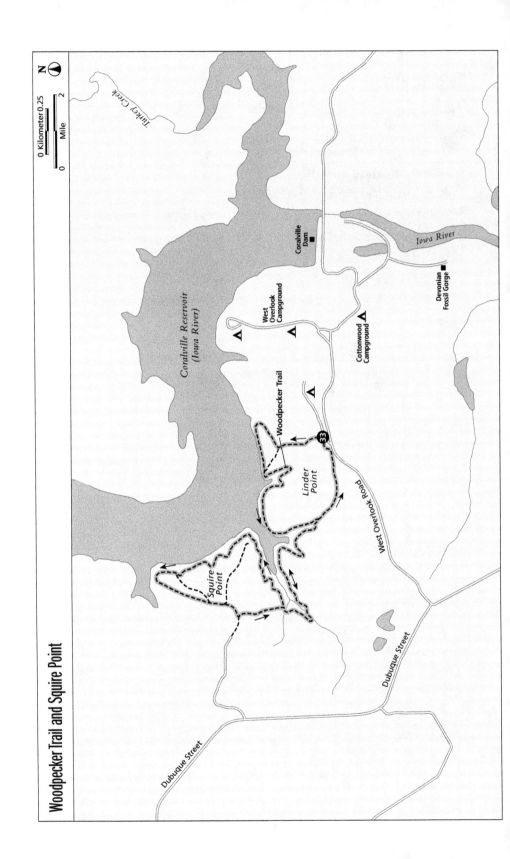

N

0 Kilometer 0.25

0   Mile   2

Turkey Creek

Coralville Reservoir
(Iowa River)

Coralville Dam

Iowa River

Devonian Fossil Gorge

West Overlook Campground

Cottonwood Campground

Woodpecker Trail

Linder Point

West Overlook Road

Squire Point

Dubuque Street

Dubuque Street

the downy, and its call is a sharp "peek," while the downy has a slightly larger bill and calls a flat "pick."

Descending to the lake, the forest structure changes as trees that are tolerant of fluctuating water levels dominate: cottonwood, black willow, and basswood. Here you'll have the best chance to see the rare pileated woodpecker, the largest woodpecker left in America, hammering on large snags for insects. Cavity-prone tree species such as basswood, silver maple, and black cherry may also house northern flicker, red-headed woodpecker, barred owl, and eastern screech owl.

When snow is on the ground, the trails provide ungroomed cross-country skiing. (Hikers and snowshoers are asked to steer clear of established ski tracks.) Winter bird residents include black-capped chickadee, brown creeper, blue jay, northern cardinal, and tufted titmouse. Ringed-bill gulls live at the lake year-round and can be seen from almost anywhere patrolling overhead. Bald eagles will occasionally fly over the lake; they winter along the Iowa River, which, unlike the Coralville Reservoir, remains unfrozen year-round. Watch for gray and fox squirrels digging for stashes of acorns when snow is heavy and all edible plants are covered.

Miles and Directions

0.00 Start from the Linder Point parking area.

0.20 At the fork, turn right (northeast).

0.30 At the fork, turn right (northeast).

0.45 At the point, continue around the contour of the lake.

1.80 At the fork, stay right and continue around the contour of the lake.

2.70 You've reached the northern boundary of the USACE property. Follow the trail left (west) and ascend the ridge to the Squire Point Trailhead and parking before descending back down to the contour trail around the lake.

3.20 At the fork at the bottom of the hill, turn right (southwest) onto the contour trail.

3.90 At the fork, turn right (southeast) to return quickly to the trailhead via the long staircase, or follow the contour trail for a little more distance.

4.40 Arrive back at the trailhead.

34 Mill Trail and Canyon Ridge Trail

The cats for which the park was named were mostly killed off in the mid–1800s, although rumors of bobcat sightings float around often enough. You can still see the Pennsylvanian sandstone outcrops, more than 300 million years after their deposition. Along Pine Creek, just a mile upstream from its confluence with the Mississippi River, you'll find exposed Devonian bedrock with a host of crinoid, brachiopod, and coral fossils. A delight to geologists and fern lovers, Wildcat Den State Park is the place to take your time on a slow walk so that you can enjoy the diversity of everything that's going on there.

Start: Mill Trail Trailhead near Pine Creek Grist Mill

Elevation gain: 341 feet total gain; 581 (lowest) to 715 feet (highest)

Distance: 2.05-mile out-and-back

Difficulty: Easy to moderate

Hiking time: 1–2 miles

Seasons/schedule: Park open from 4 a.m. to 10:30 p.m. daily, year-round

Fees and permits: None

Trail contact: Wildcat Den State Park, 1884 Wildcat Den Rd., Muscatine 52761; (563) 263-4337; Wildcat_Den@dnr.iowa.gov; iowadnr.gov/Places-to-Go/State-Parks/Iowa -State-Parks/Wildcat-Den-State-Park

Dog-friendly: Yes, on leash

Trail surface: Natural

Land status: Wildcat Den State Park (Iowa DNR)

Nearest town: Muscatine, 12 miles to the west

Maps: USGS Montpelier, IA, IL, and USGS Illinois City, IL, IA 2021; park map available online

Other trail users: None

Special considerations: Be aware of poison ivy and ticks.

Amenities available: Restrooms and water in the state park

Maximum grade: 15%; the hike climbs from the creek bottom to blufftop three times, each approximately 100 feet gain

Cell service: Reception may vary depending on provider; below average reception under tree cover and at the creek bottom

Finding the trailhead: Finding the trailhead: From the junction of IA 92 and 22 in Muscatine, drive northeast on IA 22. Drive along the Mississippi River, through the town of Fairport, and turn left (north) onto Wildcat Den Road. GPS: N41° 28.021' W90° 52.147'

   Trail conditions: The trails are well maintained and marked. The forested footpaths and wooden stairs receive heavy traffic.

The Hike

The Blackhawk Purchase, signed in 1832 by the Sauk and Fox tribes and the federal government, ceded tribal land to the government, opening up the Upper Midwest to white settlement in mid–1833. Benjamin Nye, Muscatine County's first white settler, arrived in 1834 and within a year had opened a trading post. Within fourteen years he had built a sawmill and two grist mills along Pine Creek. The presence of the mills

Punch Bowl

and an influx of agrarian settlers set the tone for the native ecosystems—the surrounding terrain was logged, and much of it was cropped and grazed.

The second mill that Nye built still stands on the banks of Pine Creek within the park and was added to the National Register of Historic Places in 1979. During the 1960s, the Melpine Country School was moved to the park for preservation. Local organizations hold interpretive tours at both of these buildings. (Check with Friends of Pine Creek Grist Mill for times.)

Park at the eastern end of the park near Pine Creek Grist Mill. Head west on Mill Trail toward the Pine Creek Overlook. Continue on the trail following the signs for Punch Bowl Trail to Devil's Punchbowl, a large bowl sculpted by a seasonal creek and the most visited formation in the park. Here is the best place to view the Pennsylvanian sandstone of which most of the bluffs in the park are made. Look in the sandstone for cross-bedding and ripples, suggesting that it was deposited by a shifting river channel.

The park houses a broad array of twenty-five types of ferns; on the sandstone you'll find polypody, cliff, Goldie's, and walking ferns. Look for rock-dwelling moss, liverwort, and lichen communities, especially in places where water trickles down the rocks. These nonvascular plants can go dormant during dry spells and the cold of

Mill Trail and Canyon Ridge Trail

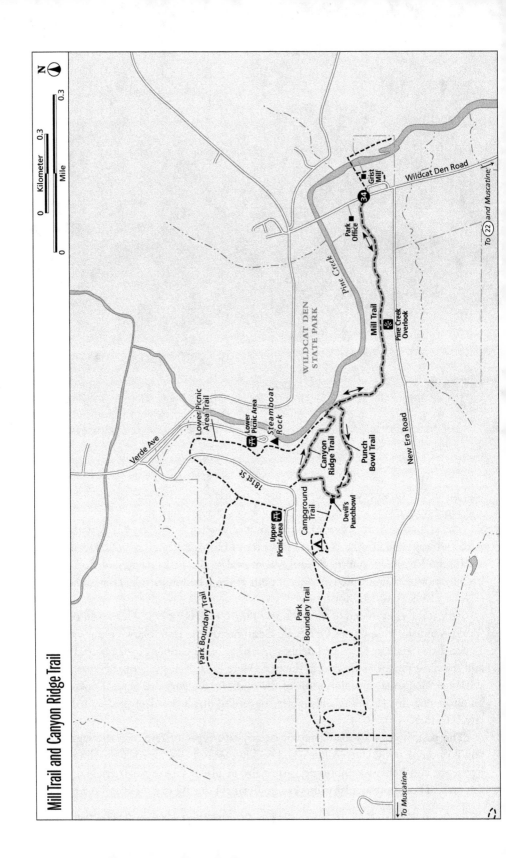

winter; however, the first spring rains and warmer days bring them back to life. Take a break to sit in the cool shade of an overhang, examine the plant communities on the rocks, and listen to the echo of dripping water as it tumbles off the sandstone shelves into pools below.

After exploring Devil's Punchbowl, head toward the Upper Picnic Shelter Area. Take Canyon Ridge Trail heading southeast downhill. Once you reach the creek bottom, follow Mill Trail back to the trailhead on the eastern end of the park to complete the 2-mile loop. However, consider the option to explore the upland section west of the state park road. The upland portion of the park provides a good opportunity to view the park's landscape, as the bluffs rise significantly above the surrounding terrain (200 feet in some places). The northwestern part of the park was grazed and logged until the 1970s, and though the black oak and ironwood trees are young, you'll find a rare orchid, oval ladies' tresses (*Spiranthes ovalis*) here. At midsummer, search beneath the colonies of white pine on top of the cliffs for rattlesnake plantain (*Goodyera pubescens*), an orchid that likes the acidic conditions formed by decaying pine needles.

You can use the Lower Picnic Area Trail to hike to Steamboat Rock, named for its shape, then rejoin Mill Trail along Pine Creek. To the north of Steamboat Rock, you'll discover a passageway known as Devil's Lane. Here you'll find carved graffiti dating from 1861, although earlier graffiti at the base of the cliffs may have been destroyed by erosion. Fat Man's Squeeze used to be located near Devil's Lane. A small opening in the rocks once wide enough to shimmy through, it has recently succumbed to erosion and collapsed.

Miles and Directions

0.00 Begin at Mill Trail Trailhead.
0.34 Pass an alternate trailhead.
0.66 Turn left (southwest) onto Punch Bowl Trail.
1.00 Campground Trail junction.
1.11 Turn right (east) onto Canyon Ridge Trail.
1.34 Turn right (southeast).
1.37 Turn left (southeast) onto Mill Trail and cross the footbridge.
2.05 Arrive back at Mill Trail Trailhead.

35 Sam Rodgers Educational Trail

Eddyville Dunes Sand Prairie protects one of the rarest ecosystems in the state of Iowa. Rare species such as prickly pear cactus and ornate box turtles call this prairie home. The pleasant 1.5-mile Sam Rodgers Educational Trail is superbly maintained and has numerous interpretive panels describing the unique ecosystem. This is one of the best prairie hikes in a state where less than 1 percent of remnant prairie remains.

Start: Parking area at 23125 182nd St., Eddyville, IA 52553
Elevation gain: 72 feet total gain; 736 (lowest) to 793 feet (highest)
Distance: 1.43-mile loop
Difficulty: Easy
Hiking time: About 1 hour
Seasons/schedule: Trails open daily year-round
Fees and permits: None
Trail contact: Wapello County Conservation, 1339 US 63, Bloomfield 52537; (641) 682-3091; pioneerridge@wapellocounty.org; wapellocounty.org/conservation/parks/eddyville_sand_dunes_prairie/

Dog-friendly: Yes, on leash
Trail surface: Crushed rock and natural (dirt, grass, and sand)
Land status: Eddyville Sand Dunes Prairie (Wapello County Conservation)
Nearest town: Eddyville
Maps: USGS Kirkville, IA; park map available online
Other trail users: None
Special considerations: None
Amenities available: None
Maximum grade: 5%; there are no notable inclines on the loop
Cell service: Adequate

Finding the trailhead: From Eddyville, take CR G77 east to 232nd Avenue, the first gravel road east of Eddyville High School. Turn south onto 232nd Avenue to 182nd Street, then west to the road closure gate. The parking lot is on the north side of the road. GPS: N41° 9.080' W92° 37.010'

   Trail conditions: The trail is easy to follow as there are no intersecting trails. It is well maintained and well marked with interpretive signs. The surface is mostly crushed rock with some sections of dirt, grass, and sand. There is plentiful prickly pear cacti just off-trail, so avoid hiking off-trail to protect your feet and legs and the ecosystem. The trail receives light traffic.

The Hike

Eddyville Dunes Sand Prairie is only 55 acres, but it would be difficult to find another place in Iowa with more plant diversity than this unique ecosystem. There are very few sand prairies left in the state. Find rare plants and animals here, like prickly pear cactus, pale green orchid, six-lined racerunner lizards, and ornate box turtles. The dunes were formed between 12,000 and 15,000 years ago by strong winds that deposited sand along the Des Moines River valley.

   The sand is largely covered by prairie grasses, but don't venture over the dunes to get a closer glimpse, as they are covered with prickly pear cacti. The bright yellow

Prickly pear cactus

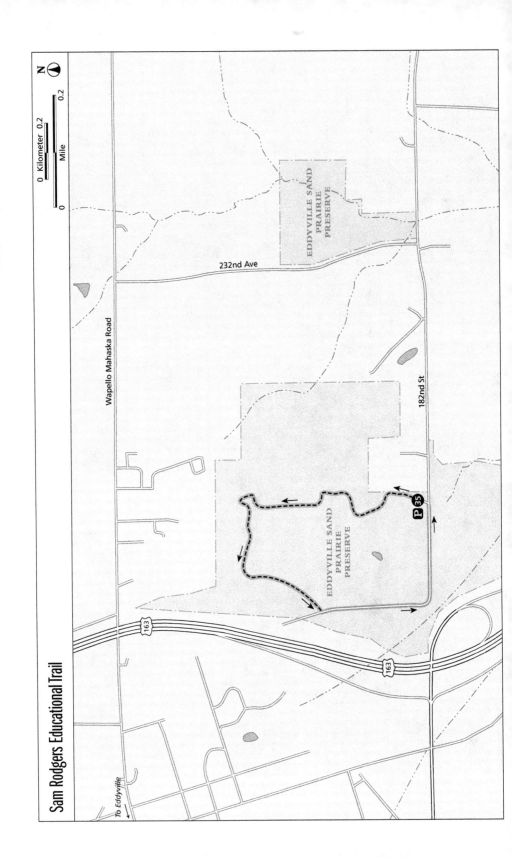

Sam Rodgers Educational Trail

flowers bloom from May to July, so time your visit to Eddyville Dunes Sand Prairie to see the dunes covered with blooming cacti. Prickly pear cactus is found in a few Iowa counties, as it prefers dry, rocky, or sandy prairies with well-drained soil. Even though the southeast corner of Iowa receives on average the most precipitation in the state, the conditions at Eddyville have converged to encourage prickly pear cactus at the sand prairie. Prickly pear cactus is so rare in Iowa that it is on the list of endangered, threatened, and special concern plants administered by the Natural Resource Commission and the director of the Department of Natural Resources.

A simple yet thoroughly enjoyable 1.5-mile loop explores the sand prairie on the southeastern edge of the town of Eddyville. The Sam Rodgers Educational Trail is named after an educator, long-time board member of Wapello County Conservation, and enthusiast of the Eddyville Dunes Sand Prairie. There is a picnic shelter at the parking area, which provides nearly the only shade in the preserve (there are short sections under brief tree cover). The crushed rock trail heads north through the sand prairie, then comes across a small wetland area. There is an interpretive panel and wooden platform overlooking the wetland. There are several well-designed interpretive panels along the trail that describe the rare species that call the prairie home, as well as invasive species that pose a recurrent problem. One panel explains that the presence of ornate box turtles at the Eddyville Dunes Sand Prairie was the principal reason for protecting this land, as they are an indicator species of the extremely rare sand prairie ecosystem.

Northwest of Eddyville, Cedar Bluffs Natural Area has 2 miles of trails that take you across prairie and oak savanna restoration areas, down into a box canyon, along a 100-foot-high bluff overlooking Cedar Creek, past a several-thousand-year-old burial mound, and through forests that house spring-blooming wildflowers galore. Visit Cedar Bluffs in early May to forage for wild edible mushrooms, but make sure to keep your spot a secret!

Miles and Directions

0.00 Start at the trailhead and head north.

0.14 Wetland viewing deck.

0.94 Keep left (south).

1.20 Turn left (east).

1.43 Arrive at the gate to the parking area.

36 Brinton Timber

Perched on the hills overlooking the Skunk River, 320-acre Brinton Timber is part of a 1,000-acre swath of forests along the riparian corridor. Mature oak-hickory forests cover the hills, and in springtime the understory is an explosion of blooming wild-flowers. To help hikers avoid getting lost, trails are named and labeled with colored symbols painted on trees. The trails are a favorite among cross-country skiers when the snow is deep.

Start: 2980 Fir Ave., Brighton, IA 52540
Elevation gain: 699 feet total gain; 617 (lowest) to 735 feet (highest)
Distance: 5.3-mile loop
Difficulty: Moderate
Hiking time: 3-4 hours
Seasons/schedule: Trails open daily, year-round
Fees and permits: None
Trail contact: Washington County Conservation, Conservation Education Center, 2943 IA 92, Ainsworth 52201; (319) 657-2400; wscounty conservation@gmail.com; washingtoncounty .iowa.gov/170/Conservation
Dog-friendly: Yes, on leash
Trail surface: Natural

Land status: Brinton Timber (Washington County Conservation)
Nearest town: Brighton, 5 miles to the south
Maps: USGS Brighton, IA; trail map available online and posted at the trailhead
Other trail users: Equestrians
Special considerations: Flip signs are installed to close the trails to horses during muddy conditions to help protect the safety of patrons as well as the resources.
Amenities available: Modern latrine, pit toilets, and primitive camping
Maximum grade: 13%; there are three climbs of approximately 100 feet
Cell service: Average to weak

Finding the trailhead: From IA 1/IA 78, take CR W21/Fir Avenue north (1 mile west of Brighton). Brinton Timber is at the north end of Fir Avenue from this direction. GPS: N41° 13.428' W91° 51.130'

   Trail conditions: Trails are well maintained. There are several stream crossings that might be difficult to cross if water is present. The trail receives heavy horse traffic.

The Hike

Six different loops, each named and associated with a symbol (painted onto trees along the trail), traverse the forested bluffs overlooking the Skunk River. The total combined length of the loops is 6 miles, but you can choose your hike depending on the amount of energy you have. At each trail intersection there is an area map posted; an arrow points to where you are, so you won't get lost amid the maze.

   From the parking area, take the Grandfather Trail (red feather) down to the creek and cross it, following Indian Ridge Trail, marked with orange arrowheads, to the right (northwest). Almost immediately you'll turn right (north) onto the Wood Duck Trail (dark blue wood duck). You'll follow the creek down into the forested

A subterranean stream emerges from the rock at Brinton Timber. ZACH ROZMUS

bottomlands of an old Skunk River terrace. During early spring, ground-nesting wild turkeys will wait until just before you step on them to flush, startling the whole forest with a great commotion. Be respectful of the nests by leaving quickly so that the females can return to their eggs.

The name of this trail reflects the fact that riparian forests are favored by wood ducks, which require cavities in trees to lay their eggs. By the early 1900s wood ducks were close to extinction because of habitat loss and extensive hunting for their plumage and eggs. The discovery in 1937 that wood ducks readily adapt to laying eggs in nesting boxes, and a surge of nest box programs since then, have enabled populations to grow steadily.

At the intersection of Wood Duck and Bent Rock Trails (light blue half moon), turn right (north). This trail loops south and connects with the Tall Timber Trail (violet double tree). Though the hills have been logged multiple times since first being settled by the Brinton family in the early 1800s, this swath of forest along the Skunk River still serves as habitat for many birds. Listen for pileated woodpeckers drumming on large snags and the echoing, metallic song of the wood thrush. Large numbers of warblers use Brinton Timber during migration. During spring look for cerulean and Kentucky warblers, Louisiana waterthrush, and northern parula.

Brinton Timber Trails

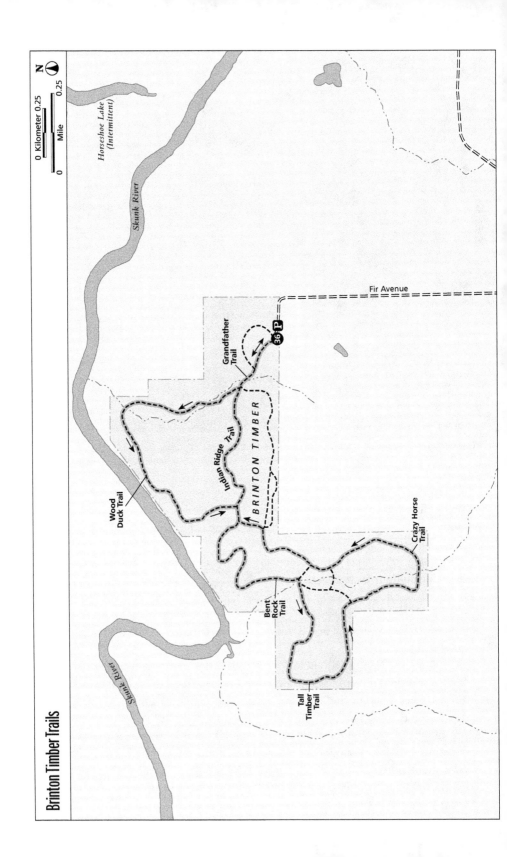

Follow the Tall Timber Trail around to the Crazy Horse Trail (yellow horseshoe). When you reach the intersection with the Bent Rock Trail, turn left (west) and walk down to the drainage to find the "bent rock," an outcrop exposed by erosive powers of the small creek.

Backtrack to the Bent Rock Trail and head northeast toward the parking lot. Spring wildflowers abound on the slopes. In April you'll find small clusters of hepatica blooming before anything else. The flowers emerge before the leaves and range in color from white to soft pink and purple to a deep lilac. Also look for Dutchman's breeches, bloodroot, nodding trillium, and spring beauty just as the trees are beginning to leaf.

You'll encounter two successive forks that diverge back onto the south part of the Indian Ridge Trail to walk through the shrub area on your way back to the trailhead. Walk just a little farther to take the north part of the Indian Ridge Trail, past three vernal pools that are home to several species of breeding frogs during spring. Listen for the spring peepers' short, loud "peep," repeated every one or two seconds. You may also hear western chorus frogs' fingernail-on-a-comb call, or the banjo-tuning notes of green frogs. Cross the creek, hop back on the Grandfather Trail, and cruise up to the trailhead.

Miles and Directions

0.00 Start from the parking area and follow Grandfather Trail (red feather) down to the creek.

0.30 At the fork, turn left (north) onto the Indian Ridge Trail (orange arrowhead), and make a quick right onto the Wood Duck Trail (dark blue wood duck).

1.50 Arrive back at Indian Ridge Trail; turn right (west). You'll quickly approach another fork.

1.60 At the fork turn right (northwest) onto the Bent Rock Trail (light blue half moon).

2.20 At fork, turn right (west) onto the Tall Timber Trail (violet double tree). Cross the creek and climb up to the ridge.

3.00 At the fork, turn right (south) onto the Crazy Horse Trail (yellow horseshoe).

3.90 At the fork, continue straight (north) onto the Bent Rock Trail.

4.30 You'll come to two successive forks; stay left (north) at both of them. **Option:** If you turn right at the first fork, you'll wander through a shrubby area, rife with birds, on your way back to Grandfather Trail and the trailhead.

4.40 At the third fork, turn right (east) to check out the vernal pools.

5.10 Cross the creek and follow Grandfather Trail back up to the trailhead.

5.30 Arrive back at the trailhead.

37 Flint River Trail

The preserve is split in half by Flint Creek, which cuts through a nearly vertical 100-foot-high escarpment of fossil-rich Mississippian limestone. Starr's Cave is 300 feet long and home to several species of bats, but is closed to the public to protect the bats from white nose syndrome. Crinoid Cavern, a man-made cavern opposite Starr's Cave, draws explorers while forest and prairie areas of this 184-acre preserve host diverse wildflowers and birds. The trail to Starr's Cave is accessible for wheelchairs and strollers.

Start: Flint River Trailhead north of Starr's Cave Nature Center
Elevation gain: 213 feet total gain; 541 (lowest) to 666 feet (highest)
Distance: 2.2-mile loop
Difficulty: Easy but with a steep climb from Starr's Cave to Flint River Trail
Hiking time: 1–1.5 hours
Seasons/schedule: Park hours are 6 a.m. to 10:30 p.m.
Fees and permits: None
Trail contact: Starr's Cave Park and Preserve, 11627 Starr's Cave Park Rd., Burlington 52601; (319) 753-5808; desmoines county.iowa.gov/conservation/parks/ starrs_cave_park_and_preserve/
Dog-friendly: Yes, on leash

Trail surface: Crushed rock and natural (dirt)
Land status: Starr's Cave Park and Preserve (Des Moines County Conservation)
Nearest town: Burlington
Maps: USGS West Burlington, IA; park map available online
Other trail users: Mountain bikers on Flint River Trail; foot traffic only on hiking trails
Special considerations: No collection or destruction of plants, mushrooms, animals, fossils, rocks, or artifacts
Amenities available: Restrooms
Maximum grade: 13%; the trail climbs over 100 feet over one-third mile from Starr's Cave to the bluffs on Flint River Trail
Cell service: Adequate

Finding the trailhead: From US 61, take Sunnyside Avenue or Upper Flint Road to Irish Ridge Road. Follow signs to Starr's Cave Park Road. The nature center is at the end of the road. GPS: N40° 50.978' W91° 8.114'

Trail conditions: Flint River Trail is a multiuse trail open to bikers and hikers (bikers must yield to hikers). The trail is easy to follow and there are trail markers at junctions. The hiking-only trails are clearly marked. These trails are narrow, dirt single-track trails that take hikers closer to the bluffs overlooking the Flint River. The trails receive moderate to heavy traffic.

The Hike

There are three caves within the preserve. The largest was named for a previous land-owner, the preserve's namesake. As with most caverns in Iowa, Starr's Cave is rumored to have been used as a hideout by Jesse James and his gang; it's also thought to have been a stop on the Underground Railroad. Previous explorations describe the cave as

Starr's Cave is closed to protect brown bats.

750 feet long, and even older stories claim it once extended as far as the Mississippi River, more than a mile away.

Today an assortment of bat species enjoy the constantly 55-degree F temperature of Starr's Cave, which serves as a hibernacula during winter and breeding grounds during summer for big and little brown bats and quite possibly the endangered Indiana bat. In the past, Starr's Cave was accessed by trail from a parking area on Irish Ridge Road. It's now reached by taking the paved trail along Flint Creek and crossing the new bridge that spans the creek and leads to the mouth of the cave. The cave was previously open to the public, however, access to the cave is now restricted to protect the bats from white nose syndrome.

From the parking area in front of the nature center, walk west up the hill where oak-hickory forests form an extensive canopy. Eight species of oaks and three species of hickory live within the small preserve, a testament to its topographic variance and habitat diversity. Within the upland forests you'll find white, black, bur, and red oaks intermingling with shagbark, bitternut, and mockernut hickory, among others. The delicate spring wildflowers are in full bloom during April and May. Look for Dutchman's breeches, spring beauty, hepatica, rue anemone, bluebells, and trillium.

Flint River Trail

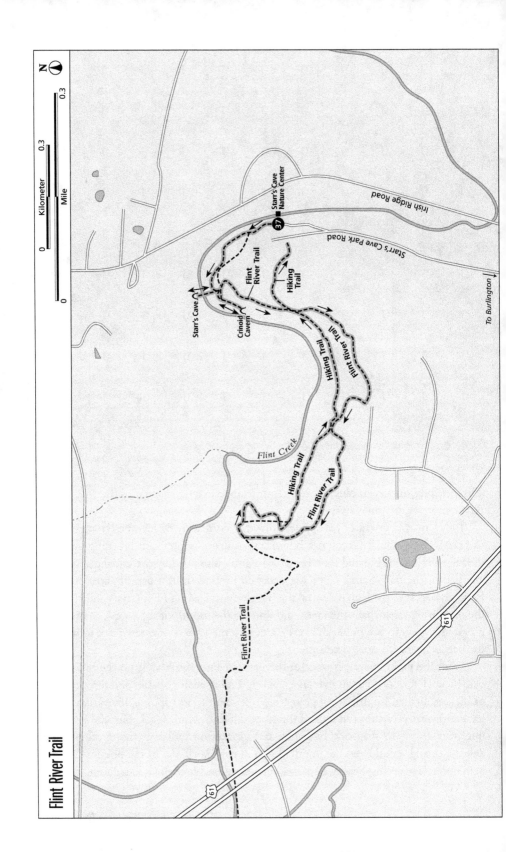

The accessible trail leads to the footbridge over Flint Creek. Before crossing the bridge, find the footpath along the south bank of the creek to reach Crinoid Cavern. You'll have to scramble up the bluff to reach Crinoid Cavern, a small cave/room facing the creek—a good place to enjoy a snack. Check out the ceiling for fossils of brachiopods, crinoids, and cup corals, as well as a gray-green crustose lichen that can survive in environments with little light. From here you'll see black-capped chickadees flitting along green ash treetops, while belted kingfishers and great blue herons make hunting pilgrimages up and down the drainage.

After visiting both the cavern and cave, continue south on the Flint River Trail. The multiuse trail leads along the ridge that towers 100 feet above Flint Creek, where eastern red cedars, redbuds, blue ash, and chestnut oaks hang onto the rocky bluff amid a moss and lichen bed. While the bike/hike trail is a wide and gentle hiking trail, don't walk too close to the edge of the steep bluffs on the hiking-only trails—the rock is somewhat unstable, and it's a long way down to the bottom of the canyon.

Flint Creek is framed by tall sycamore and cottonwood trees, as well as thickets of peachleaf willow. Horsetails, wood and stinging nettles, and wild grapes occupy the creekside understory. Long ago, the flint deposits for which the creek was named were collected by Sauk and Fox tribes to make tools.

Miles and Directions

0.00 Head north at the trailhead.

0.07 Keep right (north).

0.17 Turn right (northwest) onto a natural surface trail.

0.28 Crinoid Cavern; return the way you came.

0.34 Turn right (southeast) to follow a footpath uphill to the footbridge.

0.35 Turn left (northeast) onto the footbridge toward Starr's Cave; return the way you came.

0.63 Continue straight (south).

0.66 Continue straight (south).

0.96 Continue straight (west).

0.99 Keep left (southwest).

1.34 Continue straight (north) onto the hiking trail.

1.74 Turn left (east) onto Flint River Trail.

1.78 Turn left (northeast) onto the hiking trail.

2.00 Turn left (north) onto Flint River Trail, then keep right (northeast) onto the hiking trail.

2.11 Continue straight (east).

2.20 Arrive at the nature center.

38 Lake Trail

Take a creek walk in Geode State Park, named for Iowa's state rock, and you may find several of the beautiful stones—but it's illegal to take them home with you. Early spring and summer are the best times to visit, when wildflowers blanket the forest floor and migratory ducks find themselves at home. A 7-mile trail around the lake drops in and out of small ravines and is popular with hikers and bikers.

Start: Picnic area to the northeast of the beach

Elevation gain: 653 feet total gain; 587 (lowest) to 702 feet (highest)

Distance: 7.0-mile loop

Difficulty: Moderate to difficult

Hiking time: 2–3 hours

Seasons/schedule: Park open year-round, 4 a.m. to 10:30 p.m.

Fees and permits: None

Trail contact: Geode State Park, 3333 Racine Ave., Danville 52623; (319) 392-4601; Geode@dnr.iowa.gov; iowadnr.gov/Places-to-Go/State-Parks/Iowa-State-Parks/Geode-State-Park

Dog-friendly: Yes, on leash

Trail surface: Natural (forested footpaths)

Land status: Geode State Park (Iowa DNR)

Nearest town: Burlington, 17 miles to the east

Maps: USGS Lowell, IA; park map available online

Other trail users: Mountain bikers

Special considerations: Geodes are on display in the park office, but it is prohibited to remove geodes from the park

Amenities available: Water, restrooms, shelters, picnic areas, and camping in the state park

Maximum grade: 12%; there are numerous inclines and declines, the steepest a 100-foot climb over one-tenth of a mile

Cell service: Average to weak under tree cover

Finding the trailhead: From the junction of US 34 and 61 on the north side of Burlington, drive west on US 34. At the fork, when US 34 turns to the northwest, continue straight ahead on IA 79, which will take you directly west to the park. GPS: N40° 49.688' W91° 23.035'

Trail conditions: The trails are well maintained, well marked, and easy to navigate. The hike is shaded for the overwhelmingly majority of the hike. The trails receive moderate traffic.

The Hike

Geode comes from "geoides," the Latin word for "earthlike," and some exceptionally beautiful specimens can be found within a 35-mile radius of Keokuk, Iowa. Located in tributary valleys of the Des Moines River, geodes are spherical rocks with usually hollow cavities lined with mineral crystals. World-famous Keokuk geodes originated in the clays of the Mississippian seafloor, around 340 million years ago. Their enigmatic formation validates how unique they are. Iowa adopted the geode as its state rock in 1967. It is illegal to remove any geodes from the state park.

From the parking area northeast of the beach, you'll see a small peninsula jutting out into the lake that serves as an annual nesting ground for Canada geese. During very early spring you may flush common goldeneye, greater scaup, bufflehead,

Trailhead at Geode State Park ULF KONIG

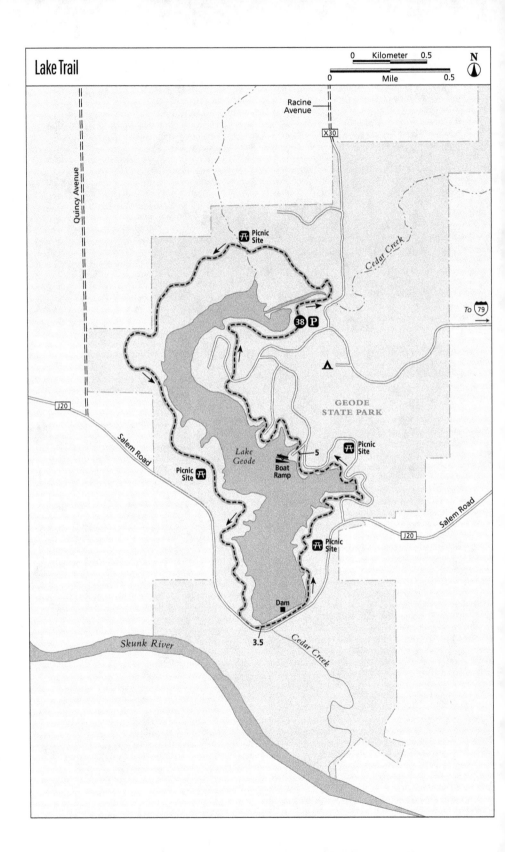

Lake Trail

0 Kilometer 0.5
0 Mile 0.5

N

Racine
Avenue

X30

Quincy Avenue

Cedar Creek

To 79

Picnic
Site

38 P

GEODE
STATE PARK

J20

Salem Road

Lake
Geode

5 Picnic
Site

Boat
Ramp

Picnic
Site

Salem Road

J20

Picnic
Site

Dam

3.5

Cedar Creek

Skunk River

common loon, or northern shoveler. Blue-winged teals, wood ducks, and mallards spend the summer in the lake.

Follow the trail south along the developed side of the lake, following a contour in and out of the inlets. You'll pass the beach, the boat ramp, and several picnic shelters before crossing the dam. A small interpretive trail leads from the beach up to the campground (brochures available at park office), where you'll find a display of Keokuk geodes.

Continue west, across the dam that was built in 1950 just before the park's opening. The introduction of nonnative carp and their subsequent predation on native fish, along with the siltation of Lake Geode, compelled the Department of Natural Resources to drain the lake in 1981. The silt was removed and the lake was refilled and restocked with fish. However, the siltation problem returned so the lake was renovated from 2017 to 2020, removing silt. The lake was also restocked with fish in 2021.

Following the west side of the lake back up to the parking area, you'll find a much more diverse forest habitat. Instead of following a contour, the trail dips in and out of ravines and can get very muddy during rainy periods. Water from runoff and many small springs drains into Lake Geode, with several species of ferns hanging over the small riparian areas. Dense mats of mosses flank the sides of the trail. During April and May look for wild blue phlox, wild geranium, Jacob's ladder, and downy yellow violet.

Honeybee Hollow Trail is a 2-mile out-and-back, hiking-only trail established in 2018. It begins at the park office parking area and heads north through a mature woodland area. The trail leads to three different pond areas that were constructed to control silt entering the lake. The pond areas have become wildlife magnets—many birds and mammals can be observed at these locations. Honeybee Hollow Trail is not listed on the park map, but it begins and ends at the park office.

Miles and Directions

0.00 Start at the picnic area to the northeast of the beach. The trail leaves from the north side of the parking area and heads east.

3.50 Cross over the dam and follow the trail along the lakeside.

5.00 Cross over the boat ramp.

6.10 Walk past the beach and continue north.

   Option: Turn to the east to follow the Fallen Oak Interpretive Trail up to the campground.

7.00 Arrive back at the trailhead.

39 Des Moines River Trail

The unparalleled beauty of the forested bluffs rising from the huge horseshoe bend in the Des Moines River reveal each season's spectacular show. Winter's snow cover forms a contemplative silence followed by spring's diverse wildflower display and budding trees. The shade of the tall forest canopy is a perfect respite from the heat of summer, while autumn yields one of the most vividly colorful scenes in Iowa.

Start: Near Shelter #1
Elevation gain: 341 feet total gain; 568 (lowest) to 707 feet (highest)
Distance: 3.31-mile out-and-back
Difficulty: Easy to moderate due to steep trail to the Des Moines River
Hiking time: 1.5 hours
Seasons/schedule: Park open year-round from 4 a.m. to 10:30 p.m.
Fees and permits: None
Trail contact: Lacey-Keosauqua State Park, 22895 Lacey Trail, Keosauqua 52565; (319) 293-3502; Lacey_Keosauqua@dnr.iowa.gov; iowadnr.gov/Places-to-Go/State-Parks/Iowa-State-Parks/Lacey-Keosauqua-State-Park
Dog-friendly: Yes, on leash
Trail surface: Natural (dirt) and paved roads
Land status: Lacey-Keosauqua State Park (Iowa DNR)

Nearest town: Keosauqua, 2 miles to the northeast
Maps: USGS Keosauqua, IA; park map available online
Other trail users: None (there are multiuse trails in other areas of the state park)
Special considerations: A series of Native American burial mounds from the Woodland Culture overlook the Des Moines River. These are sacred locations, so please avoid walking on or disturbing the mounds.
Amenities available: Restrooms and water throughout the state park
Maximum grade: 15%; the biggest climb is at the end of the hike from the Des Moines River up to Shelter #1, gaining 125 feet over one-quarter mile
Cell service: Average to weak, especially under tree cover

Finding the trailhead: From Keosauqua, head southeast on IA 1. After crossing the Des Moines River, turn southwest onto State Park Road. Continue for 1.4 miles, then turn north toward Shelter #1. After 0.2 miles, reach the parking loop; the trailhead is located on the western end of the loop. GPS: N40° 42.992' W91° 58.333'

Trail conditions: The trails are well maintained and waymarked. The trail along the Des Moines River is wide but too rough for strollers. The trails will be soft and muddy after rain, so turn around if your activity leaves a mark. The trails receive moderate to heavy traffic.

The Hike

Walking along the Des Moines River at 1,653-acre Lacey-Keosauqua State Park elicits Van Buren County's motto: "The rush of life races the blood, but the quiet life restoreth the soul." For reasons unknown to geologists, the Des Moines River decided to slow down a little here at Keosauqua, deviating from its normally linear course to form the largest oxbow in southeast Iowa. Lacey-Keosauqua lies on the

Ely Ford Mormon Crossing on the Des Moines River

south side of the oxbow, almost 49 river miles from the Mississippi River at Keokuk. Across the river from the park, sandy alluvial deposits underlie the terraced farmland inside the river's bend. The park sits atop deeply cut older bedrock.

When the former Big Bend Park was dedicated in 1921, it was renamed Keosauqua. A good deal of controversy surrounds the origin and meaning of Keosauqua, first used as a second name for the Des Moines River on Charles de Wards's 1835 map. It is believed that Keosauqua is a Fox word, though there are varied speculations of its meaning. Several theories, taken from early settlers' accounts, include "the stream bearing a floating mass of snow, slush, or ice," "clear broad river," and "great bend." In 1926 the name Lacey was added to the park in honor of Major John F. Lacey from Oskaloosa. Lacey fought in the Civil War, was a member of the Iowa House of Representatives and the US Congress, and campaigned for and wrote conservation legislation.

The River Trail extends west from the highway over the Des Moines River, past Shelter #1, then stopping at a beautiful picnic area at Ely Ford Mormon Crossing. Ely Ford, named for the Mormon expedition that crossed the Des Moines River here, is a popular picnicking and birding spot along the River Trail. Sit in the shade of the tall sycamore and elm trees and look for such exciting birds as northern parula; yellow-throated, worm-eating, cerulean, Kentucky, and hooded warblers; summer

Des Moines River Trail

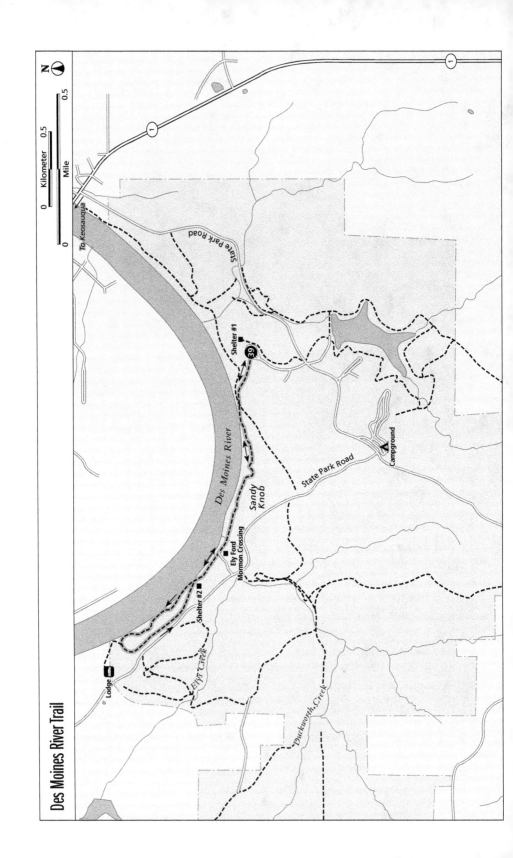

N

Kilometer 0.5

Mile 0.5

To Keosauqua

1

1

State Park Road

Shelter #1

39

Des Moines River

Sandy Knob

State Park Road

Campground

Ely Ford
Mormon Crossing

Shelter #2

Ely's Creek

Lodge

Duckworth Creek

and scarlet tanagers; ovenbird; and Louisiana waterthrush. Follow a small trail south of Ely Ford up a forested ravine where Ely Creek has dissected the terrain to expose the Keosauqua sandstone formation hidden beneath alluvium in the rest of the park.

Continue west on the River Trail, climbing the river bluff and passing burial mounds before approaching the day-use lodge. Late Woodland peoples buried their dead in the conical mounds they built atop the bluffs along the river. Nineteen are visible now. Pottery shards and tools such as spear points and animal-bone scrapers have been discovered by recent archaeological explorations in the beds of Wesley, Ely, and Thatcher Creeks.

Before reaching the lodge, take the trail toward the Lacey Monument. This trail will loop back to Shelter #2 and then the Ely Ford Mormon Crossing. From there, it's a leisurely hike along the river, then a 100-foot climb up to Shelter #1. Several connector trails access the 1-mile upland forest loop in the northwest section of the park, a 2.5-mile loop trail around Lake Lacey, and a 3-mile trail connecting Lake Lacey to Lake Sugema Wildlife Management Area and camping area. These all ascend the forested bluffs and meander over the rich upland oak–hickory forest that dominates the park. If you want a lengthy hike, park at Lake Sugema and walk all the loops in the park, including the snowmobile trail that winds through the Keosauqua Unit of Shimek State Forest. Leave early, and spend the whole day enjoying the Big Bend; you can even stop in Keosauqua for a midday treat.

Miles and Directions

0.00 Begin at Shelter #1 and head northwest on River Trail.

0.16 Turn left (west).

0.26 Continue straight (west) toward Ely Ford.

1.02 Ely Ford Mormon Crossing.

1.18 Continue straight (west).

1.27 Continue straight (west) toward the lodge.

1.70 At the sign for Lacey Monument, keep left (west).

1.75 Keep left (south).

2.00 Continue southeast on the road toward Shelter #2.

2.10 Continue southeast around Shelter #2.

2.15 Turn right (southeast).

2.40 Ely Ford Mormon Crossing.

3.10 Turn right (east).

3.31 Arrive back at the trailhead.

40 White Oak Lake Trail

One of the largest blocks of contiguous forest in the state, Shimek was named for one of Iowa's most important conservationists. The first unit was purchased in the 1930s after a century of logging and farming had left it infertile. In the late 1930s, the Civilian Conservation Corps planted thousands of evergreen and hardwood trees to demonstrate a reforestation regime for state parks and private landowners. An old railroad bed serves as the main thoroughfare in the adjoining Farmington and Donnellson Units, the designated hiking-only units. Mowed firebreaks and several dirt roads spur off onto small loops through tree plantings and to Shagbark, Black Oak, and White Oak Lakes.

Start: Black Oak Lake parking area
Elevation gain: 488 feet total gain; 567 (lowest) to 712 feet (highest)
Distance: 9.1-mile loop
Difficulty: Difficult
Hiking time: 3–4 hours
Seasons/schedule: Open daily year-round
Fees and permits: None
Trail contact: Shimek State Forest, 33653 Route J56, Farmington 52626; (319) 878-3811; Shimek_forest@dnr.iowa.gov; iowadnr.gov/places-to-go/state-forests/shimek-state-forest
Dog-friendly: Yes, on leash
Trail surface: Portion of the trail is an old railroad bed; mowed firebreaks and gravel roads form the rest of the trail system
Land status: Shimek State Forest, Farmington and Donnellson Units (Iowa DNR)
Nearest town: Farmington, 2 miles to the west

Maps: USGS Farmington, IA; trail map available online
Other trail users: None
Special considerations: Hunting is allowed in the state forest, so check season dates and dress accordingly. Nonpoisonous snakes are common and the two poisonous species, the rattlesnake and copperhead, are known to exist on the east side of the Des Moines River between Farmington and Bonaparte. Rattlesnakes have been found in the northern part of the Farmington Unit.
Amenities available: Campgrounds in Lick Creek Unit, Farmington Unit, and Donnellson Unit. Only the Lick Creek Unit campgrounds have water; all have restrooms.
Maximum grade: 13%; the biggest climb is 125 feet over one-half mile
Cell service: Average to weak

Finding the trailhead: From the junction of IA 2 and IA 1 south of Keosauqua, take IA 2 east. Cross the Des Moines River and enter the town of Farmington, where IA 2 turns southeast. Look for CR J56 and turn left (east). This will take you out of town, become a gravel road, and pass the Shimek State Forest Headquarters. Just after the headquarters, turn right (south) toward the Black Oak Lake parking area. GPS: N40° 38.461' W91° 42.739'

Trail conditions: Expect some overgrown trails, especially in summer. Ticks will be abundant in summer. There are a lot of trails, some unmarked, so take a map and GPS device to navigate. With high water, the creek crossings may involve some wet feet.

The Hike

The southern boundary of Iowa is formed by a straight line following the approximate arc of parallel 40° 35' north latitude. When the line intersects with the Des Moines River, the river becomes the state boundary. The bulk of Shimek State Forest is located just east of the intersection, 34 river miles north of the Mississippi River.

Among Iowa's ninety-nine counties, heavily forested Lee County has the highest amount of rainfall and the lowest elevation. Such tree-friendly conditions are exactly what the state was seeking when it first purchased the land. The Civilian Conservation Corps (CCC) began planting demonstration plots with softwoods, many of them nonnatives such as eastern white, red, jack, and Virginia pines, as well as several spruces and larches. Sit down and have your lunch in one of the plantings, where shafts of light break the thick canopy and the smell of sunlight on pine will tickle your nose.

Wild turkeys were abundant in the state during presettlement times (the Turkey River in northeast Iowa was named for high gobbler populations). Rampant hunting led to near extirpation of the birds, and by the early 1900s there were only random sightings. After several attempts to reintroduce game-farm birds failed, eleven wild turkeys were obtained from Missouri and released in Shimek in 1965. The population exploded, and less than ten years later, a limited hunting season was opened. Today wild turkey populations are enormous and the birds can be found almost everywhere in the state.

Three trailheads provide access to the Farmington and Donnellson Units, open to hikers and mountain bikers only. You'll have to do a little bit of road-hiking and backtracking to traverse the unit, but it's worth it. The old railroad bed that runs east-west through the unit serves as its backbone, and the bulk of the spur trails are mowed firebreaks. Visible from the railroad bed trail are wet lowlands housing walnut, swamp white oak, silver maple, green ash, hackberry, and elm trees. You'll cross Lick Creek, which is shaded by willow thickets and tall cottonwoods. Three lakes are located within the unit, and just southeast of Shagbark Lake there's a primitive campsite available to backpackers.

To the south the Lick Creek and Croton Units house one of the most popular trail-riding systems in the state, a maze of paths surrounding Lick Creek just before its confluence with the Des Moines River. The trails are extensive; however, many are seriously eroded muddy swaths rather than footpaths. On weekends during summer, the horse traffic can be substantial. Exploration by foot in early spring and late fall or on cross-country skis in winter is your best bet at avoiding the crowds and scat. The Croton Unit has long been known as a birding hot spot—ten of the twelve warblers you may see are annual nesters here, and both scarlet and summer tanagers can be found.

White Oak Lake Trail

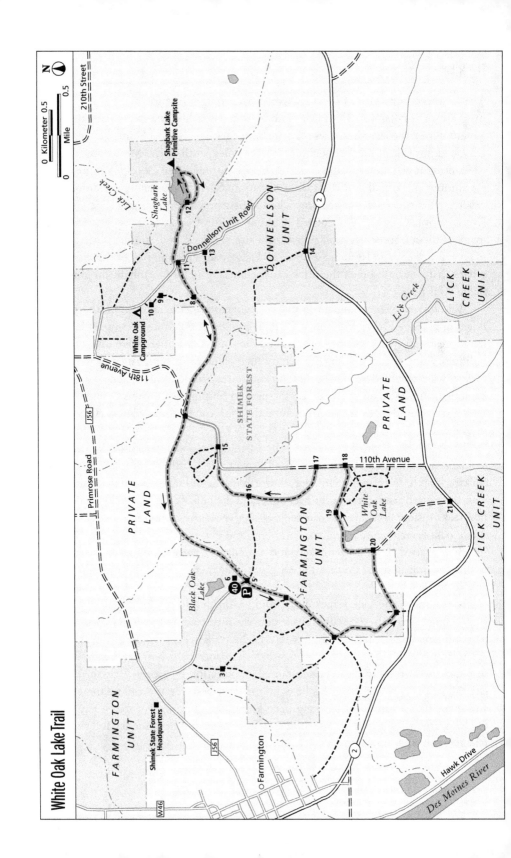

Miles and Directions

0.00 Start at Black Oak Lake parking area; walk south on the trail until you arrive at the railroad bed. Turn west (right) at Signpost 6.

0.82 At the fork (Signpost 2) turn south (left).

1.34 At the fork (Signpost 1) turn left (east). (*Note:* Turning right here would take you to the IA 2 trailhead/parking.)

1.75 At the fork (Signpost 20) turn left (northeast) and cross the dam at White Oak Lake.

2.24 At fork (Signpost 19) turn left (east). *Option:* Follow any of the trails that wind through a pine planting. They all loop around to Signpost 18, where you want to end up.

2.46 At the fork (Signpost 18) turn left (north) onto a dirt access road; walk 0.25 miles.

2.63 At the fork (Signpost 17) turn left (west) and walk through pine planting.

3.15 At the fork (Signpost 16) turn right (north). *Option:* Loop around another pine planting, or just continue on the main trail.

3.50 At the fork (Signpost 15) turn right and emerge onto dirt access road once again; walk north.

3.90 At the fork (Signpost 7) turn right (east) back onto railroad bed.

5.00 At Donnellson Unit Road (Signpost 11) turn left (north) and then make a quick right (east) onto the access road for Shagbark Lake. This will end at a parking lot.

5.40 From the parking lot walk due east over the dam and turn left (north) onto the small footpath that fringes the southeast side of the lake. At the fork walk left (west) for the last 50 feet before the campsite.

5.70 Arrive at Shagbark Lake primitive campsite. To return to the parking lot, backtrack and take the left (east) fork around in a small loop before climbing back up on the dam and walking into the parking lot.

6.00 Arrive back at the Shagbark Lake parking area. Follow the access road back down to the Donnellson Unit Road.

6.50 Hop back onto the railroad bed and take this all the way back to the trailhead.

9.10 Arrive back at the trailhead.

Honorable Mentions

M Amana Nature Trail

Located outside the village of Homestead, the Amana Nature Trail winds through forest to a bluff overlooking the Iowa River. In the river below the overlook, there is an Indian fish weir made of rocks that was used to trap fish when the water level was low in the river (the fish trap is no longer visible due to a change in the river's course). Spend the morning in the Amana Colonies, then walk off lunch on the 3-mile nature trail.

Start: Trailhead near the Amana Sportsmen Club off US 151
Elevation gain: 164 feet total gain
Distance: 3.5-mile loop
Difficulty: Easy
Hiking time: 1.5-2 hours
Seasons/schedule: Closed during deer hunting season
Fees and permits: None
Trail contact: Amana Society Conservation Committee; conservation@amanas.net
Dog-friendly: Yes, on leash

Trail surface: Natural
Land status: Amana Society
Nearest town: Amana, 3 miles to the north
Maps: USGS Middle Amana, IA; trail map posted on the nature trail
Other trail users: None
Special considerations: The trails are open for cross-country skiing in the winter.
Amenities available: None
Maximum grade: 6%
Cell service: Average

Finding the trailhead: From Amana, head south on US 151. After the junction with US 6, turn north at the sign indicating the Amana Nature Trail. GPS: N41° 45.891' W91° 52.594'

Trail conditions: The trails are easy to follow and in generally good condition despite overgrowth and tall grasses in the summer. The trail receives moderate traffic.

N Port Louisa National Wildlife Refuge

The adjoining Lake Odessa State Wildlife Management Area and Louisa Division of Port Louisa National Wildlife Refuge together encompass more than 10 square miles of public land along the Mississippi River Flyway, one of North America's most important corridors for migrating birds. Because the Odessa-Louisa Complex is dedicated to providing ample habitat for animals and plants and caters mainly to boat recreation, it offers only one designated hiking trail. However, with a little imagination you'll be able to find suitable walking areas from which to observe migrating birds, as well as diverse mammals, reptiles, amphibians, and invertebrates.

Start: Muscatine Slough Trailhead
Elevation gain: None
Distance: 1.5-mile
Difficulty: Moderate
Hiking time: About 1 hour
Seasons/schedule: Portions are closed from Sept 15 to Dec 31 for migrating waterfowl.
Fees and permits: None
Trail contact: Port Louisa National Wildlife Refuge, 10728 CR X61, Wapello 52653; (319) 523-6982; fws.gov/refuge/port-louisa
Dog-friendly: Yes, on leash
Trail surface: Mowed grass or bare soil
Land status: Port Louisa National Wildlife Refuge (US Fish and Wildlife)
Nearest town: Wapello, 5 miles to the southwest
Maps: USGS Wapello, IA
Other trail users: None
Special considerations: The trail may flood if waters are high.
Amenities available: Visitor center, restrooms
Maximum grade: Level-grade trail
Cell service: Unreliable; reception may depend on carrier

Finding the trailhead: From Wapello, head east on CR 99 for 1 mile, then turn north onto CR G62. After 3 miles, turn north onto CR X61 and continue for 1.5 miles until reaching the visitor center at the wildlife refuge. GPS: N41° 12.854' W91° 7.702'

   Trail conditions: The trail can be muddy and flooded if waters are high. Overgrown trails can also be encountered at the height of the growing season. The trails receive light traffic.

○ Chief Wapello Trail

Spend a day checking out Garrison Rock, a Wapello County Conservation Board property, where bluffs of Pennsylvanian sandstone (the same formation exposed at Cedar Bluffs Natural Area to the north in Mahaska County) tower over the Des Moines River.

Start: 6951 Cliffland Rd., Ottumwa, IA 52501
Elevation gain: 272 feet total gain; 636 (lowest) to 780 feet (highest)
Distance: 1.7-mile out-and-back
Difficulty: Moderate due to rugged terrain and overgrown trails
Hiking time: 1–2 hours
Seasons/schedule: Trail is open daily, year-round
Fees and permits: None
Trail contact: Wapello County Conservation, 1339 US 63, Bloomfield 52537; (641) 682-3091; pioneerridge@wapellocounty.org; wapellocounty.org/conservation/
Dog-friendly: Yes, on leash
Trail surface: Natural
Land status: Garrison Rock Resource Management Unit (Wapello County Conservation)
Nearest town: Ottumwa, 4 miles to the northwest
Maps: USGS Agency, IA
Other trail users: Equestrians and mountain bikers
Special considerations: Poison ivy and ticks
Amenities available: None
Maximum grade: 20%; there are two 100-foot climbs
Cell service: Below average

Trailhead at Garrison Rock Resource Management Unit

Finding the trailhead: From Ottumwa, head southeast on E Main Street. Less than 1 mile after crossing over US 34, turn southeast onto Old Agency Road/Cliffland Road. Continue for nearly 2 miles until reaching the small parking lot on the east side of the road. GPS: N40° 59.140' W92° 21.559'

    Trail conditions: The trail can be overgrown and is not well marked. Wear long pants, protect yourself from ticks and insects, and take a map and/or GPS device. The trails receive light traffic.

Hike Index

Printed in the USA
CPSIA information can be obtained
at www.ICGtesting.com
CBHW071307220524
8849CB00001B/1